Praise for
The Rifle 2

"A wonderful, powerful tribute to the very last warriors of the Greatest Generation. This is an important and extremely valuable book."

—**ALEX KERSHAW,** multiple nationally bestselling author of *The Longest Winter: The Battle of the Bulge and the Epic Story of World War II's Most Decorated Platoon*

"Honest and brutal, heartbreaking and moving. From Peleliu to the cockpit of a P-47 over Germany, to the Battle of the Bulge, to a gun turret of the *USS Ommaney Bay*, to hunting U-boats in the Atlantic, to the Siegfried Line, to the skies over Normandy, to stories from the last of the Mohawk code talkers, Biggio captures first-person histories from World War II in a book that does not shy away from the long-term impacts of a generation sent to war. He goes beyond the stories of heroism and valor that so often define the Greatest Generation and humanizes the men who lived it. They endured capture and surrender, heard the crying of drowning comrades, witnessed the horrors of concentration camps and the reality of shallow graves. Biggio reminds us that the realities of combat are sometimes overshadowed by the glory of war—glory tempered by the blood of their brothers and the deaths of those young men in opposing uniforms sent to stop them."

—**JACK CARR,** former Navy SEAL sniper and the #1 nationally bestselling author of *The Terminal List*

"Biggio has had terrific success in eliciting details from World War II survivors—shared with him because of his own status as a USMC combat survivor of twenty-first-century warfare. He's a superior writer and storyteller."

—**MARK A. BANDO,** 101st Airborne historian and bestselling author of *101st Airborne: The Screaming Eagles in World War II*

"A must-read for any history buff! A book full of interesting stories that have never been told. Biggio brings to light the soldiers of every background and every caliber whose stories might otherwise have been lost through time."

—**SAMMY L. DAVIS,** U.S. Army Vietnam War veteran and Medal of Honor recipient

Praise for
The Rifle

"Andrew Biggio stayed true to his warrior ethos by not forgetting those who fought before him. I am beyond impressed and . . . grateful for the service he has rendered a new generation of veterans."

—**ROBERT O'NEILL,** U.S. Navy SEAL and New York Times bestselling author of *The Operator: Firing the Shots that Killed Osama bin Laden and My Years as a SEAL Team Warrior*

"Stories that all Americans, especially veterans and the families of those who fought in World War II, have been waiting to hear. Biggio tells emotional and heartwarming stories punctuated with accounts of the terror of war and the thrill of combat. This book honors every Marine and soldier who never lived to share their stories."

—**MAJOR SCOTT HUESING, USMC (RET.),** bestselling author of *Echo in Ramadi: The Firsthand Story of US Marines in Iraq's Deadliest City*

"Andrew Biggio is a loud and effective voice for veterans. . . . His experience as a combat veteran gives him credibility. I applaud him for relating these stories."

—**TOM KELLEY,** co-author of *The Siren's Call and Second Chances*

"*The Rifle* is not just a story of the heroism and abiding patriotism of the Greatest Generation, it is a fine recounting of forgotten history. Andrew Biggio is . . . able to bring the trials and tribulations of armed combat to life."

—**MICHELLE McPHEE,** bestselling author of *Maximum Harm: The Tsarnaev Brothers, the FBI, and the Road to the Marathon Bombing*

"Andrew Biggio has travelled the world to find specific World War II veterans to honor them. This book belongs on everyone's coffee table as a tribute to our World War II veterans."

—**CHARLEY VALERA,** National Indie Excellence Award–winning author of *My Father's War: Memories from Our Honored WWII Soldiers*

"Andrew Biggio has a remarkable ability to form meaningful connections with veterans of wars that were fought decades before his birth. *The Rifle* is his way of thanking those men for their service, and we all owe him a debt of gratitude."

—**JIM "DOC" McCLOUGHAN,** combat medic for the U.S. Army and Medal of Honor recipient

The Rifle 2

The Rifle 2

Back to the Battlefield

ANDREW
BIGGIO

FOREWORDS BY
Donald Halverson, 34th Infantry Division;
Louis Zoghby, 17th Airborne Division;
Ed Cottrell, 48th Fighter Group; and
Gerhard Femppel, 2nd SS Panzer Division

REGNERY
HISTORY
Washington, D.C.

Regnery History™ is a trademark of Salem Communications Holding Corporation
Regnery® is a registered trademark and its colophon is a trademark of Salem Communications Holding Corporation

Cataloging-in-Publication data on file with the Library of Congress

ISBN: 978-1-68451-506-6
eISBN: 978-1-68451-512-7

Published in the United States by
Regnery History, an Imprint of
Regnery Publishing
A Division of Salem Media Group
Washington, D.C.
www.RegneryHistory.com

Manufactured in the United States of America

10 9 8 7 6 5 4 3 2 1

Books are available in quantity for promotional or premium use. For information on discounts and terms, please visit our website: www.Regnery.com.

This book is dedicated to the thirteen U.S. service members who gave their lives on August 26, 2021, at Hamid Karzai International Airport in Kabul, Afghanistan. Their bravery, dedication, and discipline in the face of chaos will never be forgotten. Semper Fi.

Marine Corps Lance Cpl. David L. Espinoza, 20

Marine Corps Sgt. Nicole L. Gee, 23

Marine Corps Cpl. Hunter Lopez, 22

Marine Corps Lance Cpl. Rylee J. McCollum, 20

Marine Corps Lance Cpl. Dylan R. Merola, 20

Marine Corps Lance Cpl. Kareem M. Nikoui, 20

Marine Corps Sgt. Johanny Rosario Pichardo, 25

Marine Corps Cpl. Humberto A. Sanchez, 22

Marine Corps Lance Cpl. Jared M. Schmitz, 20

Marine Corps Cpl. Daegan W. Page, 23

Navy Hospital Corpsman Maxton W. Soviak, 22

Army Staff Sgt. Ryan C. Knauss, 23

Marine Corps Staff Sgt. Darin T. Hoover, 31

When politicians fail and the generals miscalculate, you send a 20-year-old to fix the problem.

CONTENTS

CONTENTS

Author's Note

The stories in this book each came from a veteran's memories and personal experiences nearly 80 years after the events occurred. While every effort has been made to verify the facts of battle, some minor facts may have been lost with the passing of time. The veterans interviewed were between the ages of 96 and 104 years old. Statements have been cross-referenced with historical documents, division histories, and other firsthand accounts. While most of this generation is gone, its members' opinions and experiences still mean a great deal.

To protect the privacy of some veterans, multiple names have been changed.

Forewords

In Cassino, Italy, 1943, we had just set up a bivouac area at the bottom of a mountain. I watched as an Italian man and his son came down the hill to beg us for food. We gave them what little we had, but his son was distracted by a pair of boots that seemed to be stuck in a bush. The boy grabbed the boots, but they were attached to a mine. It was booby trap set by the Germans. The explosion killed the boy and another G.I. I watched as the father threw the boy's carcass over his shoulder and walked back up the mountain, saying nothing to no one. At age one hundred, I stood at the bottom of that hill again with Andrew Biggio, seventy-eight years later.

My memories of serving in Italy soared, thanks to the rifle project. I joined the 34th Infantry Division in Naples, and we had three crossings of the Volturno River. My first major battle was Mount Pantano. It took one week to defeat the Germans; we exchanged grenades at close range, while others engaged in hand-to-hand combat. Mount Pantano was very difficult—I remember four companies making their way through this area at different times. This was the winter of 1943. We hiked the mountains in the rain and snow, our clothes were soaked, bedding was soaked, you sat on your steel helmet, there was mud everywhere and it was hard to make trails. Yet Monte Cassino was the most difficult of the battles.

Monte Cassino I can say nothing good about. We crossed the base of the hill in the dark, not talking, and dug in. The Germans thought we were their own replacements and let us come in close. We had 160 in the company, and they had about 70, so they surrendered. However, when daylight broke, we found that we had to run across a ravine to capture a castle. The Germans dropped mortars up and down on us. There was nowhere to hide. We finally got across there—only *four* of us were left out of forty in my platoon.

Andy's work traveling all over the United States and interviewing former World War II vets, collecting their stories, is admirable. I was happy to help his project by signing books in Italy, Iowa, and Boston. It's interesting to read their stories and know that we were all going through the same things in World War II. No one should ever forget those that served and what they did to preserve our freedom. Thank you, Andy, for your kindness and thoughtfulness, for these interesting trips and telling the stories. I never dreamed that I would be able to go back and see Italy. I never thought I'd live this long. I'm glad I lived this long to get to see this stuff. I feel very lucky.

Donald Halverson
Tech Sergeant, U.S. Army, 168th Infantry
Regiment, 34th "Red Bull" Division

When Andy Biggio called me for an interview four years ago, I was thrilled. He explained that he was collecting stories of soldiers who carried the M1 Garand rifle in World War II, which he hoped to be published. Andy flew to Denver, Colorado, and interviewed me and had me sign the M1 rifle. I was the 199th signature. I served as a gliderman in the 17th Airborne Division. Fortunately the 17th did not have to participate in D-Day. However, we were called into the Battle of the Bulge, which was the biggest battle of World War II, lasting forty days. The weather was very cold and snowy. Within a couple of days, soldiers were complaining of frozen feet. I myself did not feel my feet for three weeks.

The 194th Glider regiment that I served in (F Company) was charged with recapturing the Belgian town of Flamierge. It was a fierce battle, taking three days. We had to cross a ridge that was fully exposed to the enemy. We lost almost one thousand men a day. After the Bulge, we spent February resting, receiving replacements, and most of all, preparing for the biggest drop in World War II.

Operation Varsity was launched on March 24, 1945, in cooperation with the British 6th Airborne. Over 17,000 paratroopers and glidermen were involved. We were dropped behind the German army and fought until the end of the war on May 8, 1945. An experience never to be forgotten. I was ecstatic to know the rifle project led to the construction of the first 17th Airborne monument in the town of Wesel, Germany. This town was the main objective of our airborne operation that day. Like the 82nd and 101st Airborne Divisions, the world should know our drop zones and the sacrifices made by the least known airborne division in World War II.

Louis Zoghby
194th Glider Infantry Regiment,
17th Airborne Division

As a World War II veteran it is my privilege to be a part of *The Rifle 2.* I started my flight training at Visalia, California, my basic flight training at Chico, California, and received my pilot wings after finishing advance training at Luke Field, Phoenix, Arizona. I was assigned to do transition tracing at Wendover Field, Utah. It was there that I was introduced to the P-47 Thunderbolt aircraft.

This is the plane in which I flew sixty-five missions with the 48th Fighter Group, 493rd Fighter Squadron.

I am proud to be a part of *The Rifle 2* along with other World War II veterans who share their war experiences. Andy's first book, *The Rifle*, along with this second offering, helps U.S. citizens understand the adventures and pitfalls the Greatest Generation faced as they fought the war.

In addition to inclusion in the book, Andrew Biggio gave me the opportunity to visit my airfield located in St. Trond, Belgium, four times, and provided a visit to the gravesite of my roommate, Ted Smith, who was hit by flak, crashed, and died. Ted was hit on January 1, 1945, and is buried in an American cemetery in Holland. We have also made several visits to Bastogne, Belgium, where the historic Battle of the Bulge took place.

Many of the stories found in *The Rifle 2* relate to that furious battle. I am sure that you will find these interesting and find the book difficult to put down.

> *Ed Cottrell*
> *48th Fighter Group*

Born in 1925, I volunteered for the Waffen-SS at the age of seventeen and became a very young lieutenant (Untersturmführer) in the 2nd SS Panzer Division Das Reich in 1942. We soldiers were Germans and not "Nazis." I was proud of my squad! On Christmas Day 1944 my company commander was killed in the Ardennes offensive, and I became his successor. I led the company on to Hungary and Vienna until the last day. After the end of the war I walked home and was not taken prisoner.

Fighting the American soldiers was difficult because my family had numerous expatriate relatives in the United States. Today I am happy about the friendly contact with former American veterans. Similar youth experiences connect us. We regret together that our two countries fought two world wars against each other. But even now, more than seventy-eight years after the end of the war, recognition and respect are only granted to former American frontline fighters. The millions of fallen German soldiers, on the other hand, are officially thought of only half-heartedly and bashfully.

My generation rebuilt the country after the war. I set up two companies in the U.S.A. more than fifty years ago and have always had good experiences with Americans. I do not have the same views that I did when I was young. I hope there will be no more war between us. Through their respectful attitude, may readers help all to be proud of their country, and always recognize the dedication of their veterans appropriately.

Gerhard Femppel Stuttgart, March 2023
2nd SS Panzer Division Das Reich
To learn more about Gerhard's story,
visit www.Karstwehr-Versand.de.

Prologue

I told myself I was done chasing ghosts after completing this book's predecessor, *The Rifle*. The signatures on the rifle continued to mount, however, well after the book was written. The once walnut-stained M1 Garand became white, covered with signatures from the barrel to the buttstock. The ink on the rifle didn't just create a new paint job on the gun, it symbolized more stories, stories I could not just bury. These stories needed to be told, and I could not yet call it quits.

This was not my idea alone. Readers demanded more, and there was plenty more to tell. There are hundreds of names on that rifle, after all. Writing a book about World War II seventy-five years after the war's end was very difficult when I did it the first time. If you want to tell these stories correctly, having a survivor recount his story is not always enough. So many books have already been written about World War II in the 1960s, '70s, '80s, and even '90s. These were times when a World War II veteran's memory was in its prime. Now most of those men are in the later portion of their nineties.

To tell a man's story correctly I had to listen carefully to his recollection, corroborate it with historical documents, and, if I were lucky enough, speak with another survivor and hear *his* side of the story, too. It took me nearly five years to write *The Rifle*, this book's predecessor. When it was released on June 1, 2021, it soared to number one on Amazon in multiple categories. The book went viral—not just in America, but in Belgium, France, and the Netherlands.

I loved every second of this. I loved giving World War II buffs what they wanted. More important, I loved bringing light to the veterans whose lives I wrote about. But after its publication more World War II veterans with stories to tell came along.

The rifle itself was no longer guiding me to World War II veterans—the book was.

The Rifle took me on a journey of signings, speaking engagements, and nationwide travel. I started to meet more and more World War II veterans. They, too, wanted me to sign their books, knowing that *The Rifle* was already written and they were not in it.

Soon after, I found myself back in Europe with American World War II veterans who hadn't returned since the war. These men were there thanks to the book. Thousands of people wanted *their* books signed by the same veterans who had signed the M1 Garand. The book was creating even more phenomenal experiences. Although I'd told myself I would no longer chase ghosts, here I was, six months after the release of *The Rifle*, gearing up to write *The Rifle 2*. Yet how could I not?

On a darker note, on my post-publication journey I learned that stolen valor is not a new phenomenon. The vast majority of those who signed the M1 Garand are members of the Greatest Generation. A very few proved to be the greatest fabricators. In my search for World War II veterans to sign *The Rifle*, I always kept in mind that the average age would have to be older than ninety-five. Deciding whom I would interview was a challenge. I was desperate to find these rare individuals, but in my excitement and naiveté, as I'll recount in one chapter included here, skipping due diligence in my background checks came back to haunt me.

My rifle project gained massive attention on social media, especially after the book was published. I was approached by some people with good intentions but no facts. They would say something like, "There's a guy who lives on my street who was in World War II," or, "This guy I know, George, was in the Battle of the Bulge, and he got shot, too! You should have him sign your rifle!"

I must have heard that a dozen times. Still, I would approach every veteran with a: "Honored to meet you, sir. What division were you in?"

"Uh. . . . The 29th. . . ?"

At that age, dementia could easily have set in. For most men, however, not being able to remember what unit or division you were in during the war is like not knowing your own name.

The stolen valor guys were good storytellers, and I fell for some of their tales. But once I requested official records, the truth began to come out. It turned out your neighbor George had been lying for the last seventy-five years. He was actually in the Army Band—not the Battle of the Bulge. Nor did he get shot. He didn't hold an M1 Garand in battle. He played the tuba.

I once had an elderly gentleman gather his entire family, nearly three generations of bloodlines, into one living room. He proceeded to tell me about life as a ball-turret gunner in a B-17 during World War II. His family stared, captivated by his story, yet I knew something was off. He signed my rifle, and although I couldn't prove in that moment that he was lying, it was not long before I figured out he was a mechanic who'd never left England.

I spent a few nights scrubbing phony signatures off the rifle with paint thinner, causing damage to the wood. I cursed myself.

But it eventually dawned on me why they had been lying all these years.

More than sixteen million Americans served during World War II. Who the hell wanted to be the one who *didn't* see action?

Let's face it, someone had to peel the potatoes—yet I never met one person who admitted to doing so. Fixing and repairing vehicles was a much needed job to run the mighty war machine; however, I never ran into one mechanic. While some lied through their teeth, others were

respectable enough to tell me about desertion, faking injuries, and causing self-harm to get off the front lines. That I could respect. While the
tuba player and mechanic I met may have technically been World War
II veterans, these particular men made the decision to lie to me. Worse,
it was not just me they were lying to. They'd lied to their own families
for seven decades.

I did not expose them. What was the point? At their age, what good
would it do? Plus, I didn't want to embarrass their families, who viewed
grandpa as a war hero. All I could do was sit at home and scrub their
names off the rifle to make room for veterans who had an honest story
to tell.

Yet I never turned down a signature of any World War II veteran
on the rifle. It did not matter what their military occupational skill was,
so long as they were telling the truth.

"Are you sure you want me to sign the rifle? I only fired it once in
basic training. I was just a truck driver." Those words spoken to me by
one veteran instilled in me what it meant to be a humble, honest man.

"Of course, sir," I replied. "If it wasn't for you how would our troops
have moved around Europe? Or gotten food, ammo, and other supplies?"

Comments like these made these men feel appreciated, even after all
those years. As they should. But the M1 Garand is no place for liars,
fabricators, or stolen valor. The stories you are about to read are testa-
ments of men who will forever remain, at heart, war fighters. And even
if you're in your late nineties, war never leaves you.

CHAPTER ONE

Ninety Seconds of Hate

On June 26, 2021, I had just returned from a motorcycle ride from Winthrop, Massachusetts, to New Hampshire and back. I made it home in time to join my wife and kids for a swim at the beach. I threw on my bathing suit and decided to put the family in the truck for the drive to the ocean. Having my own truck with me was important. I had a toolbox full of SWAT team equipment in the bed. As a member of SWAT, you were on call 24/7. If a situation erupted, you could leave from wherever you were and head straight to the incident. And such situations did happen on occasion.

As I made my way out of town, my cell phone began to ring repeatedly with calls and texts. Messages appeared such as:

"Are you ok?" And, "I heard some of your guys are getting shot at?"

I answered the next call from a fellow police officer in my department. My town was experiencing its first active shooter situation, and there were casualties.

I turned my truck around and drove to the vicinity of the situation. I jumped out of my truck, popped open my toolbox, and put on my vest and slung on my SIG Sauer M400 rifle. I told my wife to head straight home with the kids.

I continued to walk several blocks to where the incident was unfolding.

However, when I arrived, it was over.

Multiple bodies lay in the streets surrounded by pools of blood. A commercial-sized box truck continued to smoke where it had crashed through a residential home. The remains of the house had fallen down around it. My little town of Winthrop, Massachusetts, looked like a war zone.

I recognized a policeman I knew, Officer Dutra, and ran with my rifle toward him. "What the fuck is going on?" I asked him.

"It's over. Bettano killed the guy," he replied.

I looked over to see Sergeant Bettano sitting in the rear seat of the police chief's car. His head hung low as the deputy chief handed him a bottle of water to drink. He had just taken the life of another person.

"I love you buddy," I called over to Bettano.

He raised the bottle of water to acknowledge me. He had done his job, killed a domestic terrorist, but he would only be allowed to communicate with the police union and other investigators from here on to protect himself legally.

Paramedics were loading a body into an ambulance when I heard a bystander exclaim, "Officer, there is another body over here!"

I walked over to an alleyway. There, an officer from another jurisdiction was looking over yet another victim. The man had been shot half a dozen times at point-blank range. His eyes were wide open. He lay on his back and seemed to stare at the sky. A blue surgical mask, worn as a COVID precaution, covered his mouth. It was a precaution he no longer needed. He had been shot multiple times in the head while on his back. Perhaps he had already been dead when he hit the ground. Perhaps not. His brain matter was all over the vinyl siding of the home just a few inches away. As I looked away from the gory scene, I realized it was the first time I'd seen that bright pink brain matter since Afghanistan.

A pistol and shell casings surrounded the man's body. His killer had emptied the gun into him, leaving the empty pistol behind, and departed with a second gun to look for his next victim. He wouldn't reach his next target. Winthrop police sergeant Bettano had intercepted the shooter and eliminated him. The shooter's body was at that moment being carted away by ambulance with multiple rounds in his torso and one in the neck.

According to Officer Dutra, while the suspect was spurting blood from his neck he was still trying to charge Bettano. It was evident he may have been on some sort of drug during the murderous rampage. He also was the operator of the box truck that had been intentionally slammed into the home.

Witnesses later reported that the crazed gunman had exited the smoking truck and opened fire on onlookers. The shooter killed two innocent people before being dispatched to hell himself—all in a span of approximately ninety seconds.

Back in the alleyway with the deceased body, my deputy chief walked over to me.

"Let's find out who this guy is," he said as he rummaged through the victim's pockets.

He pulled out the man's wallet and checked the identification. This victim was a retired state trooper and an Air Force veteran, according to his ID. He had been enjoying a summer day, minding his own business on his front lawn, when he probably heard the crashing of the box truck. He went to see how he could help, and this had ultimately cost him his life.

Seeing that this man was not only a retired cop but a veteran, I vowed to stay with his body as the crime scene tape went up. It was going to be a long day and night as local and state law enforcement agencies arrived to conduct investigations, collect evidence, and take witness statements. Minutes turned into hours on the hot summer day. While I had a heavy bulletproof SWAT vest on with my rifle slung across it, I was, luckily, still in my bathing suit.

With the heat, and with the victim's bodily fluids leaking in the street, it was only a matter of time before flies came. While the brain matter had been a minor trigger of memories of warfare, it was the flies that sealed the deal. As the flies began to land on the face of the deceased man, I had my first ever flashback.

I was in Afghanistan again. Like I'd entered a time portal, I found myself back on a day I'd looked over the bodies of Afghan police who had been killed by an IED. Flies in Afghanistan were an instant occurrence after any kind of exposure of blood or food. They would come seemingly out of nowhere.

Sure enough, on that bloody day in Winthrop, as soon as that fly touched down on the face of the murder victim there was no stopping my mental transportation to ten years before. I was having an out-of-body experience watching twenty-four-year-old me, in 2011, open an MRE (meal ready-to-eat). The same flies that had been buzzing around dead carcasses during the day were the same ones landing on my food that night. I was so hungry, I swatted them away and ate anyway.

I snapped back to the current scene—and suddenly I was satisfied. With what I'll admit was a trace of gruesome satisfaction, I was relieved that some of my coworkers had finally gotten a taste of what I'd experienced before becoming a police officer. Then my thoughts turned to anger. I hated myself for not being the guy who took out the shooter. My emotions bounced up and down. What was happening to me? Then my guilt was interrupted.

"Hey officer, can I get through here? I have an appointment to get my hair done?"

A female bystander on the other side of the caution tape was asking me if she could cut through the crime scene. She had zero respect for the lives lost there that day. This startled me out of my trance. I blew up.

"Get the fuck out of here now!"

I screamed so loudly that everyone at the crime scene from different agencies was staring at me. I wasn't even the one who had fired the fatal shots that killed the bad guy, yet here I was acting like a loose cannon.

"Get a hold of yourself, Andy," I told myself.

Other onlookers began to take photos of the murder victim. He lay there for hours. At times, the wind would blow the sheet from his body, providing an opportunity for people to take out their iPhones and grab pictures.

My rage was growing. I protected the dead state trooper as much as I could, blocking the alleyway from the paparazzi with my body. After nearly eight hours, the crime scene was ready to be broken down. The hearse came to pick up the body and I rendered the veteran his final salute as they loaded him in. My job was done. I'll never forget Trooper David Green, nor the heroic actions of Sergeant Nicholas Bettano.

Yet, the next morning, I could hardly move out of bed. I wasn't the cop who had returned fire, but I felt paralyzed. Was it my flashback playing tricks on me? Had I done enough? I am not a pussy. I had seen this kind of stuff before. Why were my body and mind doing this to me now? I was once again angry.

All the hard work with the rifle and hundreds of World War II veterans who had given me advice seemed almost washed away in a day.

"This can't be," I thought to myself. I was done with that war.

And why now? It had been ten years.

Snap out of it, I told myself.

My wife brought me a coffee. I watched as she placed it on the windowsill. I stared at the coffee for hours. There was only one group of people capable of getting me out of this funk: my World War II veteran buddies. I went downstairs, buttoned up the rifle, and hit the road. It was time to start over again.

CHAPTER TWO

The Old Breed Still Exists

With the Old Breed, by Eugene Sledge, is every Marine's unofficial Bible. Sledge's account of fighting in the Pacific brought not just every Marine but every reader into the macabre world of what became known as the "island hopping campaign." At times, Sledge's stories seemed so crazy, one had to sit back and wonder, "Wow, can that be true?" His stories were surreal enough to help spark HBO's miniseries *The Pacific* and leave the world yearning to learn more about the World War II fighting Marine.

During my travels promoting *The Rifle*, I always wished I'd been able to write about the island of Peleliu. I could never find a survivor, however. It was my firm belief that the reason this was so hard was because the battle lived up to its reputation as one of the harshest ever fought in the Pacific. Even if a Marine was not killed there, most didn't live into their nineties.

Then I met Emilio. Emilio Magliacane served with A Company, 1st Battalion, 5th Marines. Author Eugene Sledge Served with K Company, 3rd Battalion, 5th Marines. I was never going to get a closer account of

Emilio R. Magliacane, 1st Battalion, 5th Marines

Peleliu than this, which I collected in 2021 when I began working on my next set of stories.

Emilio was a second-generation Italian who came from the Boston area. Like all Italian Americans during the Great Depression, his father had to journey outside of Boston to get work.

"We ended up in Gardner, Massachusetts. My dad worked for the Heywood-Wakefield Company building furniture. It was here in Gardner that I learned the Japanese attacked Pearl Harbor," Emilio told me.

In 1942, a seventeen-year-old Emilio was sitting in the movie theater watching Tyrone Power in *Blood and Sand*.

"It was something about that movie that made me want to enlist. I was already jacked up from the attack on Pearl Harbor, so, when the film ended, I went right into the recruiting station and joined the Marines!" he exclaimed.

At the time, I had no idea what *Blood and Sand* was about. Assuming it was a war film, I thought I had a good idea why Emilio had built up that motivation to fight. Then I watched the movie, and it turned out to be not a war movie but the story of a young matador in a bullfighting ring. Tyrone Power's character is ultimately gored by a bull and dies in front of a crowd doing what he loved. The film inspired Emilio. The kind of man who could die for something he loved so much—and sacrifice everything without hesitation—is the kind of man Emilio strived to be.

"When my mother found out I joined she was livid. I told her, 'It's better I choose where I want to be than be drafted into something I don't.'" Not long after displeasing his mom, Emilio was on the same coal-powered train car as many other young American boys from the East Coast bound for Parris Island, South Carolina. "We were up all day and night, the smoke filled the train cars, we were covered in black soot. But we got to see the nation's capital, so that was nice."

The pleasantness would come to a swift end when Emilio's bus entered the gates of Parris Island. "We rushed off the bus and were put into different ranks. This big drill instructor introduced himself. He said 'Listen to me and listen to me carefully. My name is Drill Instructor Staff Sergeant Moses. *I may have not created the Commandments, but I sure as hell broke every fucking last one of them!*'"

No sooner had the words left Drill Instructor Moses's mouth than the largest recruit began to laugh. Drill Instructor Moses ran up to the big recruit and snatched him by the throat.

"I swear he did that as a test!" Emilio said.

The recruit keeled over, gasping for air. This tactic demonstrated to every recruit in the platoon that Moses meant business. Regardless of a recruit's stature, size, attitude, or ability to intimidate, the drill instructor was in charge.

"All I could think of was, 'My God, where is my mother to protect me now?'" Emilio added.

The torment of becoming a Marine went on for the next twelve weeks. After boot camp Emilio attended advanced infantry training at what is today Camp Lejeune.

"There was no break. After infantry training we were rushed to the West Coast, then eventually to the Russell Islands to a replacement depot," he remembered. "We needed to fill in 1st Marine Division's empty spots from the Battle of Guadalcanal."

The island on which Emilio would meet his new unit was called Pavuvu. Here would be his introduction to Able Company, 1st Battalion, 5th Marines, fresh off the chopping block from battle in Cape Gloucester, and before that the wicked island of Guadalcanal. It was time for the 1st Marine Division to replenish its ranks with fresh new Marines and then continue the activity there could never be enough of—training.

As Emilio debarked his ship on Pavuvu he walked through the maze of tents. "You could not walk without stepping on a rat or a coconut," he told me.

"The *whole island* was rats and coconuts!" he added, annoyance in his voice. "I don't know how they could call it a 'rest area.' The entire place did nothing but stress you out!"

"How did the veteran Marines treat you as a new guy?" I asked Emilio.

I always asked this question of every Marine I met. How hazing developed in the Marines intrigues me. Most Marines will agree that joining a new unit after graduation from boot camp could be scarier than war itself. Emilio gave me an answer that surprised me.

"They treated us fine. If the guys really experienced combat, they appreciated life. We got along. They never raised hell with us new guys," he answered.

The veterans in Company A made it crystal clear to the new Marines they would be going into combat. They trained repeatedly on Pavuvu with LSTs (Landing Ship Tanks) and amtracs, preparing to invade the next island. Eventually, that island would be revealed to the 1st Marine Division: Peleliu.

"Were you nervous to go into combat?"

"Not at first, and no one else admitted to it, either. It wasn't until that morning when we boarded the LSTs, made our way to the belly of the ships, and loaded the amtracs that guys seemed quiet," he recalled.

On the morning of September 15, 1944, Emilio's LST lowered its ramp, and the first amtracs holding separate platoons of A Company rolled off the ships and plunged into the ocean, their engines roaring.

"This is when I was finally scared. The Japanese had our amtracs zeroed as we got closer to the island."

From land, enemy artillery was lobbed into the ocean. Some shells were direct hits. One seemed to kill every Marine on an amtrac next to his, from what Emilio could see. His amtrac passed by several sinking flaming amtracs with no sign of human life or anyone trying to escape. As his amtrac pushed forward, Marine F4U Corsairs soared overhead. The pilots strafed what they could on the island, but the enemy fire did not lighten up. Navy Avenger fighter planes also strafed.

The smoldering island got closer and closer, until finally Emilio's amtrac jolted back and forth. The amphibious vehicle had made contact with the ocean floor. The beach was approaching. It would soon be time to debark this "bullet magnet" of a vehicle.

"We bailed off the side of the amtrac, and we had to wade in the water to shore." Emilio's amtrac was unable to beach itself on the sand due to overcrowding. He had his M1 rifle and bandoleers of ammo slung around his torso as he quickly waded through the thigh-deep water.

"As I ran up onto the land, I passed one dead Marine. This was the first dead Marine I ever saw. I'm sure there was more but I didn't stick around to find out. I needed cover. I was on the beach not more than five minutes before I took shelter behind a coconut tree. As soon as I did that a bullet whizzed by my head."

The enemy round impacted the tree and sent bark into Emilio's face. Temporarily blinded by debris in his eyes, he dropped to a knee to shake it off. "There were no officers I could find or anyone taking control of the situation," Emilio continued. "I just kept moving through the trees until I saw everyone assembling on the edge of an airfield."

With temperatures raging to almost 115 degrees, there was one crucial item lacking among the men as they advanced off the beach towards the airfield. For some reason, drinking water had not caught up with the men of Emilio's battalion.

"Apparently, they put our water in drums which originally had diesel fuel in them, so no one had any clean water," he said with disgust.

Without water, the men of Able Company began to dehydrate. Combat maneuvers in cool temperature require hydration, never mind the triple-digit temperatures the island of Peleliu produced in September. Having no water was also murderous to morale and showed lack of proper planning by the commanders.

The desperation of some Marines led to stealing. "One thing you learned quickly the first day was to keep your eye on your canteen, because if you didn't, it could disappear."

Cloudy white stains began to form all over the Marines' uniforms. This was the salt being extracted from their bodies in the extreme heat. "It was hard to tell another Marine 'No' when he asked for a sip of water from your canteen. But you knew if you gave out your water you would have none for yourself," Emilio stated.

The numbers of arriving American troops began to mount outside the airfield. By midday, most Marines were hoping to dig in and await orders. The heat felt unbearable, and the boys wanted to rest in the shade if possible.

Instead, someone shouted "*Jap tank!*" Emilio did a double take.

"Several Japanese tanks came screeching across the airfield. They could move fast because they were much smaller than our tanks. Behind them Jap infantry followed. Some were even riding on tanks and shooting rifles at us," he recalled.

Not far from Emilio, a Marine dropped down quickly and closed the hatch to his own Sherman tank.

"He let loose one round from his 75 mm cannon and one of the Jap tanks went two to three feet in the air!" Emilio stated excitedly, as if the event had taken place a week ago instead of seventy-five years ago.

The Imperial Japanese Type 95 "Ha-Go" tank was no match for a Sherman. The Sherman not only blew the enemy tank apart but sent the

Japanese troops riding the tank into the air in different directions. Japanese infantry, witnessing what was happening to their tanks, began to fan out from behind the tanks that were racing across the airfield.

Emilio fired his M1 Garand into the enemy troops. Other Marines joined in as well. More Sherman tanks rushed up from the beach to join the fray, firing their cannons and .50 caliber bullets into the Japanese tanks and approaching troops. Marine bazooka teams chased after the Japanese tanks that were trying to weasel away from the Shermans.

"The Japanese tanks had no sense of direction, it seemed," said Emilio, describing the onslaught.

One tank remained aimlessly driving around the airfield. One Marine's motivation got the best of him and he ran out to take on the tank by himself. This was eighteen-year-old Harold Dixon. He was a personal friend of Emilio's. "I don't blame him. He was just doing what we were taught. We were instructed that if we shot out the tank's periscope, the driver would no longer be able to see."

Without the driver's seeing device, the Japanese Type 95 tank would be even more of a sitting duck. Harold Dixon fired rapidly with his M1 at the periscope, but he failed. He waited until the last minute in an attempt to jump away but was pulled under by the tank's tracks. Emilio's description of seeing Dixon's body still made him sick seventy-six years later. "He waited too long and the tank ran him right over. He looked like a piece of cardboard when it got done with him. . . . Ugh."

The view of Dixon's body being crushed had replayed in Emilio's mind so much that it had erased his recall of the later moments that transpired on the battlefield. He couldn't remember how the assault was stopped or when the last tank was destroyed, but he remembered how dreadful it was to cross the airfield the next morning when they went on the offensive. Many veterans' combat memories are like this. It is the fog of war.

"We were given the command [to] open fire towards the other side of the airfield. The whole company opened up on where we thought the Japs might be, then before you know it we sprinted across," Emilio said.

Although he was just a rifleman, Emilio was given two boxes of machine gun ammo to carry across the airfield. "I had to stop and play dead multiple times. Enemy bullets kept landing in front of me. I watched them hit the dirt in front of me. I could tell they were coming from an elevated position. The Japanese held all the high ground outside the airfield."

After playing dead and rising up three times, Emilio made it to a large tank trap on the other side of the airfield and dove in headfirst. The large man-made gulley had been dug by the Japanese to stall American tanks, but it worked as great cover for the Marines during their advance.

As Emilio slid down the slope of the tank trap he became frozen with horror. It was the closest he'd come to a Japanese soldier. However, this enemy soldier was beyond dead. "He was perfectly cut down the middle of his body. It looked like as if someone had performed surgery on him," was how Emilio described the grisly, puzzling sight.

The Japanese soldier's body had no arms and no legs, and the center of his body was opened, exposing his heart, lungs, and organs, as if he was purposely on display. "I feel like his own guys did it to him; it didn't appear to be caused by shrapnel, it was too perfect." The gruesome memory of the sight still leaves Emilio perplexed.

Climbing out of the ditch from hell, Emilio linked up with Able Company's lieutenant. "We entered a small administration building on the other side of the airfield; inside the building was a shower room the Japanese had been using."

As Emilio cleared the shower room, he spotted what appeared to be a small green puddle of water in the corner by the drain. "I didn't care that it was green, all I cared is that it was wet!" Emilio and his lieutenant began to fill their canteens with the old Japanese drain water. In that moment, Emilio felt justified in doing so. "All I could picture was some Jap cleaning his rump with this water, but you can't imagine what you will do when you're that thirsty," he said. "I just added a couple Halazone tablets to the water and drank away—something I would never do today, boy, I'll tell ya."

Halazone tablets were commonly distributed to U.S. troops during World War II to purify drinking water.

Nightfall set in on the airfield. Thousands of Japanese troops were still missing, and the only place they could be was in the cliffs and hills throughout Peleliu. U.S. intelligence had not discovered that some of the coral rock caves in Peleliu's mountainous region could hold up to five hundred Japanese soldiers at a time.

Once the airfield was secured, the 1st Marine Division was tasked with a clean-out mission that would be harder than its original objective. There would not be the extent of major banzai charges and suicide rituals that there had been on other island campaigns, but the Japanese were in Peleliu to stay, and they had the perfect defense network of natural caves and hills to their advantage.

Planes began to take off from Peleliu's captured runway. These flew a short distance, about five hundred feet, before unleashing napalm on the hills that had proved to be initially uncapturable. Thousands of Japanese occupied these coral cliffs, and they had plenty of ammunition. Flame was a brutal tactic, but a necessary weapon to defeat the enemy.

"Did you guys have a flamethrower in your company?" I asked.

Emilio shook his head in regret. "Oh, yes. Ugh. Now that's something you do not want to be up against. It is just the worst thing you can do to a person, is hit them with a flamethrower," Emilio said.

"Did you see it used?" I'd hardly completed the question before Emilio shot back a quick "Yes."

After a moment, he continued. "They would fry the Jap right there in the bunkers. Awful, awful thing."

A series of concrete bunkers was strewn throughout the island, reaching to the lower hillsides. Emilio's platoon crept up to a blockhouse bunker after it had been shelled, ready to have the company's flame-thrower released on it.

"A buddy of mine fixed his bayonet. He was going to stab the Japanese soldier if he came running out away from the flame. I didn't see the need for that kind of brutality. What for?" Emilio said, shaking his head in disgrace at the memory.

As the flamethrower released a burst of flame, sure enough a smoldering enemy soldier with his clothes still smoking came running out of the bunker entrance.

Emilio positioned himself in front of the other Marine and shot the Japanese soldier once, causing him to fall to the ground with his clothes still cooking. "The only reason I shot him is because I didn't want to see him bayoneted. He may be a Jap soldier, but he was still a soldier. After I killed him, what I often thought, years later, is he had a family, or parents. He didn't need to be stabbed to death."

Emilio was satisfied that he had found some sort of dignity in the hell that surrounded them. "Of course I couldn't just let him run away. He could kill another Marine the next day. As a soldier you have to do what you have to do, and that's the end of it." After all these years Emilio was still trying to make sense of the violent nature that had emerged within him at the age of nineteen. I could tell that our interview was becoming hard for him.

Not wanting to revisit the topic of killing, I asked my final uncomfortable question. It was a topic I'd learned much about from previous Marines: human war trophies.

"Did you ever take any gold teeth?" I asked. Emilio knew the question was coming. His answer was a swift "Nahhh."

He didn't understand why guys would do such a thing to another human, but he then told me about a demented game some Marines would partake in, an activity known as "burping." By then thousands of dead Japanese littered the island. Their bodies bloated in the island heat to the utmost extreme.

"Some of the guys were sick in the head. If they saw a dead Jap body that was bloated, they would step on them. The body would release a burrrrrrrrrrrp," Emilio said, laughing and shaking his head at the same time. I was happy to get a chuckle out of him, even if we were doing so reflecting on how twisted combat Marines could become.

By the third day of advancement, the Marines on Peleliu had suffered more casualties than during the entire Tarawa Campaign. The intricate defense systems embedded in the coral rock cliffs proved murderous for the 5th Marines.

"Our artillery had to be dragged up those cliffs. They fired howitzers at point-blank range into the openings of caves. It was easier to seal the caves shut, instead of trying to fight every Jap inside." Tanks that could get close enough to a cave would do the same. "The objective was to try to seal them shut, trapping hopefully hundreds of your enemy," said Emilio. "You just never knew where the other side of the tunnel came up."

Recalling the anxious fighting, he added, "You could be doing all this work to try to defeat one cave and the Japanese could just exit elsewhere along the cliffs and fight you from a new location. You could never tell where the enemy fire was coming from."

The casualties mounted for the 5th Marine Regiment. Japanese snipers were scoring their best shots, having the advantage of high ground. Tanks and infantry closed on the enemy. Tanks could bulldoze caves shut, while amtracs equipped with flamethrowers could toss flame further and higher than the portable ones on a Marine's back. This was new and terrible warfare for the 1st Marine Division. A campaign that was supposed to be less than a week long had now extended a whole month. Finally the Army's 81st Division came in to relieve the 1st Marine Division.

"Were you glad to hear you would finally be getting off Peleliu?" I already knew the answer to that question.

"Yeah. But it always burned me they never used that island for anything meaningful," Emilio replied sadly.

Most islands during the Pacific Campaign were ultimately used as airstrips for heavy bombers to attack Japan or other strategic locations. The Marines were always told that the island of Peleliu would be utilized by General Douglas MacArthur to invade the Philippines. In actuality, however, he would conduct his famous waltz in knee-deep water up to

Philippine soil before the Peleliu battle was even over. This was a hard blow to morale for the troops on Peleliu.

To add insult to injury, neither the U.S. Army Air Corps nor the Navy would ever use Peleliu for any major air operations. Many Marines viewed this as a waste of life and evidence that the island could have been bypassed. Nearly 1,300 Marines were killed in action on Peleliu, and another 5,000 or more were wounded. The mental scars alone were enough to haunt some veterans forever.

"There were no good memories there," Emilio concluded.

Emilio's war wasn't over yet. He still had to take part in the 1st Marine Division's next mission, the major Battle of Okinawa. "We expected enormous casualties on the day of landing on Okinawa, but it never happened. We marched through the north side of the island, but we had nothing to shoot at. I found one civilian woman in a cave. Her skin was black with fleas—and while trying to nurse a child on her nipple. I couldn't believe the flies on this woman, either. She was covered in insects," Emilio said, shaking his head.

The Okinawan civilians were petrified by the Marines. It had been false propaganda spread by the Japanese Army that had led the woman and child to live in a cave in a state of utter filth. Emilio's next memory was of his unit's push south. Here the 5th Marine Regiment would assemble on the Shuri line, one of the largest strongholds of the Japanese Army during World War II.

"On the first morning I was dug in on the Shuri line I was in a one-man foxhole when the Jap artillery came in. A shell landed just a few feet from my foxhole, but it was enough to send me flying in the air," Emilio explained, his surprise at the time still reflected on his face.

The enemy artillery barrage at first hit in front of his location. Japanese spotters then walked the shells right into Able Company's position. The explosion catapulted Emilio out of his fighting post, landing him a few feet away. He lost consciousness and suffered a severe concussion. He was covered with enough scrapes and scratches to earn his Purple Heart.

"From there a Navy corpsman evacuated me. I was in the field hospital for a week, and they shipped me back to the States eventually."

Emilio's war was finally over. He was shipped to a naval hospital in Idaho to recover from his injuries.

Like so many others, Emilio taught me something during this interaction. He was around the two hundredth World War II veteran I had met by this point. Across the board, every veteran I'd met who had served in the Pacific could never forgive the Japanese. These men still carried hate or distaste for them to this day. The feeling expressed itself in never buying a Japanese car, or, even more extreme, in boycotting their own division reunions on Saipan or Pearl Harbor because they learned that the Japanese veterans were invited.

Emilio shocked me when I asked if he would ever forgive the Japanese soldiers. "You know what? I may be an exception, but I would, and I do forgive them. I would forgive them personally if I had the chance. They were just soldiers, like me."

Perhaps he felt guilt for the beating the 1st Marine Division gave the Japanese, or maybe he was just being a good Christian. I am not sure. One thing I know is that I was proud to finally bond with the old breed.

CHAPTER THREE

Our Mary

"**W**ell, here goes nothing. . . . Tell my wife I love her!"

The golf instructors began to laugh. Their students had gone home for the day and they had a bet going on who could hit the first hole in one.

The group of colleagues continued to chuckle as one of the instructors practiced his swing. He'd bet one of his buddies that if he missed this shot he would walk home from Duke University. It was a comment insinuating that his wife would leave him for coming home late. The instructor's punch line was clearly meant to be humorous, but the words caught Ed Cottrell up short, and he did not share the laughter.

"Tell my wife I love her" was the last radio transmission his dear friend Ted Smith had sent before crashing his P-47 fighter plane into German soil on January 1, 1945.

It was the early 1970s now. Ed was a college golf instructor at Duke and had put the war behind him. However, as many veterans have found, no matter how successful you become in life, the war never leaves you. Ed worked with some of the best young golfers in the country. His

Ed Cottrell, 48th Fighter Group

students, many of whom became very successful, never forgot their mentor.

Most did not know that their teacher had fought in the skies over Belgium and Germany with the 493rd Fighter Squadron.

I had never heard of Ed Cottrell before my book signing at the Veterans History Museum of the Carolinas. It was there that our worlds collided. I had brought the rifle with me on the book tour and was unloading it from my car when a silver-haired man drove into the parking lot. He exited the car and opened the door for two elderly women. It was 100-year-old Ed. This was the summer of 2022, and despite his age he was in great shape. He'd not only driven himself to the museum but had brought along two female World War II veteran nurses.

I could hardly believe it when someone else in the parking lot told me that all three people in the car were World War II veterans. As I followed him into the museum, I couldn't wait to ask him to add his name to the rifle. I spoke with him before the presentation. He sounded amazing for his age. He still possessed his coach-like mentality, telling me what a great job I was doing and that I should be proud of myself.

Ed signed the rifle with intense pride, becoming the first fighter pilot to do so. The rifle represented not just infantrymen but the whole war and everyone who took part in it. After basic training, most airmen like Ed would never fire the rifle again, but his legacy was just as important and deserved to be etched on it forever.

I had to know more about this remarkable man driving women to my book signing as if he were going to the drive-in theater back in the day. Ed agreed to let me interview him. I knew at the time that I was only scratching the surface of this modern marvel.

Ed, being older when he entered the Army, had a different experience of indoctrination into military service. First of all, he was already in college when Pearl Harbor was attacked. He was older than the typical high school class of '44 veterans I was meeting.

"The first time I heard the sound of airplane engine was not in the military. As a sophomore in college, I was in a pilot training program flying Piper Cubs. I'd completed thirty hours and that was it. This was all before December 7, 1941."

Ed was destined to be a pilot. After the Japanese attack in Hawaii, he'd received a draft notice. He decided to pick his own branch of service before the government did it for him.

"I went with the Army Air Corps of course, it made most sense to me having already been training to fly," he explained.

"In February of 1943, nearly a thousand of us were sent to Miami Beach for basic training. We took over all the hotels along the water and made them into barracks for new recruits. That lasted a month, and I was off to Beloit, Wisconsin."

Newly trained men from the U.S. Army Air Corps took a series of tests while stationed at colleges around the country. Ed was given the ability to choose among three options for flying in the Air Corps: fighters, bombers, and transport planes. He chose fighters, followed by bombers and transport. "They didn't promise we would get our top choice," he told me.

Luckily, Ed was ordered to report for fighter pilot training at Luke Field in Arizona. Flying in the cockpit of an airplane wasn't new to Ed. He began his general and primary flight school with both the T-6 "Texan" and the P-40 fighter planes. His tested capabilities were enough for the U.S. Army to advance him from flight school to the next stage. He had proved he could fly fighter planes—but could he conduct air combat?

Training was not over. His next assignment was Wendover Field, Utah. It was here he would meet the last and final aerial beast that he would be assigned, the P-47 "Thunderbolt." "I had no idea what plane I would be flying; there were a few possibilities. When I saw the brand new P-47s lined up on the airfield in Utah, I was jumping for joy!"

There was no time to waste for the new pilots. Gunnery school, bombing courses, and combat maneuvers were still part of his final passage to becoming a legitimate U.S. Army fighter pilot. It was also May 1944, and unbeknownst to the newest pilots of the Air Corps, the invasion of France loomed.

Ed's first gunnery course was a blow to his confidence. "A T-6 plane would tow a large sock in the air. Kind of like the advertisements you often see in the sky while on a beach. Except this was our target."

While in midair, Ed would engage the flying target with eight .50 caliber machine guns, four on each wing. "We flew in formation. Each plane had different colored paint on our bullet tips. After engaging the target during flight, the plane towing the target would land. Each pilot could inspect to see if their rounds made positive contact with the target," he explained.

To Ed's frustration, the green paint he was assigned from his .50 cal rounds were hard to spot on the aerial target.

"If you continue to shoot like that you will be out of the P-47s in no time," one instructor snarled at him.

Ed took to air the next day and adjusted his lead on the target. After his shooting runs, he landed his P-47 and walked nervously over to the aircraft that was just beginning to land while towing the sock. A glorious feeling came over him. The banner was covered in green paint. He'd nailed it.

Next was one of the most important tasks for Thunderbolt pilots: bombing runs. "We would dive into the desert valleys dropping 500-pound bombs filled with water on giant haystacks. The haystacks would have circular targets on top of them. Fortunately I was much better at this from the beginning," Ed laughed. One after another the P-47s dove into the valleys of Utah dropping water-filled dummy bombs on targets. Over and over again the pilots repeated the runs until the process was second nature.

Training at Wendover Field became more intense when the rookie pilots had to combine all the above, but do it in formation. Flying as a team was key to the success of the predator-type missions they would be assigned in the future. They were tank hunters, vehicle killers, train destroyers, and serving as best friend to the infantry on the ground. "They told us that on every mission we will ever be on, we will be in close formation until we approach the target." The pilots became a cohesive group.

June 6, 1944, came. It would not only become one of the most famous days in history, but it also marked graduation day for Ed and the rest of the new P-47 aviators. There was no secret where these pilots would end up going. Immediately upon graduation it was off to New York, then embarkation for Europe. "All of us from Wendover stayed together after finishing our last course. We went from Utah all the way to France," Ed remembered.

While the men had passed the Army's most advanced fighter pilot school, they were still rookie pilots. Their uniforms were neatly pressed and clean. Their lieutenant bars shined as they debarked from their transport in Le Havre, France. They took their bags and loaded on to a truck. "We were trucked up to Calais, France. This was the new airfield for the 48th Fighter Group, which we were now members of," Ed recalled.

The pilots of the 48th Fighter Group were experienced. The group consisted of the 492nd, 493rd, and 494th Fighter Squadrons, which had been fighting the air war starting in England and then in Normandy. By the time Ed and the new pilots joined them it was September 1944. As they unloaded from the trucks to the air base in Cambrai, France, the pilots had just come back from flight. Their leather jackets were wrinkled, with bombs painted on the back of them. Their planes featured pinup girls painted on the side. Some had the markings of swastikas, enemy trucks, trains, and tanks that they had destroyed. The pilots were salty.

"Right from the get-go, all of us were assigned to a veteran pilot. We had to follow them around after they got back from each mission to find out how it went. We kept notes on what these pilots took away from each mission."

Ed was assigned to First Lieutenant George Pullis, an experienced pilot who had been with the squadron since its first days flying in England. Ed scribbled feverishly in his notepad as he followed Lieutenant Pullis back to his P-47. When he raised his head from jotting down his last note, he looked up and saw a sexy pinup model painted near the nose of the plane. The caption read *Our Mary*.

"When it's time this will be your plane," Pullis said, slapping the pinup model as if she were a real woman. *Our Mary* was a plane Ed could get used to. He felt this was what he'd been destined for since flying Piper Cubs as a sophomore in college.

A few days later *Our Mary* had her propeller roaring and Ed was in the cockpit, ready for his first aerial flight in the Second World War. "Our first flight out of Cambrai was to see how all the new guys flew in formation. There were twelve planes on each mission, the most experienced guy led the mission. Younger pilots flew on the wings. They took us up and gave us commands on how to fly in combat. Eventually they showed us the bomb line."

"What's a bomb line?" I asked. Nearly three hundred veterans had signed my rifle, and this was the first time I'd heard the term.

"It was the last recorded front line for friendly troops. All bombs should be dropped beyond the bomb line to not kill friendly forces. Any tanks around the bomb line had markings on top so we could distinguish them from German armor."

A few short weeks later the 48th Fighter Group was on the move. The 9th Army was advancing into Belgium, securing more runways that Ed's fighter group could use for takeoffs. The farther the U.S. Army moved towards Germany, the more it needed close and quick air cover to support it. The 48th Fighter Group now called a former German airfield in St. Trond, Belgium, home.

The senior pilots flew their planes to St. Trond, while the younger pilots trucked over with the rest of the Air Corps personnel. The enlisted men hopped off the trucks and assembled their tents not far from the airfield. The officers were trucked a mile farther to a schoolhouse, where they slept seven pilots to a room.

The next four months on this airfield would forever change the lives of the men in the 493rd Fighter Squadron. Ed's first combat mission was conducted from here. The men proved the P-47's worth in removing Nazis and their supplies from planet Earth. But by the end of the operations, Ed would find himself staring at multiple empty beds in his schoolhouse bunk room.

The airfield at St. Trond began to be developed into a complete base of operations. While old buildings on the airfield were occupied, the Army put up tents and other structures to operate the 48th Fighter Group. A burned-out B-17 and damaged B-24 were pushed into the center of the airfield. They were planes that had previously made emergency landings but would now serve as diversionary targets if the base came under attack. The 494th and 492nd Fighter Squadrons would take the north side of the airstrip, and the 493rd the southern side.

The new air base was up and operational within days. Ed and his two close roommates, Art Sommer and Ted Smith, were picked up in a Jeep from their living quarters and brought to the airfield. Their first flights over occupied enemy territory began, but the more experienced pilots led the formation.

It was finally time for those hunting missions Ed had heard about. Squadrons of P-47s roamed the sky in search of anything related to the German army. No truck, train, or anything without United States Army markings was safe.

"What was it like to pull the trigger on eight .50 cals all at once?" I asked. I assumed the feeling had been exhilarating but produced moral qualms. Many World War II veterans reminisced with regret about shooting guns and causing chaos. Ed began to smile ear to ear.

He seemed once again a twenty-one-year-old fighter pilot. It was evident that even seventy-seven years later the feeling of unleashing holy hell from the sky was as exciting as ever. Squeezing that trigger in combat for the first time was something he'd never forgotten.

"It feels just like you would think it would feel," Ed replied, his triumphant smile broadening. "If it was trucks we were strafing, you could see soldiers jumping out and running into woods before we went into a dive. They knew we were coming."

Ed and the others from his fighter squadron would take turns descending from the sky and onto their target, unleashing steel rain one formation at a time. Ed squeezed the trigger to his weapon system. Fifty caliber machine guns on each of his wings pumped rounds into the German column.

"You knew you were hitting the vehicles when smoke began to come from the engine and the trucks would halt," he continued. "Germans were running into the tree line to the left and right or diving on the side of the road."

His first mission was a success. The Germans attempted to return fire with small arms, but all American planes were accounted for and returned to St. Trond airfield. "When I returned to base I thought, 'That was easy, they didn't even shoot back.' When I walked around my plane I found six or seven bullet holes in it. I had no idea. Small arms fire had little effect on the P-47."

Ed, Art, and Ted safely parked their planes in the usual spot and went to their debrief. All three roommates waited for their Jeep to bring them back to their living quarters. Shoulder slapping and congratulations for completing their first combat mission were kept to a minimum. They knew the war was far from over.

"Our next target when we went back in the air was a train." This was one of the P-47 pilots' favorite targets, German locomotives. "Our fighter group would receive intel of trains in the open. The pilots would scramble to their planes and head towards the last known coordinates. One by one, formation by formation, the 493rd Fighter Squadron would drop out of the sky, turning enemy trains into twisted steel," he said. "The steam engines would erupt with a billow of dark smoke if you hit them right."

Another easy mission completed, or so it seemed to Ed. The members of the 493rd Fighter Squadron were living their best lives, attacking convoys and trains with little resistance from the ground. Any bombs that were not dropped during missions were released on the city of Aachen. "I don't know why, but we couldn't return with any bombs. We were always told to drop any ordnance before returning to St. Trond on Aachen. I did this a half a dozen times."

By early December, strategic missions were being assigned to the fighter group whose pilots had gained more combat flying time. Supporting the infantry was key, and the next mission would require a tactical approach, not just strafing trains hauling supplies. "Our destination was Jülich, Germany. Apparently the 9th Army was locked in stalemate with the enemy troops occupying the town there."

On December 7, 1944, Ed's morning briefing reported that members of the 29th Infantry Division were bogged down fighting the Germans. The only thing separating the two armies was a soccer field. "We were informed that one end of the soccer field was the Americans, and the other was the Germans."

The 29th Infantry Division needed close air support. This would be Ed's first time delivering a "danger close" bombing run. "When we approached the soccer field we came in low and released our bombs in the center of the field. This was known as skip bombing. Because of our speed and elevation, we could drop our bombs and watch them skip across the soccer field and into the German lines."

Thunderbolt after Thunderbolt came over at treetop level and released their 500-pound bombs onto the soccer field. First Art, then Ted, and finally Ed. Their bombs slammed into the dirt at high speed, tumbling rapidly into the tree line at the end of the soccer field. After soaring through the smoke, Ed looked back at the damage and saw clouds of dirt and flame arise from the tree line.

"Looks like good hits!" Art called out over the radio. "Everyone ok?" Ted Smith replied. All fighters were accounted for.

Upon returning to St. Trond, Ed's plane was surrounded by the aircraft maintainers as he parked in his usual spot. They appeared concerned that he might be hurt. "Little did I know, I had the most small arms bullet holes all over my plane yet. I had no idea, but that's just how close we were to the ground to perform that kind of bombing run." Ed spoke with a smile on his face, still astonished by his own accomplishment after seventy-seven years.

"We must have did a pretty good job because the commander of the 9th Army called over to our airbase to commend us on our success. They finally were able to take the town of Jülich!"

Ten days later, word was moving fast through the 48th Fighter Group that a major German offensive was taking place. "We were called in for an emergency meeting, and they explained that units were being overrun all over the place. They told us to be prepared for anything because we were the closest airfield to support the units under siege."

It was by now no secret to the airmen in St. Trond that something major was going on regarding enemy movement. Dire calls for air support rang through the 48th Fighter Group communication center. Waves of enemy tanks and vehicles had pierced the American lines all over the Ardennes region of Belgium. "We were told that if the Germans were successful in breaking through and reaching our airfield we would be prisoners of war. The most senior pilots would fly the planes back towards France and we would have to surrender," Ed recalled.

The German counteroffensive, also known as the Battle of the Bulge, was conducted using the Army Air Corp's weakness, poor weather. While the heavy bombers of the 8th Air Force that operated at high elevations were useless, fighter planes could sometimes get away with operating in poor weather thanks to their maneuverability, speed, and other flight characteristics at low level.

After the emergency briefing, the fighter pilots were put in the sky that very day. On December 17, 1944, Ed's mission was to scan the area between Koblenz and Cologne. "We were told there were Tiger tanks on the move in this vicinity."

The P-47s took off from their airstrip. For forty-five minutes to an hour they buzzed through cloud cover at the highest elevation possible. The P-47 only had two and a half hours of fuel, so a belly tank with extra gas was necessary for this mission.

"We got towards Cologne; we dropped our belly tanks in the woods." The squadron leader gave the command for the planes to drop down to three hundred feet. Enemy tanks had been spotted in a clearing.

As the P-47s lowered themselves through the clouds they found themselves on the outskirts of Cologne. "As my formation began to dive, the flak started." Anti-aircraft guns in place to protect the enemy armor rattled Ed's plane. Twelve planes, split in three formations of four, dived towards the Tiger tanks.

The Cologne area was heavily populated and defended. It was open season on the American fighter planes. "I could see three to four tanks located in a clearing in the woods. I dropped a thousand-pound bomb and began to climb back into the sky."

"*Bandits! One o' clock!*" someone screamed over the radio.

As Ed was pulling *Our Mary* out of her dive, a German Me-109 was descending on him.

"When I saw the plane I didn't have time to think. I could see his 20 mm cannons blinking. He was firing right at me."

Ed was staring right into death. His plane jolted violently, and oil exploded all over his windshield. He was hit, and blinded. The radio shrieked with orders and with pilots yelling out locations of more inbound enemy fighter planes. The Allied squadron had been ambushed by eight Me-109s. The dogfight was on.

Ed threw back the canopy of his cockpit in order to see. His squadron commander noticed he was disoriented and told him over the radio to turn ninety degrees and head west.

Ed's engine was chugging. He was unsure if he could make it back to Belgium, but he turned to 270 on his compass and attempted to do so. "I can't bail out because my plane isn't high enough, nor will it gain altitude."

Our Mary was a sitting duck. Her attempts to limp home made her easy prey for the Me-109s. As Ed desperately sputtered in the sky, frantic to escape the onslaught, his roommate Art Sommer had already slammed his plane into Germany territory. Unbeknownst to Ed until later, Art had been shot down in the initial ambush as part of the third foursome that attacked the tanks.

As Ed fought to control his failing aircraft, Art was being dragged from his cockpit by SS troopers on the ground. He was then shot in the back of the head and buried in his flight suit in a shallow grave next to a small church. The SS removed his dog tag to keep it for their own records.

Ed would not learn of this for seventy-seven years. At this moment his only concern was to get back to St. Trond. His prayers seemed to go unanswered as a German pilot swept in on *Our Mary*. Then another enemy plane did the same. They both followed, and to Ed the end seemed near.

"The planes assembled behind me, then they crisscrossed with one another. They usually did this before the final kill." Ed said goodbye to his pregnant wife in his mind, but the Me-109s did not blast him out of the sky. As the seconds turned into minutes it appeared as if they were escorting him.

"One of the German pilots pulled up alongside of me. He made the "A-OK" symbol with his hands. They followed for a little longer, then peeled off. By this time I knew I must have been over friendly skies," Ed recalled.

To this day that Ed was sharing his story with me, he wondered why his life had been spared. "I would do anything to meet those pilots and thank them today. They could have easily shot me down. If they wanted to save ammo they still could have forced me down. They could have flown on top of me and forced me right down to the ground, but they didn't do that either!" He spoke with relief he still felt.

Just before *Our Mary* made it to the runway in St. Trond, Belgium, her engine stalled for the final time. Ed had hydraulics but no power. He was able to "dead-stick" the plane and land her before it was too late.

On the runway he climbed out of the plane and immediately kissed the ground. It was during the debrief that they realized one Thunderbolt was unaccounted for, Art Sommer's. He was classified as missing in action, and they hoped he had been taken prisoner. Little did anyone know his true fate.

Ed was shaken up. He had been scared half to death by his experience—rightfully so. He found himself staring at the empty bed of Art Sommer as he recalled what had just happened. The next morning there was a knock on the door. It was Major Stanley Latiolais, someone Ed admired and thought one hell of a pilot.

"I looked up to him. He, too, was shaken up from the dogfight the day before. He'd had a bullet enter his cockpit and graze his head," Ed recounted.

"We are going back in the air today," Major Latiolais said. "It's not a mission, but only a little hop, a reconnaissance around the airfield. We need to shake off the jitters and not be afraid to fly again." On December 18, just one day after they had both been nearly killed, Major Latiolais and Ed were buzzing around St. Trond. The enemy must not be allowed to win the battle of the mind.

Ed landed his plane before the weather got worse. This little buzz helped him tremendously in overcoming the nervousness from the day before. The major's remedy proved to be beneficial, and he was lucky to get the flight in. The next eight days no planes were able to take off from St. Trond. It was the worst winter in many years for that area of Belgium.

Everyone on the airfield was instructed to burn personal letters and effects. "All we were allowed to keep were our dog tags. This was a plan in play if the German army had overrun the airfield. Every day we listened to intelligence officers on what the infantry divisions were reporting. We were waiting each day [to see] if the infantry units were able to hold the line."

On January 1, the 48th Fighter Group was cleared to fly again. The 493rd Fighter Squadron was given a mission, but Ed and three other P-47s were assigned to "runway alert." Ed tipped his hat to Ted Smith, one of his remaining roommates, telling him "Happy New Year," and proceeded to watch Ted take off.

"Four of us had to stay back with our engines going at the end of the runway. We were kind of a quick reaction force to defend the base if necessary."

Ed's assignment was to stand by, twiddling his thumbs, waiting at the end of the runway for his squadron to return. Due to the weather, it had been nearly ten days since many of the men had seen action.

The boredom ended abruptly. The airmen on St. Trond were taken by surprise when seven Focke-Wulf 190s came soaring in at ground level. Ed was sitting in the front seat of his plane, feeling frozen. If he tried to take off he would be eliminated. He'd already played this game once.

"Our anti-aircraft guns were going crazy," he said. The German planes made a second pass over the Allied airfield, blazing away at the burned-out B-17 and B-24 in the middle of the airfield. The skeleton aircraft had proved their worth as distraction tools.

"On the third pass, our anti-aircraft gunners were scoring amazing hits and sending multiple Focke-Wulf 190s smoking down to earth," Ed remembered.

It was time for Ed to get better cover. Sitting in his taxied P-47, he was a big shiny target. "I saw another German plane coming in. I jumped out of the cockpit and into a ditch at the end of the runway. A quad .50 caliber anti-aircraft gun emptied what seemed like hundreds of bullets into the Focke-Wulf 190. The pilot never dropped his belly tank."

As Ed slid into the ditch the enemy plane slammed into the concrete runway. Ed raised his head to watch as the German pilot was ejected from the cockpit and rolled thirty feet away. Mechanics, pilots, and air crew ran over to the German's lifeless body.

"As I ran up to him, I would see a hole right through the middle of his head. He'd been shot through the skull. He must have been sixteen or seventeen. Which explained why he didn't drop his belly tank. This pilot had little to no experience."

Anti-aircraft gunners shot down four of the seven German aircraft. St. Trond was not the only base attacked that day. What remained of the entire Luftwaffe struck every Allied airfield reachable from the fatherland. This attempted blitz from the sky ended what was left of the Nazi air force.

The attack on St. Trond's airfield was a mixed success for the Germans. They had destroyed ten aircraft and damaged thirty, but no U.S. service members had been killed on the airfield. Enlisted men on the base were also able to capture one German pilot alive.

The returning squadron returned to a fiery scene at St. Trond. With them they brought bad news. Lieutenant Ted Smith had been shot down flying low back in Germany. Ed was down another roommate. Yet Ted's death hit him differently. Ted Smith had been with Ed since training in the United States. The pair had come to Europe together.

The other pilots detailed Ted's last moments to Ed. He had been hit by flak and was unable to bail. He went down fast and his last words over the radio were "Tell my wife I love her, goodbye!" He slammed into the ground and was killed on impact, according to future reports.

Ed was assigned to go through Ted's belongings before mailing them home. "I had to check all of his personal effects before they were sent back to his family. I was instructed to remove anything top secret or anything that shouldn't be sent home to his wife. This was very hard for me." In the present, Ed became teary-eyed. Nearly one hundred years old, he was still filled with sorrow as he recalled rummaging through Ted Smith's personal gear. Ted was gone.

After the attack on New Year's Day, the war became a blur for Lieutenant Ed Cottrell. As the 9th Army advanced into Germany, so did the 9th Air Force. Ed wouldn't see a large airbase again until the end of the war, in Nuremberg. "After we left St. Trond, we leapfrogged through Germany, taking off and landing only on metal strips," Ed remembers.

The strips could be thrown down in villages or clearings nearby. They were not long, just long enough to land a P-47 and take off again. The pilots would seek shelter in whatever abandoned homes were nearest to their temporary landing strips. "We would eat chickens, eggs, whatever we could find. A few days later the strip would be rolled up and we would be on to the next that was put down."

As Ed followed the Allied advance into Germany, the ground fire was low to nonexistent. His last duty station would be in Nuremberg, Germany. *Our Mary* had served her purpose, and Ed was getting a new plane. This time, it was up to him to name it.

"My wife sent me a letter, telling me I was now the father of a beautiful baby girl. She sent me the little footprints of my firstborn daughter Carol. I decided to copy the footprints onto the nose of the plane. I named this new Thunderbolt *Feet of Heaven*."

Ed retuned home and put the war behind him. The names and memory of Art Sommer and Ted Smith were not gone, but they were placed on hold in his recollections. He went on to have two daughters, a wife of seven decades, and to hold various teaching and athletic jobs at various colleges, including West Chester and Duke University.

As our interview wound down, it was time to ask Ed my golden question. "Would you ever go back?" I had to blurt it out. He was ninety-nine years old, but looked as if he were in his late seventies. I found that I had bonded with Ed as much as with the infantrymen I had met.

"I have been back to Europe, but not to St. Trond," he responded. The light bulb over my head began flashing. A month later, Ed and I—along with several other veterans—were heading to Belgium. While in Belgium, I told local historian Reg Jans about Ed's experiences. Reg was familiar with the St. Trond airfield. It was still an active runway.

Reg had contacted the commander of the airport, a Belgian air force officer. After hearing whom we had as a guest, the commander allowed us access to the entire runway. Ed was our guide. Ed led us around the airport. He was familiar with and remembered everything. Yet something was off.

"We have to go over there." Ed pointed to a large mound of dirt and grass. "I would take off just beyond that mound."

The Belgian officer assured us there was no access over the dirt mound and nothing on the other side. Ed was adamant. We loaded back in the cars and diverted around a large wooded area of the airport to get to the other side of the mound of dirt. Sure enough, on the other side there was a small section of runway left. This runway portion was old, from the 1940s. Grass was now protruding through cracks in the cement.

Ed jumped out of the van. "Here, this is what I remember. I would park my P-47 right here," he said, out of breath from the exertion. The near one-hundred-year-old man was getting quite excited. He stopped dead in his tracks on the section of runway and pointed to the ground. "Here is where I would park *Our Mary*, right here."

I couldn't believe what I was seeing. The salty fighter pilot was back at St. Trond seventy-five years later. And Ed wasn't finished. The group continued to trail him as he brought us to the ditch still dug in the earth at the end of the runway.

"This is the ditch I dived in when we were attacked. The Focke-Wulf 190 dived in on us from over here. The pilot landed over here with a hole in his head." Ed pointed in many different directions, reliving New Year's Day 1945.

I took a stone and smashed a piece of the runway off for him. This was a souvenir he should go home with. Soon we were back in the van and heading to one last destination I'd kept secret—the grave of Ted Smith.

Ted's body had been recovered from his crash site in 1945. He was ultimately buried in Holland at the Netherlands American Cemetery in Margraten. When we arrived, Ed and the other World War II veterans walked around in astonishment at the beauty of the cemetery. In my experience, it has always amazed veterans to see that these cemeteries in Europe were better kept than cemeteries in the United States.

I led Ed down a row of graves, pretending I was locating fallen soldiers from Massachusetts. I was well aware that halfway down the row was his former roommate, Ted Smith. Ed studied each grave. He was making comments to himself about each man. "Here's one from the 17th Airborne!" he said, while signaling to veteran Bob White, who was also with us.

Suddenly Ed stopped in his tracks. "Oh," he said, as if he'd stepped on a cactus.

Ed rushed to the grave. It read "Theodore Smith 48th Fighter Group." He gripped the top of the headstone and fell to one knee. He was crying. He held his head down as he lost control of his emotions. He kept one hand on the grave the whole time as he cried. He was remembering his brave roommate.

Ted Smith was a person Ed had never forgotten but had put in the back of his mind as Ed went on to conquer life. Now the two had met again. Ed collected himself and immediately reached for his daughter, Susan, who was along with us. The pair had a moment. After he introduced his daughter to Ted, it was my turn.

"Come here, you!" Ed said, grabbing me with a hug. "Thank you for this."

"You don't ever have to thank me, brother. This is what we do for one another," I replied, trying not to choke up. The experience at the Margraten Cemetery seemed similar to the graveyard scene in *Saving Private Ryan*—except this one was the real deal.

As we boarded the van to leave, it began to rain. We were cold and wet. I glanced over at Ed. He was still looking at all the graves in the distance as we departed. I felt that accomplishing this task was one of the best moments in my life—because I was sure it was one of the best moments in Ed's life, as well.

CHAPTER FOUR

The Lobster Man

It was a warm and sunny day in Gloucester, Massachusetts. The city is by the sea, and known for its fishing history. To say the downtown area was vibrant this day would be an understatement. As on typical summer days, there were hardly any parking spots. Fishing vessels, tugboats, and private ships were coming and going in the harbor. I closed the door of my pickup truck and removed the carrying case of the rifle.

I was standing outside of a restaurant known as Gloucester House. It was once a well-known restaurant in the area, serving a range of fresh seafood and other American food. I walked into the entrance of the restaurant and approached the entry station. A hostess behind it asked, "How many people?" with a stack of menus in her hand.

"Actually, I am not here to eat," I said, unsure how to explain my purpose. "I am here to see Mr. Linquata."

"Oh, right this way," she replied, and led me through the busy restaurant interior and into a private room. "I'll let him know you're here."

As I surveyed the walls of the room, I could see Mike Linquata's medals and a brief history of his life displayed in frames. He was the

Michael Linquata, 35th Infantry Division

ninety-six-year-old proprietor of Gloucester House restaurant, which he'd owned since 1958. Before I could read the citations hanging on the wall, the door opened and in came a silver-haired man with glasses. He was wearing a black button-up shirt and still dressed as if he were running the whole seafood operation.

"Thank you for agreeing to meet with me," I stated, extending my hand. He shook my hand, then sat down, obviously considering what to make of me. I had just brought a rifle into his restaurant, after all. I decided to break the ice using something he and I had in common. "So Mike, we're both alumni of Suffolk University!" I said excitedly.

His eyes lit up. "You went to Suffolk? I graduated in 1950 with a business degree, and I am still a trustee there," he replied.

Our connection to Suffolk University got our interview on the right track. "I helped create the mascot of the school, ya know," he added.

"Really?" I exclaimed, remembering the Suffolk University ram. Mike began to share a hilarious story of when he was tasked with picking up a live ram two hours away from Boston in 1949. "This was before Eisenhower was president, so there was no real highway then. It took us forever to get to Attleboro, Massachusetts. The only farmer we found who was willing to part with a ram was living down there." According to Mike, the ram had stunk, was filthy, and was very irritated. "A bunch of my friends had to wrestle it into the auditorium when we got back to the campus," he said, chuckling at the memory.

As much as I found the history of my old college fascinating, I wanted to dive into Mike's military experience. I slid in a question to get this started. "Did you always want to serve in the military? Or did you feel compelled because of the attack on Pearl Harbor?"

"I came from a patriotic town. We were raised very patriotic. I remember seeing the last Civil War veteran marching in our parade. He was probably the age I am now." Mike painted the bigger picture for me. Joining the Army had seemed as natural as going to high school back then.

In Massachusetts, most twelfth graders who would have been class of 1944 had their senior year cut in half. It was an agreement between the school committee and the government that the students would be joining the military. In January of 1944, Mike Linquata found himself with nearly one thousand other eighteen-year-old kids of all shapes and sizes in an industrial garage in Boston. Everyone was stripped down to his socks and underwear. They were undergoing physical and mental examinations before their entry into the service.

Mike stood in line with other kids from Gloucester. His friend Jack Curley stood behind him. One of their first examinations was a color chart. "Oh shit!" Mike exclaimed. "What's the matter?" Jack asked. "I can't see the numbers we are about to read. I am color-blind," he whispered. As Mike approached the table to read the numbers of the color chart, Jack whispered from behind the correct answers. He passed the test and was on to the next examination.

Being color-blind was not Mike's only hurdle. He was nearsighted, and even Jack couldn't save him on the next test. But being nearsighted was not enough to disqualify you from service. It just meant you would be placed in a non-infantry role or one that did not require decent eyesight. "About a month later I was shipped to Rockford, Illinois, Camp Grant. It was medical camp, to teach new draftees to become medics. That was their solution to my vision issues."

"Did you want to be a medic?" I asked. It had always been important to me to find out if a World War II veteran enjoyed the job he was assigned.

"I didn't mind it, but what bothered me was I was stuck with conscientious objectors, Seventh-day Adventists, and other religious soldiers who did not want to fight. That's who the Army placed as medics," Mike said, a note of regret in his voice. "I was going to fight if need be."

Not long after completing training as a medic, Mike and the others were rushed to Europe aboard the RMS *Queen Mary*. "There were thirteen thousand of us on the ship. When we docked in Scotland we had to wait. We had no idea Winston Churchill was on the vessel with us. He walked off first and on the dock he gave us the 'V' for victory hand sign. All the guys on the ship gave him a great big cheer!"

Thousands of replacement troops were placed on trains and pushed south towards England. Several weeks went by while the men awaited their units. "A notice went around that if we gave a pint of blood we would be granted a twenty-four-hour pass to London. Naturally, I volunteered to give a pint of blood."

Mike and another soldier excited to see London hailed a cab from their base. "Can you show us around London?" Mike asked eagerly. The cab driver seem unamused, but continued to drive. He traveled several miles, then stopped.

"Here, get out and take a look," the driver said.

Mike and the other soldier looked around. For fifteen blocks in each direction was nothing but waist-high rubble of what used to be a neighborhood. "It wasn't until then did I realize the hell England had been facing with the unmanned V-2 rockets," Mike said.

On Thanksgiving Day 1944, Mike's transport ship left Dover, England, bringing him to Le Havre, France. "I ate sardines and tomato sauce in the bottom of the ship. That was my Thanksgiving dinner."

The replacements were marched into Camp Lucky Strike, where they received more inoculations and equipment. It was here Private Mike Linquata was assigned to the 35th Infantry Division. "They placed us in six-by-six trucks and brought us towards the front lines. This was early December of 1944 now. We were being rushed right up!"

The chilly winter wind began to nip at Mike in the back of the truck. The distant sound of artillery fire grew nearer. He was being introduced to the elements of combat.

"We were not far from the Luxembourg border. I was rushed off the truck and placed into the battalion aid station. Walking through the aid station I was clumsy and bumped into the outstretched arm of a soldier on a stretcher. I apologized to him, but realized he was long dead."

"Move him outside onto the sidewalk," a surgeon told Mike. It was the first time he had seen a dead American soldier. He and another soldier picked up the stretcher and put him in line with the rest of the bodies waiting on the side of the road to be picked up by graves registration.

While Mike and another aidman placed the fallen soldier on the sidewalk, incoming German artillery struck the surrounding area. "One shell hit a barn across the street from us. Heavy shingles from the roof began to rain down to the ground. If any one of us were under it [they] would have cut us to pieces."

Multiple weeks went by while Mike worked at the battalion aid station, exposed to the dead and dying. His job consisted of assorted tasks such as stacking the dead for pickup, moving stretchers, and cleaning up old bandages. Once while relocating a dead soldier outside for graves registration to pick up, he noticed something gruesome.

"The man had the back of his head shot off. His brains were right next to him, as if they just fell out. So I collected his brains, put them back inside his head, then wrapped his head with a bandage. I placed a helmet back on him too. I don't know why I did it. I just wanted him to be all in one piece for his burial."

As Mike continued to navigate life as an aidman, he and the surgeons and doctors worked day and night, always under threat of being shelled. As the war grew closer, duty in the battalion aid station ceased, and Mike was assigned directly to a frontline rifle company. "The time came where I was to be reassigned. They needed a medic for Company D, of the 134th Regiment. I was happy to assist them," Mike recalled cheerfully.

This was what he had wanted from the beginning—to be on the front lines with the men, assigned to a specific platoon where he could give direct care to the soldiers fighting. Little did the new medic know, the Battle of the Bulge was about to commence, and he was about to go from a simple stretcher bearer to a mass casualty combat "doc."

On December 29, Mike's company was assigned to make its way towards Marvie, Belgium. It was time to reinforce adjacent units such as the 101st Airborne, 10th Armored Division, and those who had been besieged throughout the Christmas holiday. He was now the medic for 2nd Platoon, D Company. His orders were to always be the last man in a squad formation during an advance.

"Company B was ahead of us. We received orders to link up with them for whatever reason, when suddenly we came under fire." German forces occupied a section of the thick Ardennes Forest to Company D's right flank. From across a road they opened fire with burp guns on Mike's platoon. The platoon huddled in a ditch, waiting for the right time to make its next move.

"I never liked being in the rear of the platoon, because I never knew what was going on, so I decided to crawl up to see what the holdup was," said Mike. As he crawled on his knees and elbows to the front of the pinned-down platoon, he saw that men of his platoon had taken a German prisoner.

"Apparently this German soldier walked across the street to locate us, and we trained every gun on him. He had no choice but to give up." Mike asked the other soldiers if they had searched him well. They replied that they had.

"For some reason I didn't trust that our guys had given him a good pat down, and sure enough I found a pistol on him." Mike kept the pistol as a souvenir. The men of 2nd Platoon stealthily made their way back from the enemy encounter and towards friendly lines, bringing with them their new German captive.

"They immediately put him on the hood of a Jeep and began to parade him around like a trophy," Mike said. The victory was short-lived. The new year had arrived, and orders were straightforward and brutal. All new units who were helping to break the bulge were to locate and

THE LOBSTER MAN   45

eliminate any remaining enemy in the surrounding Bastogne area, including its villages, suburbs, and woods. Now that reinforcements, supplies, and air support were flowing, the United States military was attempting to turn the Ardennes defensive into their own counteroffensive.

Company D was occupying a small hill outside the town of Marvie when they observed two German snipers wearing white camouflage making a dash for the woods. "I assumed they were snipers because they had longer rifles than usual, with scopes," Mike said. "They were perhaps the same men who ambushed us early on."

Mike's platoon opened up with a machine gun on the pair of snipers as they were attempting to relocate themselves in the tree line. The snow was roughly a foot deep, and the enemy soldiers were not able to run fast. One German was struck in the leg, and his white uniform began to turn red as blood spurted from his leg. The enemy sniper limped into the woods with a blood trail following him. Mike spoke insistently to his platoon sergeant. "Let's go get him!"

"Yeah right, so his buddy can lie in wait for us," the platoon sergeant replied. "We stay put here."

Mike saw his point, but they were not spared from the danger in any case. Enemy mortar rounds rained onto the platoon. No sooner did the first rounds hit than cries for a medic rang out. Mike ran over to attend to two men, both hit seriously. One soldier had both legs below the knee blown off. Mike jumped on the man and applied tourniquets to his legs along with plenty of bandages. As the injured soldier squirmed, Mike put all his body weight on the man's legs. "I had to sit on his legs because he kept digging his nubs into the ground, causing the bandages to come off."

"Once that soldier was situated, I focused on the soldier next to him. He was thrashing on the ground in pain. I could tell by his hair who he was. He was the most handsome man in the company. I remember him distinctly because he was always combing his hair back, had a great jawline, and was an all-around great-looking guy. He was someone you could tell the ladies would just flock to. But now, shrapnel from the mortar round tore his nose off, part of his jaw, and a significant amount of his face. Just like that, he lost all of his handsomeness. No plastic surgery even with today's technology would have been able to make this guy look normal again," Mike recalled sadly.

Mike did what he could, wrapping bandages around the man's head and face. "Don't cover my nose, I can't breathe!" the soldier screamed. Mike looked at me and shook his head sadly as he remembered this. "I am not sure what he was talking about, because I couldn't locate a nose if there was one."

Mike hit each man with morphine and began the process of rushing them back to the battalion aid station. "I think about these men often. I wonder what kind of lives they led after the war. Maybe they just were not destined to live normal lives. I don't see how they could hold a job. They were both great young men."

The next day the men of Company D left their elevated position and made their way into the woods. Orders had been given to root out the Germans from their positions in the thickly entrenched tree line. "We made it about a mile or two into the woods, and our company major had a map. He was pointing us where to go when we reached a clearing in the woods. That's when all hell broke loose," Mike explained.

The German defenders opened with every gun they had. Tracers bounced off trees while bullets impacted the snow around the men, who huddled together for safety. "The major ran in the other direction and left us directionless," Mike recalled with distaste.

Mike ran past several soldiers paralyzed with fear and unable to move. They had been back far enough to avoid being killed. Mike looked at them and ran farther into the fray to look for more injured soldiers. "I was informed there was another soldier closer to the front of the patrol who was hiding behind a log. He was so shell-shocked he couldn't move. He was actually from Boston."

Mike scurried up to the clearing where he could see the soldier. The man was frozen with fear. He ran up to the soldier, put his arm around him, and guided him back to the rear of the company. "I did this a few times with others, but now the order was to stay put and fight," he told me.

The battle continued to rage in the woods between the men of the 35th Division and their foes of the 167th Volksgrenadier Division. The snow seemed deeper in the woods, with a layer of ice underneath. If soldiers were lucky enough to get a footing, it would still be impossible to dig in. Temperatures continued to plummet into the single digits. Mike watched as his platoon's weapons began to malfunction and freeze. American guns soon became quiet.

"I was lying next to a rifleman from my platoon. The M1 Garand seemed to be the only weapon still working. Unbeknownst to me, there was a German soldier advancing on us. My buddy swung the rifle around my head and killed the German solder. The burst of rifle fire ruptured my eardrum. That's how close he took the shot from my head." Pus would flow from Mike's ear for the remainder of the war.

Company D was left leaderless. With weapon systems down, the casualties mounted. Mike darted between the wounded men, searching for those who were injured the worst. The more blood they lost, the greater the chance they would freeze to death. The walking wounded were directed out of the woods. This still left over twenty men lying in the wooded area too hurt to be able to self-evacuate.

"One of the company commanders from Company C found us. The captain was very brave for seeking us out. He informed us that the battalion was giving us the order to fall back. He told me and two other medics to stay back with the wounded who could not walk."

Mike was now left with twenty wounded men. This included his own sergeant, down with a bad stomach wound. Sergeant Babcock asked him what to do, as Mike recalls. "Here was this sergeant—he was three to four years older than me—asking a private what to do. I told him to pray, make his peace with God, because I didn't see how he could survive the night."

Mike scrambled from patient to patient getting an idea of what their exact injuries were. The men were too badly wounded to evacuate, but was there a point to their suffering and dying slowly? Was there a possibility of surrendering the wounded and himself to the Germans in hope these men might live? Mike battled with these thoughts as he rocked back and forth to keep warm.

He hesitated to mention these ideas to the other medics, as the plan seemed absurd. But the groans of the wounded men grew louder. The cries continued, and some GIs were slipping in and out of consciousness. As sundown neared, the thought of waking up with twenty frozen corpses in the morning sat uneasily with this nineteen-year-old medic, who now had the weight of the world on his shoulders.

"You think you could surrender the men?" Mike blurted out to one of the senior medics.

"Me? No way."

The other medic replied, "Someone's gotta do it."

With confidence Mike ran to each of the soldiers clinging to his life. He gathered opinions on the idea of surrendering to the enemy. The injured American soldiers all agreed. Mike began to pray.

He said his last prayer while gazing over the clearing into German territory. "I prayed they wouldn't just tear me to pieces with machine gun fire," he said. After making his peace with God, Mike raised his hands and began to walk away from the American casualty collection point, deeper into enemy territory.

As he crept through the woods he couldn't believe what he was seeing. "There were between fifty to one hundred German corpses strewn throughout. Most were frozen stiff, like pieces of wood. These are not made-up numbers," Mike assured me. "I know what I saw, and there were that many of them dead from our battle."

After he passed the German bodies, the terrain began to incline. Mike seemed to enter what can only be described as an out-of-body experience. His voice cracked as explained the sensation to me. "I could see myself walking up the hill, it was my own spirit watching me."

I paused the interview momentarily to think about the immense responsibility the young medic had been under. The pressure had brought on a spiritual upheaval. This experience was something most people couldn't even imagine.

Mike ascended the hill further. Then his heart sank. Two German tanks were pointing their massive guns at him. "If they had just pushed one button I would have disappeared. They had both cannons pointed at me." The Germans swarmed Mike. They searched him and began yelling at him in German. Neither Mike nor the German soldiers could understand one another due to the language barrier.

The first line of Germans grew frustrated with him. They were unable to understand his request. They sent him further into their lines until finally he met a German officer. "The officer was dressed sharply, almost as if he was ready for a parade. We certainly didn't have uniforms like this guy in combat. He didn't know English either, but he understood my sign language, that I had twenty wounded men ready to surrender."

A squad of Germans was sent to follow Mike back to the American position. He called out to the wounded before crossing back over the clearing. "Okay, boys, I'm coming back with some German friends. Everybody just keep their hands visible where they can see them, don't hold any guns, and we shouldn't have any problems!"

As soon as the Germans made their way across the clearing and into the American side of the woods they began to snatch the rings and wrist-watches off the wounded soldiers. Mike began to jump up and down in anger. "*Nein*! *Nein*! *Nein*! Geneva Convention, Geneva Convention!" he yelled.

"They must have understood me, because they stopped stripping our guys for souvenirs after that," Mike said. The Germans were not interested in whether the American soldiers could walk. They were not there to help but to accept the Americans' surrender. "If one of the guys had an injured left leg, and another an injured right leg, I would tie two of their good legs together so they could help one another walk," Mike said.

Mike rallied those who could to help all the men to the German lines. From there they were escorted by their captors into a large barn. "The barn was being used to hold other American prisoners," said Mike. The men began limping into the barn. Upon entering the barn Mike ran into Captain Denney from Company C, the man who had given him orders to stay put with the wounded. He too had been captured, along with those who were originally able to escape the clearing.

"You're lucky to be alive," the captain told Mike. "They executed six of my men with bullets to the head." Mike stood back, imagining the horror. Why would they kill the captain's men and not his? He never found the answer.

Thus began the long march. Hundreds of Americans from various units in the Battle of the Bulge were put in formation and hustled away. "We arrived at a train terminal. They stuck ninety of us in a boxcar. The car could maybe fit forty men. We were slammed in there and the Germans threw three ounces of cheese on the floor."

The train doors shut and did not open until three to four days later. When it finally did open, men fell out and began to urinate and defecate outside the train. Others ran to whatever puddle they could find and drank from it. "We had no taste buds, we could have been drinking puddles of piss for all we knew." Mike described the scene with a note of the desperation he had felt still in his voice. His story was becoming harder for him to remember and relive.

The men had reached the gates of Stalag IX-B, also known as "Bad Orb," named for the town in Germany where it was located. The camp had one of the worst reputations of all the German-run prisoner-of-war camps, primarily due to overcrowding. "It was a hellhole. It wasn't just a POW camp, it was no different than a Jewish concentration camp, as far as conditions go.

"We had no toilets. We all had to go to the bathroom in a hole in the floor. One hundred and fifty men on each side of the building sharing one big hole. We had no beds, no clothes, no heat. We hardly had water. There was a small stream of water that three hundred of us had to share, and we all caught dysentery because of it."

There were also bug infestations. "We were covered in lice the size of small grains of rice. The bugs were constant, and gave us trouble when sleeping because they were biting us all the time."

At night there was no visibility inside the makeshift barracks. Men attempting to use the bathroom would trip over men sleeping on the floors. There simply was no comfort at Bad Orb. "I learned after returning home that a boy from Gloucester died there. He was there longer than I was. He most likely died from malnourishment."

Mike swallowed hard. It made him emotional to think about another kid from his hometown dying in that hellish prison. "Any food they gave us was bare minimum. It was several of us to one loaf of bread when I got to Bad Orb, and 20 percent of the loaf was sawdust. By the end, it was nine of us to one loaf of bread that was 60 percent sawdust," he said with disgust.

After three months, a once 155-pound teenager was 85 pounds. The Bad Orb prison camp was located in the mountains. Every night a frail Mike would peer out his window, watching what appeared to be lightning. "The lightning would get stronger and bigger each night, followed by boom sounds." This was no thunderstorm. This was the war getting closer and closer to the prison fences of Bad Orb.

"We woke up one day, and the Germans had disappeared."

On April 2, 1945, members of the 44th Infantry Division, reinforced with Stuart tanks and armored cars from the 106th Cavalry Group, broke through the gates of Bad Orb. "It was a beautiful thing." Mike's mouth trembled recounting it. "We were losing about seven men a day from starvation around this time." As a medic, he was particularly aware of how grim the situation had become before the prison camp was liberated.

Within hours, trucks began to enter the liberated camp carrying boxloads of C-rations for the starving GIs. "They gave us strict orders not to eat a lot because our bodies could not handle it. Our stomachs could rupture, and we could die." Some men were too weak to leave their wooden bunks to see their fellow Americans enter the camp. Other men climbed the trucks, throwing boxes of C-rations off to their friends. The emaciated soldiers would then run off to a secluded part of the camp, acting as if they had found treasure that must be hidden. The men happily stuffed their faces—only to ask for a medic moments later.

It did not stop there. The American prisoners mobbed their healthy liberators for cigarettes, trading any personal effect they had stowed away during captivity for a temporary drag of nicotine. The cigarette did not mean gratification to them; it meant freedom.

Three thousand four hundred American soldiers were set free when a task force from the 44th Division broke into Bad Orb, Stalag IX-B. There were roughly six thousand people in the camp of all nationalities, including Russians and Brits. Most of the U.S. prisoners were from the Ardennes Offensive, which had begun in mid-December. Many were privates like Mike, since officers and non-commissioned officers were usually taken to separate camps.

In the coming days, trucks began to transport the men to another camp about fifteen miles away. "We at the U.S. camp took gasoline baths. We were instructed to wet a cloth with gas and run it through our hair, groin, and beards. This killed all the lice. I couldn't believe it was that easy," Mike reported, gleeful at the memory.

"We had our first hot showers here." Mike couldn't finish describing what it was like to bathe and be treated like a human again. He choked up remembering how happy he was to be liberated. "We got clean clothes from the Army. They weren't new or anything, but they were fine."

Mike returned to Gloucester, Massachusetts. There he had an incredible support system, something that has always been key to a veteran's success after trauma. He wasted no time, but enrolled at Suffolk University, graduating in 1949 with a degree in business. "I worked for my father at the fish pier after that," Mike reminisced. He took over his father's business and became president of his own restaurant, Gloucester House, in 1958.

As I sat in the restaurant seventy-five years later, Mike insisted I try some food. He had some haddock brought out to me.

"Did you ever have nightmares after the war?" I asked. Mike stared at my plate of food. I thought of the irony of a man who had nearly starved to death now owning a restaurant.

"I have them now even," he replied. "You may think this is dramatic, but what helps me is every night before I go to bed, I say a prayer. I say a prayer for every man I treated. Men with no legs, the man who had his face taken off. I pray that they lived some sort of normal life after the war. I pray for every teenage boy who came who was injured. I do this because I know that they came home different. I know people look at them as if there is something wrong with them, and I hope they know that there isn't anything wrong with them. There is something wrong with the person staring at them!"

I could only shake my head in wonder at Mike's perseverance, considering that what had happened to those severely wounded veterans was something that had been on his mind for over seven decades. His concern for injured service members is similar to that of every veteran from any war. I wished he could talk with the soldiers and Marines who come through Bethesda Naval Hospital today. Mike's words were deeply moving to me. Even though I'd never been wounded in battle, they still gave me great inspiration.

As I finished my meal, Mike took his walker and began to make his way around the restaurant, greeting his regulars. His staff refused to let me pay. As I was walking out the door, I was stopped by a waiter. "I think Mike has something else to tell you," he said.

Mike strolled over with his walker. "When is the next time you're going to Belgium?" he asked.

"In a few months, I believe."

"I want to give you a cooler with thirty lobsters to bring."

I found this request comical, yet he was serious.

"Please share them with Pascal, and any other Belgian people. I am grateful for them. They treated me like gold when I returned in 2014. Pascal Hainaut is a pen pal and he helped guide me in Marvie."

Michael Linquata with the rifle

I told Mike I would be in touch with him later for the lobsters. There was no way I could travel to Europe with thirty lobsters, as much as I wanted to. I said farewell to Mike, my fellow Ram, ex-POW, medic, and fisherman.

CHAPTER FIVE

Best Meatballs I Ever Had

The sounds of explosions and distant gunfire were fierce. There was no such thing as a break during D-Day on Iwo Jima, and since there was no rear echelon, the battle raged everywhere. The call for fire missions was constant, but the men of Fox Battery, 2nd Battalion, 13th Marines, had no choice; they had to pause. "Our guns were red-hot. If we put another shell in through the cannon, we risked killing our whole gun crew," John Trezza told me.

John Trezza stared at his 75 mm howitzer. It was glowing red. You could have cooked hamburgers for the whole company on it. If another shell was placed into the artillery piece it could detonate. The Marines from his battery had just run a hundred shells through it in a short period of time. The Japanese had emplacements everywhere on Iwo. There was no end in sight to the calls for fire missions. They were facing an entrenched enemy estimated to be over twenty thousand strong.

Casualty collection points and rendezvous areas developed behind the artillery units on February 19, 1945, throughout the day. Wave after wave of Marines landed, and those who were supposed to be in reserve

John Trezza, 5th Marine Division

found themselves hitting the island midday on D-Day instead of in the following days, as they'd initially supposed would occur.

Packs and supplies of those killed on the island began to pile up behind Fox Battery. Then one pack arrived that seemed to hush the sounds of distant gunfire as the Marines passed it around. Written in black ink on a piece of gear attached to the pack was the name "BASI-LONE." The Marines of Fox Battery studied it in disbelief.

"When it got to me I couldn't look at it," said John, as he sat on a couch seventy-seven years later. He was still emotional about the Italian American war hero from New Jersey who had been killed in action. The two had much in common. They were both Italians, both Jersey boys, both Marines, and, most of all, both proud Americans. John Basilone was admired by the whole Marine Corps after his actions on Guadalcanal, actions which had earned him the Medal of Honor.

"Before we left Hawaii, I got the chance to meet him. We all looked up to him. He didn't have to go back into combat. He had a ticket to stay home forever and sell war bonds. He wanted to be with the Marines and he died doing so," John added. It was amazing to see the profound impact Gunnery Sergeant Basilone still had on his Marines nearly eight decades later. These Marines were not eighteen years old anymore. Here was a ninety-six-year-old man still upset as he remembered the loss of a Marine Corps icon. This was deep admiration. No propaganda could accomplish this. Gunny Basilone was truly a legend.

Back on Iwo Jima, an eighteen-year-old John Trezza couldn't look at his fallen hero's empty pack. It would be admitting that Basilone was really gone, and that the Japanese could kill anyone. Yet John's turmoil over seeing Basilone's gear was soon interrupted. It was time to start shelling again. The infantry depended on it.

John's fatigues were powdery white, his uniform crusted by the salt from the ocean in which he had been submerged only hours before. His landing on the beach had been anything but pleasant. For all the Marines of the 5th Division, it had been hectic.

The entire 5th Marine Division was created for the purpose of taking Iwo Jima. It was the first time the Marine Corps developed such a unit with one island as its objective. John trained on Camp Tarawa in Hawaii for six months, then loaded onto the troop transport ship. It was there he met Medal of Honor recipient John Basilone. They and the other Marines aboard spent thirty-eight days on the ship, heading generally west. After landing, the two would never meet again, yet John would never forget him. Iwo Jima affected the lives of all Marines who took part for generations to come.

After a long month of zigzagging through the Pacific, the 5th Marine Division anchored near the island of Saipan. The Marines took to the decks of the transport ships. "We would watch the B-29s take off to do their bombing runs. It seemed like there was one taking off every minute," John said. This activity gave the Marines something to occupy their time, and the young men crowded the decks to view the mighty Army Air Corps fly away to strike Japan.

What they didn't yet know was that those same B-29s were most likely being used in an attempt to prevent the onslaught that lay ahead for the 5th Marine Division. But aerial carpet bombing of the volcanic island of Iwo Jima proved to be unsuccessful. Saying the Japanese were a "well-entrenched enemy" was an understatement. Their tunnels, caves, pillboxes, and artillery emplacements remained for the most part unscathed despite American bombing raids. Anything that could be moved was wheeled or pushed into a tunnel or cave. The only advantage the bombings gained for the invading Marines was to provide defilades for cover. Other than that, Iwo Jima was like every other island, a smoky flaming mess with thousands of Japanese soldiers at the ready.

After a few days the ships left Saipan, destined for their final stop: Iwo Jima. "It was February 19, a Monday morning, I'll never forget it," John said, shaking his head.

Before the sun rose, Marines were pushing their way through chow lines in the ship's mess hall. It was noisy and hectic, and adrenaline was high. The first waves of Marines made their way to the bottoms of their ships. The ship carrying John's unit was an LCT (landing craft tank). Stored inside the ship's hull were amphibious tracs and DUKW (pronounced "duck") boats that could be launched from the bow once the ramp opened. Overhead, fighter planes soared, providing covering fire for the first waves of Marines heading for the beach. The landing crafts and amphibious vehicles of this first wave chopped forward in the ocean until they reached the black sand.

"The first wave was unopposed. The Japanese wanted them to make their way inland to a certain point before opening up on them," John explained.

"Which wave were you?" I asked.

"Third wave," he replied. "All hell broke loose on the second wave."

It was John's turn to load onto the DUKW boat. "There were four of us. A Coast Guard guy was driving it," he recalled.

The DUKW is a boat with wheels extending underneath it. It does not travel fast on water, as John and the other Marines quickly found out.

John recalled the frightening ordeal. "We were drenched with water within minutes of leaving the ramp of the big ship. Mortar shells were landing on each side of us."

Landing crafts were also taking direct hits not far from John's DUKW. The ocean seemed to be crowded with burning, scuttled landing crafts. The immense enemy fire, now concentrated on the beach and ocean, was causing a traffic jam for incoming waves of troops. The Coast Guard skipper in charge of John's DUKW boat couldn't find a place to land on his designated area of the beach.

The beach was littered with vehicles and Marines. The pileup was proving to be deadly and prevented reinforcements from coming ashore. The DUKW boats' skippers were all having trouble finding openings, and when they did they risked running over Marines already present and bogged down by enemy fire.

The Coast Guard skipper of John's DUKW boat had to work fast. He powered the boat to the far left of the designated area. "He led us right into a cove," John said.

The DUKW boat full of scared Marines made its way into the natural opening. As it pulled into the cove the Marines began to jump off the sides.

"I jumped off the back and nearly drowned." Unbeknownst to John, the water here was significantly over his head. In a sheer panic, he unslung his rifle from his body. His M1 Garand sank to the bottom of the ocean. Stripping himself of his gear, John rose to the surface, gasping for air. The DUKW boat was still within arm's reach.

"I grabbed hold of it and climbed back on," he recalled. The incident still left John feeling short of breath seventy-seven years later.

John boarded the boat again. "I had no helmet, no weapon, no nothing!" The DUKW boat spun about, trying to find a spot where John and the others could place their feet. The skipper was able to locate solid earth for John to step out on. John waited for the thumbs-up, then was off.

"I ran as fast as I could to the beach. When I looked up I saw a three-hundred-foot cliff. *Should I go up there?* I thought. *What's on the other side?* I figured I would go back to where I was supposed to land first, Red Beach One."

John began to follow the beach further down before making his advance inland. "I was running around bareback, with no equipment whatsoever!" John was practically shouting as he related this to me in his living room. The extreme circumstances of his landing had lost none of their shock value over the years.

Nervous and unarmed, John scurried along the black sand. "I got to Red Beach One and there was still no possible way to get in. I don't know how all those guys got into that little pass," John said. Red Beach One was blockaded with vehicles, bodies, and equipment. There was no way around it. "That's when I decided to go to Red Beach Three."

John ran further along the sand toward Red Beach Three. At this beach a weaponless John observed a set of makeshift stairs that ran along the cliffs. "They must have been built by the Japanese. There were a couple hundred stairs and they ran all the way up." This pathway seemed the only way to link up with his unit. He began to crawl up the side of the stairs.

"All the way to the top there were dead Marines along the stairs. They were slumped over and all appeared to be shot through the head and face. They each had just a small trickle of blood running from between their eyes."

The bodies of Marines who had attempted to ascend the stairs were scattered over the hillside. They were the victims of earlier waves, and John gazed at each one as he climbed around them, the lifeless bodies serving as markers the higher he climbed.

"Every one of those guys I saw dead . . ." John had to pause. The memory of the fallen Marines still haunted him. "Every one of those guys, my heart went out to them." Nearly eighty years later, the tears still came.

"What happened when you got to the top of the stairs?" I asked.

"Then I found my outfit!" John said, a smile on his face. Reuniting with his field artillery battalion was obviously a much happier memory. "Right then and there I found my guys."

Fox Battery was set up not far from the summit of the cliff John had climbed. Their guns had been dragged into position in the earlier two waves.

"The first man I saw was a forward observer from my battery, a lieutenant. I didn't want him to know I didn't have a rifle, so at this point I'm still trying to look for a weapon. I didn't look long before we had our first fire mission."

John's attempt to arm himself would have to wait. The 75 mm howitzers were ready to fire.

"I lost count how many shells we fired. The forward observer was giving us coordinates all day, and at night we shot illumination rounds. By day two we were running out of ammunition."

John's battery was doing a historic job of keeping a steel wall in front of the grunts of the 5th Marine Division.

At night, however, things got weird. An unknown voice called out to them. "Fox Battery, where are you? Fox Battery, where are you?" The voice seemed to come from far in the distance. "We found that so strange. We were taught never to call out to one another in the night. So we hid low behind our guns and ignored it."

John believes it was Japanese soldiers testing to see if they could infiltrate. Some Marines and forward observers had gone missing. There was no way to tell if they had been tortured or killed for information by the Japanese.

"The next day, day three, we totally ran out of ammunition for our howitzers," John said. The Marines of Fox Battery made multiple runs to and from the beach trying to track down any ammo they might find for their guns.

The less they fired, the less protection the infantry had. As an artilleryman, you were the king of battle and often the hand of God. It was artillery that could knock down rows of banzai charges.

Ammunition finally reached the beachhead, and men ushered rounds to Fox Battery's position. The new high-explosive shells had arrived just in time. Enemy counterbattery fire was incoming.

"Luckily we had a time-fire radar. We could adjust quickly and knock them out."

By day seven, Fox Battery's position was known to the enemy. The Japanese zeroed in. Enemy counterbattery poured in faster than John and his gun crew could adjust. Finally their ability to return fire ceased altogether when an enemy shell exploded to their left. The Japanese artillery blew John and the other Marines off their howitzer like rag dolls.

Stunned and temporarily deaf in both ears, John lay facedown in the dirt. Other Marines were scattered around. They slowly attempted to get up and get back to the gun. John found he could not bounce back like the others. As they sat him up, he looked down below his belt line. There was smoke coming from his groin. He had a large hole in his pants. He was hit.

"I placed my hand in my pants. I was hit right by my family jewels," he said quietly.

John was bleeding heavily. As the men shouted for a corpsman, the roar of other artillery pieces firing drowned their screams for help. John tried to staunch the blood loss from his groin, but soon passed out.

"When I gained consciousness, I was in a tent hospital. I looked down at my groin. I could see they did a good job fixing me up, and I passed back out."

For a nineteen-year-old boy to know he still had his penis and testicles was a relief. Still under a considerable amount of morphine, John was transported to a hospital ship offshore for more rehabilitation. While John was out of the fight, the battle for Iwo Jima raged on.

"Dealing with my injuries was some delicate stuff. You could put three or four fingers into my wound," John explained. He would spend the next five months recovering in hospitals both in Guam and Hawaii.

John was ultimately satisfied with the healing process. He could have lost his manhood on Iwo Jima. Thanks to surgeons, he was able to have a normal life and create a family.

"I came home and later joined the sheriff's department on May 1, 1950. I retired in 1978." John retired as the deputy warden of the Essex County Jail in New Jersey. In the prison system he would run into other Marines who had chosen to go down a different road after the Battle of Iwo Jima. "It makes you think if the war contributed to the behavior of some Marines after their return home from combat."

John had a point. Like many others, he and I both had chosen law enforcement after the Marines. By doing so we were at times confronted with the fact that some Marines chose crime.

As I placed the rifle into its case, I believed my time with John had come to an end. "Where do you think you're going?" he asked.

"Well, I got a long drive back to Boston."

"You aren't going anywhere until you have some of my meatballs!"

John hobbled over to the kitchen and turned on the burners on the stove to warm up a pot. A few minutes later, he was off-loading giant meatballs on a plate for me.

I knew I had a long drive from New Jersey to Boston ahead of me, but I sat down with the Italian American Marine. I bit into one of his meatballs, and he told me I couldn't leave until I finished.

I can honestly say they were the best damn meatballs I ever had.

CHAPTER SIX

Bananas and Milk

By mid-year 2021, my book *The Rifle* had become popular among history readers and the veterans' community throughout the country. At signings, I would hold the M1 rifle covered in names in front of my live audience. The rifle took the place of speaking notes. I could look down at it, pick any name, and tell some incredible story from the Second World War featuring a memorable veteran.

In February 2022, I was in Asheville, North Carolina, ready to rock and roll. I had taken the rifle from its case and was setting up a display for it before my speech. I peered at the early crowd as they were taking their seats. My presentation was at 2:00 p.m. at a local library. I knew my audience was going to be full of retirees and senior citizens.

Suddenly a smell wafted to me. Years of working as a police officer in Boston's urban subway system had conditioned me to recognize it. It was the smell of someone who hadn't bathed in a long time, usually one of homeless status. Someone in the audience had either not taken care of himself or was unable to. My eyes scanned the crowd.

Joseph Cooper, USS *Ommaney Bay*

There he was. A bearded, white-haired man had just taken a seat. His clothes were ragged and stained. On his crusty hat were the words "WWII and Korean War Vet." The unidentified man had on layers of moldy clothes, some of which appeared to be disintegrating. As I got a closer look, I could see he was sorting feverishly through a laminated picture book.

"Hey Mike, do you know this guy?" I said in a low voice to Michael McCarthy, the American Legion official standing beside me. Mike had booked me for the event. I nodded my head in the direction of the poor fellow.

Mike was not sure. "I don't recognize him," he replied. "He must have read about this event in the local paper. He's not a member of the Legion, I don't think."

I watched as Mike approached another Legion member. This Legion member knew exactly who the man was. The Legion member stood up and announced, "This here is a neighbor of mine, Joe Cooper. Joe served on the USS *Ommaney Bay* in World War II. His ship was destroyed, and then he went on to fight in Korea. He is ninety-nine years old!"

The small audience clapped for the man. Of course I needed to know more, and to get Joe's signature on the rifle. The Legion member sat down after his announcement, proud of educating us. Still, I thought, if this guy is your damn neighbor, why would you let him live like this?

After the presentation, I went over to Joe, who was packing up his picture book. No one had come to look at it. They were most likely turned off by his stench.

"Whatcha got there?" I asked.

"This was my ship," Joe replied. His voice was high and raspy.

The book contained enlarged black and white photographs of an aircraft carrier on fire. It was, indeed, the USS *Ommaney Bay*. The mighty ship was smoldering in different images. Black clouds and explosions erupted from her in a series of still photographs taken seventy-eight years before. Men could be seen jumping overboard.

"We were hit by a kamikaze. . . . She . . . she exploded." Joe turned the pages, exposing his long and dirty fingernails. *For God's sake, Andy, I told myself, don't be selfish. Get this guy some help.*

Joe bent over the crowded library table and signed my rifle. I turned my head to talk with several others who'd been in the audience. When I turned back, the exit door was swinging and Joe was gone. Did I say something wrong? I *had* expressed interest in his story. Maybe he was self-conscious about his appearance?

"Mike! What's the deal with that guy?" I asked my host. "How come no one is helping him?"

Mike sighed. "The truth is, we have tried," he replied. "He doesn't want the help and has denied others several times. We tried."

The answer didn't seem good enough. This would never happen in Boston, I thought. I approached the other American Legion member who'd introduced Joe to the crowd. "That guy was your neighbor?"

The man was wearing a Vietnam veteran hat. I'm sure he wasn't neglecting his neighbor on purpose, but I needed to know what the scoop was.

"Well, sort of, he lives in his car."

"What?!" I nearly threw the rifle out of my hands. In all my life I had never heard of a nearly one-hundred-year-old man living in his car, not even in my time working as a cop.

"He shuts us all down, and refuses the help. Sometimes he is vicious about it," the Legion member continued.

"What the fuck does he do in the wintertime?" I growled.

The semicircle of people gathered around had no answer.

I buckled the rifle in its case, determined to see this man's living situation for myself. I also began to calm myself down somewhat.

Of course, the American Legion members were technically right. Joe had rights. Nobody could force him to do anything he didn't want to do. The Asheville veterans community is an extraordinary one. If they had looked into this situation and been frustrated, then I trusted it was a difficult issue to deal with.

The truth is that Joe Cooper, the veteran in question, was set in his ways. He demanded to be left alone. Many efforts were made by friends and family, but Joe was too proud to accept help.

"I've got to interview this guy, at least," I said to Mike.

I looked at Mike with urgency in my expression. I was heading back to Boston the next morning.

"I can see if we can get in touch with him and find out if he is willing to meet with us," Mike suggested. Mike spoke to Joe's neighbor. He was the only one who could relay the message to Joe, since Joe did not have a phone. But I heard nothing and had to leave.

A month passed by before I heard from Mike in North Carolina again. I received a text message that read, "Joe said he would meet with us at the local museum if you're still interested." I was soon on my way back to North Carolina again.

A few days later, at 10:00 a.m., I sat in the Veterans History Museum of the Carolinas waiting for Joe Cooper to arrive. Sadly, as he entered the museum, I could smell him before I could see him. Joe was wearing the exact same outfit he'd worn a month earlier at my book signing. He held the same picture book and other documents. The inner layer of clothing under his jacket looked as if it was rotted to his skin. A mix of food crumbs and mold collected around his collar, wrists, and belt line. It looked to me that if he were ever to take off those clothes, his skin would come with them.

I asked Joe the common questions I asked every veteran. I did not alert him to the fact I was concerned about his health. I wanted him to feel comfortable. But I also wanted to hear everything in his life that had led to this current situation. My end goal, I thought, would be to trick him into letting us help him.

The usual questions were asked. Where are you from? Where did you go to basic training? Were you drafted?

Then I snuck in another question I don't usually ask: "What is your exact address?"

Joe paused for a minute.

"It's just so I can mail you a copy of this interview after I write it," I added. The truth is, I never asked for addresses. I just wanted to do some reconnaissance after our interview.

Joe nodded his head and finally answered. "I live at 15 Putnam Street," he said. "I don't live far from here at all. I walk all the time."

I'd deal with that later. Now it was time to dive into the life of a sailor on the USS *Ommaney Bay*.

I wanted to hear about Joe's story of survival, but I was also curious about his childhood. As I gawked at his filthy clothes, I wondered if he'd lived an earlier life of squalor.

"Where did you grow up, Joe?"

"Right here in Brevard, North Carolina," said Joe. "My father was a World War I veteran. When he came back from the war, he opened up his own garage as a mechanic. I was one of eight kids. I have been here my whole life, and in four months I turn one hundred."

"Did you grow up poor?"

"Oh yes, dirt-poor. Well, us kids got to eat three meals a day, but it was mostly beans and corn bread." He laughed.

"Why did you join the Navy of all branches?" I inquired.

"Well, they promised me bananas and milk!" he exclaimed.

It was amazing to think that this young boy chased his branch of the service because of a promise of nutritional food. Before I could ask the next question, Joe continued recollecting his memories of food.

"Oh, yes, the Navy fed us good, they did. I never missed a meal. I went in at 104 pounds, and came out 130 pounds," he recalled.

While satisfying his quest for food, Joe became a gunner's mate in the U.S. Navy. "I attended basic training in Norfolk, Virginia, class 323. I will never forget it. I trained on various weapons systems to include the .50 caliber, 20 mm, 40 mm, and 75 mm guns that would be mounted to whichever ship the Navy was going to send me on." He spoke with the same raspy, screeching voice I'd heard at the signing.

Training with naval guns in those days included shooting floating targets and engaging targets being towed through the sky by small planes. The guns Joe operated often took a crew of three to four sailors. These men learned to work as a team to keep the guns operational during mock enemy aircraft attacks, or in the event of spotting a real enemy ship. The training never ended for the sailors.

"*General quarters! All hands man your battle stations! All hands man your battle stations!*"

This was the announcement one often heard over the intercom systems of ships docked at the Norfolk Naval Station. Sailors were expected to race towards the positions they would man in the event of enemy contact. Training was continuous.

Each man had a second position. For example, when "general quarters" sounded, the ship cooks would become assistant gunners. If the ship took damage, the electricians and machinist's mates would become firefighters. Everyone had a combat role and battle station.

After weeks of training, Joe and his shipmates from class 323 graduated Navy basic training. The men were spread throughout the U.S. fleet to places they were needed. Joe received orders to report to San Diego.

"After graduating from basic training, I got word I would be assigned to a brand-new aircraft carrier, the USS *Ommaney Bay*," Joe said with a smile seventy-eight years later. He was grinning as if he were still standing on the dock gazing at her for the first time. This sibling of eight who'd gone from eating beans three times a day to meat and potatoes in the Navy was going to receive a bunk on a brand-new, state-of-the-art aircraft carrier.

Joe walked aboard the ship, commissioned in Astoria, Oregon. He was officially a "plank owner," a name given to the original crew of a new ship. The ship got underway several days later with its crew of 800-plus. Joe became familiar with his gun position, which for now would be the dual 40 mm gun turret located on the portside stern of the ship.

With two cannons mounted together, Joe's gun required several men directing fire, reloading, shooting, and cleaning empty shells away from the turret to prevent jams. The gun could be adjusted left, right, up, and down so long as a sailor spun the wheels of the rotary alignment system. If a shell or any brass landed in the cogs, the gun might become inoperable during battle.

Joe Cooper and the rest of the sailors soon departed San Diego for the South Pacific. Little did they know that the USS *Ommaney Bay* would never return to U.S. shores again. "Our first stop was Sydney, Australia. We picked up some P-47 Thunderbolts and a P-61 night fighter," Joe recalled.

"From there we supported the 1st Marine Division and the 81st 'Wild Cat' Division during their invasion of Peleliu Island," he continued.

I found it remarkable he could remember his ship's route and the tiny islands it had to support. "We got there fourteen days before the landing craft did. We helped bomb and shell the island day and night. It was the first time I shot the 40 mm guns."

Joe was not only plank on *Ommaney Bay*, he was one of the first sailors to fire her guns in combat. After the landings, the *Ommaney Bay* provided air cover for the fleet and close support strikes for the forces ashore on Peleliu. The invading Marines and soldiers were in a vicious fight with their Japanese enemy and were lucky to have the aircraft carrier anchored offshore with its planes providing air support.

While the Battle of Peleliu raged throughout September, the *Ommaney Bay* received orders to head towards the Philippine Islands by mid-October 1944. The ship was to prepare for General MacArthur's return.

"This was the first time the Navy fleet experienced kamikazes," Joe said. "At the Battle of Leyte, they would come at us three or four at a time! Three of them would dive in on us, while the fourth plane would go and report back their findings to Japanese intelligence."

The guns on the *Ommaney Bay* lit up the sky. Other Navy vessels in the area also shot flak and bullets upward to knock out the enemy aircraft. The sky was soon black with smoke.

Joe took another photo from his binder. It was a Japanese bomber on fire soaring over the *Ommaney Bay*'s flight deck.

"Did you shoot this plane?" I asked.

"We all did. The plane set fire, flew over us, did a barrel roll, and landed in the water about two hundred meters away," he said, his voice still echoing the traces of the terror he must have felt at the time.

"The *Ommaney Bay* downed several planes during the Battle of Leyte Gulf and Samar. The USS *West Virginia* was helping shoot down planes too, but we lost the USS *St. Lo* that day," he recalled.

The *St. Lo* was a fellow aircraft carrier that sank after being struck by a kamikaze, killing 150 sailors. The sailors of the U.S. Navy were now fighting a new kind of war that hadn't been seen before—attacks by a suicidal airborne enemy.

Until meeting Joe, I had not realized the Japanese were using larger bomber planes as kamikazes in addition to the one-man fighter planes. I was used to seeing single-engine planes dive in on the ships in the movies and on black and white newsreels. I looked more closely at Joe's photos and the kamikaze bombers targeting his ship.

"These are called Betty Bombers," Joe explained, pointing to the doomed aircraft in the black and white photo. U.S. sailors referred to the Japanese Mitsubishi G4Ms and their successors, the P1Y Frances twin-engine bombers, as "Betty Bombers." This same plane would eventually determine the fate of the *Ommaney Bay*.

Joe's ship maneuvered north during the winter months toward Luzon, Philippines. At about 5:00 p.m. on January 4, approximately fifteen Japanese planes were detected on radar at a range of forty-five miles.

American fighter planes engaged the incoming Japanese aircraft and caused the enemy group to split into two groups. *Ommaney Bay* did not receive radio traffic which would have confirmed that some of the enemy planes had slipped through the cracks. As sailors from the *Ommaney Bay* casually strolled across the deck of their ship, their attention was grabbed by the sound of the guns of the nearby USS *New Mexico*. *New Mexico* was firing rapidly into the sky.

With the sun behind its back, a single Japanese P1Y Frances twin-engine bomber maneuvered into a dive. It was plunging right for the *Ommaney Bay*.

Sailors on the USS *New Mexico* witnessed the attack unfolding. They tried to fire anti-aircraft guns to protect the *Ommaney Bay*, but these shots were all misses. The bomber continued its descent.

"We didn't get off a single shot, nor did we see the Betty Bomber. The blinding sun disguised them," Joe recalled. He had just finished eating a meal in the mess hall before the attack.

The kamikaze, armed with two 1,400-pound bombs and using the sun as cover, crashed like a meteorite, virtually unopposed, into the *Ommaney Bay*. It cut through the middle of the ship like a knife through butter. One bomb penetrated to the port engine room, rupturing the fire main and knocking out the ship's power. The other bomb detonated on the hangar deck, setting the American planes parked there, full of fuel, ablaze.

"I was eating my meal and we all heard *boom!* I thought we got hit by a torpedo. All the lights on the ship went out, and smoke began to fill the chow hall." Joe's voice became agitated as he described the ship's minute by minute destruction.

Joe began his escape from the mess hall. "My buddy and I went up the smoky stairway to the hangar deck. When I got there, I saw planes exploding and their ammunition hitting the bulkhead. One sailor was missing a leg, and an officer was hit in the neck, bleeding, but there was nothing I could do for him," Joe said.

Ordnance carried by the planes in the hangar deck was now being ignited from the fires aboard ship. Joe and other sailors took cover as the ammo cooked off overhead. As they got up to run, they passed the pilots' briefing room. They could hear screaming.

"The pilots were locked in the room. They had been sitting in on a briefing when the ship was hit. The ship's structural integrity had been compromised so bad by the explosion that the doors to the pilots' room bent, and were now sealed shut. We could not pry the doors open," Joe sadly recalled.

With the fire and smoke growing, Joe had to leave the screaming pilots behind. "I returned to the hangar deck and began to throw ammunition overboard to prevent it from igniting." Sailors attempted damage control, only to have their efforts come to naught as the ship became an inferno. Men began to abandon ship.

"More explosions and bullets began to sizzle over my head. I was so scared that the ship was going to fully erupt. I decided it was my turn to go. I jumped sixty-five feet over the port side of the ship. I didn't have a life jacket on because I always left it next to my gun mount."

Joe plunged into the ocean, rising up for air as soon as he could. While in the ocean, another sailor threw Joe a life jacket. Joe tucked it under his arm and began to paddle away from the blazing ship. "I was in the water for four to five hours, and guys began to yell, 'Shark! Shark!'

Several sharks passed by me. I just lay flat and didn't move my legs. I heard stories of sailors who were sunk at Guadalcanal that said to never kick your legs if you think you're being circled by sharks. Sure enough, they went by me and didn't bother me none.

"Finally a destroyer arrived by the name of USS *Helm*. It sent small rescue boats to pick us out of the water."

The *Helm* had also had to defend itself during the kamikaze attack, and so hadn't been able to assist the *Ommaney Bay* survivors right away. Finally the *Helm* dispatched rescue boats to fish out Joe and the other sailors, some of whom were badly burned.

"When the boat came over, I grabbed the side and yanked myself up. The coxswain yelled at me and said, 'Hey, you're gonna tip the boat over.' They brought us back to the USS *Helm*, where I had to climb up a cargo net to the deck of the ship. When I climbed to the top of the cargo net, the sailors on board pulled me up by the back of my shirt because I was so exhausted. I almost didn't make it. They fed me and got me dry clothes. I was very tired."

Joe glanced back at the *Ommaney Bay*. Miraculously, she was still floating. The aircraft carrier was billowing dark black smoke and tilting to one side, however.

Approximately one hundred sailors from the *Ommaney Bay* lost their lives on January 4, 1945. While the ship didn't sink entirely from the damage, the U.S. Navy had her scuttled as unsalvageable. This was accomplished by a torpedo from the destroyer USS *Burns* in the Sulu Sea, under orders from Admiral Jesse B. Oldendorf.

Survivors from the *Ommaney Bay* were spread among other ships almost immediately. A day later, Joe was transferred to the USS *Minneapolis*. The U.S. Navy didn't care that Joe had survived the attack on *Ommaney Bay*. He was still needed. Joe went on to serve in the Battle of Luzon as a 20 mm gunner.

Other survivors, including a friend he had been eating with in the mess hall during the bombing, were transferred to the USS *Columbia* only to die in another kamikaze strike aboard that ship. In all, twenty-five men who survived the *Ommaney Bay* attack died on the USS *Columbia* in another kamikaze strike.

"I got discharged in 1945. Went back to Brevard, North Carolina, and couldn't find work, so I joined the Army." Joe served in the occupation of Germany and Okinawa, Japan, until he volunteered for service in Korea in 1950. He served as a rifleman with the 7th Infantry Division in several battles, arriving first in Pusan.

I might have continued on and spoken to Joe about his Korean combat, but I was determined to help him. I planned to scout his home address and see what his living conditions were like.

Joe picked up the rifle and we both took a photo with it. We left the museum and I plugged the address he'd given me into my GPS. It was only a five-minute drive. When I got there, I couldn't believe my eyes. I found myself at a dilapidated structure that was supposed to be a home. It was easily the worst condition I'd ever seen a house in that was still standing.

This was the home of an elderly World War II veteran?

The single-family residence looked as if a tornado had picked it up and dropped it from a great distance. The roof was collapsed, and the walls of the home were bowing. The place was uninhabitable. A single extension cord ran from the home and into a white van. This must be where Joe slept.

There were holes and openings everywhere in the house, and animals must have dwelled there as well. Joe must have still had access to the structure. Where else would he get clean water? The extension cord testified to the fact that there must also be a working electrical connection. I got back into my truck without investigating any further. I did not want Joe to catch me on his property without permission.

There was no way I could let a man nearing one hundred years of age live or die in such conditions. I got on the phone with Mike from the Brevard American Legion and we met in person to discuss a game plan for Joe. Joe's not accepting help was no longer an option, I said. He deserved more than to spend his last days on earth in the back of a van without heat.

Mike finally saw the living conditions for himself. Many people in the community had been unaware of Joe's address and did not know his true living situation.

After numerous visits they were able to persuade Joe to bathe at the YMCA. Later, he finally agreed to a haircut. One of the only good things about COVID-19 was that it hospitalized Joe. From there, friends and family were able to get him transferred to an assisted living center after his rehab. It became a success story.

In Boston, I received photographs of Joe in my email. He looked like a totally different person after his lifestyle transformation. He also no longer looked one hundred years old going on a thousand.

Discussing Joe's living conditions is not meant to embarrass him but to show the world where some of our World War II veterans have ended up in life. This country could be doing better with what we provide for elder services. Joe is not the only World War II veteran living like this, and we could all do our part by checking on our seniors who live amongst us.

I was proud that my tour with the rifle had sparked a fire in local heroes like Mike McCarthy to see that Joe was comfortable for what was left of his life. Most of us do not want to be thanked for our service, as we feel we did not sacrifice much. Joe Cooper is the epitome of a veteran for whom "Thank you for your service" should be a given.

CHAPTER SEVEN

A Case of Stolen Valor

Hunting down survivors of the 101st Airborne had never been a particular goal of mine. Since that unit earned a great deal of fame after World War II, its members were not a priority to track down. My rifle project was initially geared towards overlooked veterans from divisions that were less well-known. The 101st had long been popular due to Hollywood productions and books, and most of all because it is still an active-duty unit possessing a great public relations office.

Truly, they deserve all the praise they got for what they accomplished in Normandy and beyond. Now that my M1 Garand was full of names from less well-known divisions and units, I decided it was time to pay my respects to the 101st Airborne. It was time to get a veteran from the famous "Screaming Eagles" to sign the rifle.

I learned of an Airborne veteran living not far from me. In typical 101st Airborne fashion, the fame of the unit had led to his being featured in the newspaper every Veterans Day and Memorial Day for years. He was the grand marshal of the parades and had his own seat at the local diner. His name was Melvin B. Harris.

I got in touch with the local Veterans of Foreign Wars post over the phone. The commander there told me Mel was a member who visited from time to time.

I drove to the VFW to meet Melvin. I set up the rifle on a round table. All the veterans and associate members who were day-drinking in the bar crowded around.

I heard "Wow, look at all those names!" and "My father was in World War II." Everyone wanted photos with the rifle. Some gave me leads on other World War II veterans they knew or had heard of. The rifle brought back memories of family, and connected people wherever I went.

The vets' attention on the rifle was interrupted when the front door of the VFW opened. Everyone in the bar cheered. It was their beloved 101st Airborne veteran, Melvin B. Harris. Mel was walking with a cane. On his head sat a 101st Airborne hat with a set of jump wings. On the wings were two bronze stars representing parachute operations in both Normandy and Holland.

Mel hobbled over and sat down at my table. Everyone whipped out their cell phones and began to take photos of him with the rifle. It was a glorious scene. There was no need to wait; Melvin picked up the pen and began to sign his name on the rifle. His handwriting was perfect.

And there it was. I'd finally got a 101st Airborne vet's signature on the rifle. I felt proud, in the big league with other historians. My goal had always been to represent the whole war on the rifle, and I was a big step closer.

As it turned out, I was about to become a victim of my own hubris and the tall tales of a lonely old man.

"Where did you go to jump school?" I asked as Mel finished signing.

"In England!" he replied. He chuckled. "Those British airborne instructors were some tough sons of bitches!"

"Where did you grow up?" I continued. We were not far from my hometown, yet I'd never heard of him.

"Why don't you guys talk in private," the VFW commander said.

We proceeded down a hallway to a separate room. As I sat down at a round table with him, Mel adjusted his hearing aids.

"I grew up in Canada," he said.

"Really? How did you end up here?" I asked. Mel wasn't the first veteran I'd met who came to the United States from Canada and enlisted in the Army. However, they all had different reasons for doing so.

"Well, I have no problem discussing this now, but for a long time I never mentioned it, especially while my wife was alive. My older sister, brother, and I ran away from Canada when I was in grammar school. My father was an abusive drunk. One day we woke up and my mom said we were getting on a bus to the state of Maine."

The mother stayed behind. It was just the three children in a new country. While in Maine, Mel and his brother took various jobs working on chicken farms.

"Every morning I would have to pick up hundreds of chicken eggs and try not to drop them. It was stressful for a young kid. The farmer would get mad at me if I broke any. I would have to wake up at 4:00 a.m. and work until 7:00 a.m., then go to school. They were long, hard days for a kid my age. By the time I was fifteen years old I was sick and tired of the chicken farm."

Life in Maine began to become a hell on its own. Mel's older sister became a severe alcoholic. The police often found her passed out at railroad stations and other public spots around town. The chicken job, designed for a grown man, became very difficult for young Mel, especially after he and the owner became the only ones working on the farm.

"I began to resent my older brother. He found love, got married, and started to live a comfortable life. I was trying to fend for myself, so at seventeen years old I tried to join the Navy, but they wouldn't let me. If you were younger than eighteen you would need your mother to sign for you."

A frustrated Mel showed up to his brother's home.

"I made it no secret to him that I wanted out of Maine. He wouldn't let me stay with him and I grew angry. I told him, I would join the service right now if I could. But thanks to you and my sister I can't ask my parents because you made us run away from Canada!

"Our argument grew more heated until finally he said, '*If you need your mother to sign your enlistment papers, then ask your sister, Carol, because* she's *your fucking mother!*'"

At that point, sitting with me, Mel seemed wholly lost in the past.

"'What? What are you talking about?' I said to my brother."

Mel's older brother had finally snapped and let out the family secret. This was why Mel, his brother, and sister fled Canada. Carol, Mel's older sister, was actually his mother. Mel's father had raped his own daughter. She became pregnant and gave birth to Mel.

After the father was thrown into jail, the kids ran away to the United States. Mel's brother and sister kept the incest a secret from Mel.

When his brother revealed this startling news, Mel felt his world crashing down around him. He was upset his brother had never told him, but it also made sense as to why his sister had become a raging, homeless alcoholic while in Maine.

"I didn't want to talk to them anymore. I was disgusted, confused, and betrayed. I jumped on a bus to Boston. I quit school and work and just left Maine," Mel told me.

I couldn't believe what I was hearing in this interview. Personally, I don't think I could ever admit a thing such as he'd just told me. I think I would die with a secret like that. However, at age ninety-eight, having outlived his spouse, maybe none of that mattered anymore to Mel. Perhaps it was time to tell someone. Maybe Mel did not want to go out with such a memory held within his chest.

In Boston, Mel would turn the legal age of eighteen, which was the answer to his ongoing problem of signing up. He enlisted in the Army on the day of his birthday.

"They sent me to Camp Pickett, Virginia, for basic training. There I became a medical aid man, or medic," he explained.

Upon graduating basic training Mel was sent to England in September of 1943.

"It wasn't until I arrived at a base on a farm in Pheasey, England, that we learned the airborne divisions were looking for volunteers. They slapped posters on a bulletin board asking for volunteers to join. It was an extra fifty dollars a month, too. So me and my buddy volunteered."

The fact that Mel went to jump school in England pre-Normandy invasion left me yearning to know more. It was the first I had heard of this. An American paratrooper getting his butt kicked by British airborne instructors? This story was unique, and already blowing me away.

"Airborne school was hard. The British would run us into the ground, call us names and give us a smack if need be. When I graduated jump school I was sick as a dog. I was taken to the hospital and diagnosed with spinal meningitis."

While in the hospital Melvin found out that the American members of his jump school were now joining the newly arrived 101st Airborne in England. The doctors, however, would not clear Melvin to join his new unit.

"I spent so much time in the hospital that the next time my buddies came to visit they told me that the unit was getting ready to move out and an airborne operation was most likely planned. The doctors still refused to let me out of the hospital. So my pals stole an ambulance, backed it up to the doors of the hospital, and wheeled me into the back of it. We then went to Birmingham, where I joined my new unit and prepared for the D-Day invasion." He laughed at the memory of the ordeal.

"It wasn't until after I landed in Normandy that my commanding officer told me he received a letter from the hospital. He asked how I'd managed to go AWOL? I told him I didn't, an ambulance picked me up! He then told me that if I was crazy enough to leave the hospital to be here with the men, then I was crazy enough to stay. He said, 'I don't know a thing about it, and I'm going to pretend I didn't see this letter.' He burned it right in front of me," said Mel.

Mel had gotten to know the surgeons, doctors, and medics of the 326th Medical Company while locked behind barbed wire fences in

Greenham Common, England. Greenham Common was an airstrip guarded by military police in towers. The idea was to lock all paratroopers and glider men into a confined area before the D-Day invasion. The U.S. Army wanted to minimize all possible leaks of the operational details of Operation Overlord, and the fact that it was going to take place at all.

"They had us study sand tables with models of French towns. We learned to identify the towns by the different church steeples. Nobody could go in or out of our base until after we were airborne. Everything was top secret. We were supposed to take off on the fourth of June and land the fifth, but the weather pushed it a day forward."

"Did your C-47 take any flak?" I asked, curious about Mel's journey over the English Channel to France.

"Oh, yes. As soon as they told us to stand up and hook up, a piece of shrapnel came out through my buddy's seat. If he was still sitting, he would have been badly injured."

Mel's plane started to get hit all over by anti-aircraft fire. "One of our engines cut out and the plane went from seven hundred feet to four hundred feet off the ground when we were given the green light to jump. The plane was so low that as soon as I exited my chute opened and my feet hit the ground—almost simultaneously. That's how low we were. Or that's how it felt, at least."

Mel landed five kilometers from his objective, which was the town of Hiesville. In Hiesville he would report to his first field hospital. The building, built in 1554 and soon to be a surgical hospital, was a large chateau known as Chateau Colombière. The chateau had a castle-like appearance, with courtyards and stables. It would soon work well when the wounded were placed behind the surrounding walls for protection. The compound was spread out enough that vehicles could come and go, delivering the injured without issue. Connecting farmlands—perfect for observation posts and security—surrounded the area. Paratroopers cleared the German occupiers out of this building and by 9:00 a.m. on June 6, it became the first surgical hospital for the Allied airborne in Normandy.

Mel began work as a stretcher bearer, retrieving the wounded and bringing them back to the chateau. "The first soldier I helped had a busted leg. I splinted it and let the doctors know what was wrong with him. That was my job," he recalled.

It wasn't long before combat injuries began to flood the hospital. Broken bones and jump injuries turned into gunshots, sucking chest wounds, and shrapnel entries. Mel was taking trips to and from the chateau, bringing in wounded who were not far from the compound. The fields surrounding the hospital had wounded men scattered everywhere, it seemed.

"I was working on bandaging one fella when I heard a voice from behind me. The voice said, 'Hey doc, I need help in a hurry.' When I turned around I saw a paratrooper on the ground. I could only see from his belly button and up. I had assumed maybe he was covered in dirt from an artillery blast. As I got closer, there was nothing from his waist down. Those were his last words to me," Mel said mournfully. "I'm not afraid to tell you that I threw up what little food I had in me after seeing that," he added.

Mel's description left me stunned for a moment, considering that he'd witnessed this as a teenaged medic. So many of our country's youths saw such gory scenes at a young age. Although they were considered men, in a sense their childhoods were robbed from them.

"We had plenty of markings on the hospital, including the roof, but the Luftwaffe still bombed us," Mel said.

"You guys were bombed?"

"Yeah, a few days after the invasion. A German plane dropped two bombs on us."

Just before midnight, on June 9, 1944, an enemy aircraft swooped down on the hospital and released two several-thousand-pound bombs. One scored a direct hit on the chateau, killing twenty medical personnel and wounding sixty others, including patients. The explosion rendered a large part of the building useless or too unstable to further occupy. The second bomb landed outside the courtyard, finishing off what could still be used of the building.

"I was in the motor pool when the bombs went off. I dove under an ambulance. Luckily I survived," Mel said.

The motor pool was usually a parking area of vehicles and ambulances. Here vehicles would stage and get repaired, refueled, or undergo maintenance. As a stretcher bearer, Mel was in this area during the bombing, on standby to transfer the wounded evacuated by ambulance from battlefields.

The next morning medical tents had to be set up outside the ruins of the chateau to house the wounded. The former hospital was a disaster area. Supplies had been destroyed and the roof was caving in.

"We treated and evacuated over four hundred casualties before the bombing," Mel reported.

Mel couldn't recall details of what happened in Normandy after the bombing. A few weeks later, the 101st Airborne was sailing back to England. They would receive rest, replacements, and training for the invasion of Holland.

"My jump into Holland went well. I landed in a field and there was a farmhouse not too far away. The people came out and gave me apples and milk. I didn't take any fire that day. After that, I drove ambulances back and forth from the battlefield to Nijmegen. We took over a civilian hospital near Nijmegen and we worked alongside civilian doctors," Mel recalled.

"After I retired, I took a job driving a cab when I was about sixty years old. A man hopped in the back and I could tell by his accent he was Dutch. I told him I jumped into Holland and he said he remembered watching us from the roof of his home when he was a boy." The memory of that meeting brought a warm smile to Mel's face.

During his time in the Netherlands, Mel drove an ambulance up and down what would later be called "Hell's Highway" as he transported the injured to Nijmegen. Mel realized Operation Market Garden was not going well when the casualties began to increase. And as the number of wounded soldiers mounted, the hospital also came into the line of fire. On October 29, 1944, the hospital was hit by rockets. These blew out all the windows and killed several medics. It was time to move out.

"I drove an ambulance back to France sometime in November, us and the 82nd Airborne. While we waited for our next missions, the two divisions destroyed the bar rooms in France. Guys were out of control with drinking and wreaking havoc in the streets of France. It was later decided that the two divisions could never have liberty at the same time."

Much steam had to be blown off by both divisions. They'd lost men and failed to reach their ultimate objective—which was trying to end the war by Christmas. It was not until the offensive in the Belgian Ardennes that the 101st was finally on the move again.

"We rode in the backs of open trucks. It was December now, and we were freezing. We didn't have the right equipment either, to stay warm. Inside the trucks we were squeezed so tight that if you reached for your pocket you might be in the guy next to you's pocket. We traveled 180 miles to get straight to Bastogne, Belgium."

Arriving in the dark, the 326th Medical Company set up two aid stations in Bastogne. Mel would be stationed here during what would become the Siege of Bastogne. The main hospital itself was fifteen kilometers outside the town.

"They set up tents and surgical areas at a crossroads, out in the open. Our medical commander told General McAuliffe that this was a bad spot and that he believed it was not safe. He felt we were too far from the rest of the division. Sure enough, within twenty-four hours, the field hospital was overrun!" Mel exclaimed.

Mel had been making runs back and forth with his ambulance from Bastogne to the field hospital. On December 19, barely two days after his arrival to Bastogne, Mel was speeding with his ambulance to the field hospital when he was stopped by another ambulance traveling in the opposite direction.

"They were coming from the hospital. They told me, 'It's gone!' In the background I could see smoke, and the tents were on fire. The other ambulance driver told me Germans overran it, the hospital. He said patients were bayoneted while they lay on their stretchers, IVs still in their arms, and some had their throats cut."

Mel turned his ambulance around and went back to downtown Bastogne. The 101st Airborne was surrounded by the enemy. The second aid station in the city was soon destroyed by a German Junkers Ju 88 bomber. Melvin escaped death this time as well. Being an ambulance driver had its perks: a soldier would never be in one place for very long.

"The 326th Medical Company was never reconstructed," said Mel.

"Who were you attached to the rest of the war?" I asked.

"I was assigned to headquarters for the rest of the war. All the way to Germany. But all our documents were destroyed when the hospital got overrun in Bastogne, so I have no records that I was with the 326th Medical Company."

Mel's story included later encounters with German civilians and Jewish prisoners from a concentration camp as the war went on. He truly saw it all, from D-Day to the Nazi safe haven of Berchtesgaden, Germany. Yet after the war ended, Mel had never attended any 101st Airborne reunions.

For age ninety-seven, Mel was in incredible shape. His memory was fairly sharp, and he could walk unassisted. I was going to have a book signing on the beaches of Normandy, and I wanted to invite several veterans to join me. Mel would be a perfect fit.

"Would you come back to Normandy with me?"

"You bet!" he quickly replied.

This wasn't Mel's first trip back. I had seen his previous returns depicted in several photos on the internet. There was plenty of artwork and paintings for sale on the internet, items that Mel had autographed, most featuring iconic images of the 101st Airborne on D-Day. He was also mentioned in several books as being part of Operation Overlord. This was going to be epic for me. To return with a paratrooper to Normandy was certainly a coup.

But there was one problem: I had no records. Mel was certainly a World War II veteran, but at the end of the day I had no discharge papers from the Army, nor even a photo of him in uniform. I usually had one or the other when documenting legitimate veterans. Mel was a runaway from Canada, and his unit had been overrun in Bastogne. To top it all, there had been a fire at the National Archives in St. Louis forty years ago. Many records, including what was left of his, were destroyed. This was the case for a lot of veterans.

Nevertheless, I was determined to track down something official. He deserved to have a record with his name on it that verified his legendary service to our country.

While the federal government had already declared Melvin's original discharge papers destroyed in the 1973 fire at the archives, I knew there was a chance he'd given a copy to the state of Massachusetts when he'd returned from the war. Most veterans did this so they could claim a welcome home bonus and tax discounts.

Emails were sent; calls were made. I did not hear back from anyone. Either way, Mel, three other World War II veterans, and I were Europe-bound for my first overseas book signing. I was convinced that Mel knew too much to be making this stuff up. I had met many liars already and knew the signs, plus nobody would fake being in such an obscure unit as the 326th Medical Company.

In just seven hours we went from Boston to France and were greeted by the masses. Many still grateful French people of the Normandy countryside were ecstatic to meet the men who had liberated the region seventy-eight years ago. We were the first veterans back since the COVID-19 pandemic.

All four veterans signed hundreds of autographs. Grandparents held their grandchildren over the crowds of people so they could get a glimpse of living World War II veterans. The veterans were treated like rock stars at every public venue.

Finally it came time to visit their battlefields. Mel's was the first. I was eager to bring him back to the chateau that had hosted his initial field hospital. To walk the very grounds of his first Allied airborne field hospital in Normandy was going to be breathtaking.

Our tour guide jumped on our bus that morning. He, a local Frenchman, was as excited as I was to show Mel his old battlegrounds. The bus took us from our hotel thirty minutes away to the countryside of Hiesville.

As our bus pulled into a dirt driveway I could see where the road was leading. I must have stared at hundreds of black and white photos of this building. We were here, the chateau.

I turned my head and gawked at Mel. He was sitting two rows up from me on the bus. He was staring out the window. He was showing no emotion. There were no facial expressions from the man who was arriving at such a pivotal location for him during the war. Perhaps there were too many thoughts running through his head.

As the bus came to a stop in front of the chateau, the hydraulic door opened. Our tour guide sprang out and prepared his large binder, consisting of a photo collection for a presentation. I stood up and held Mel's arm. I escorted him off the bus, helping him balance by grasping his elbow. I walked in front, giving him my shoulder so he could support himself as needed as we got closer to his former field hospital.

Everyone else on the trip formed a semicircle around the bus. They prepared their cameras while the other veterans stepped aside to let Mel have his moment. Walking away from the bus, I gave Mel a while to take it all in. Still, he was emotionless. He stared blankly without saying a word.

There was an awkward silence until finally I had to say, "You recognize this place, right?"

Mel looked around.

"No," he said with a chuckle.

I was surprised. The building was almost entirely the same as it was seventy-eight years ago, minus the repairs from the bombing.

"Sure you do."

Mel's daughter stepped in and revealed to Mel where we were. Mel nodded his head. Still there were no clever words or any expression from him.

Our tour guide stepped in, showing enlarged photographs of the chateau from 1944. Perhaps these would refresh Mel's memory.

"Do you know where you were during the bombing?" the tour guide asked.

He brought the enlarged photograph over to Mel. It was a large black and white photo of the badly damaged chateau.

"Right there, I was in those tents," Mel said, pointing his cane at the photo, which had been plastered on a large poster board.

"But the tents were set up after the bombing. They were used to shelter the wounded when the building was no longer safe," the tour guide whispered in my ear.

This was getting weird.

"Mel, you told me you were in the motor pool, remember?"

He didn't respond to me. Maybe the flight over to France had taken a toll on him and he was exhausted. He seemed confused. We loaded back up on the bus, and nobody said a word. This did not make any sense. Mel hadn't developed Alzheimer's overnight. We came all this way to France only for him to *forget*?

That incident at the chateau was all he talked about back home.

I took out my iPhone and began to search for more photos of the chateau during World War II. Maybe there were some tents set up before the bombing. Surely the internet would have them. As I tried to salvage Mel's story, at that very moment—as if by incredible coincidence, or providence—I received a new email alert on my phone. It was from the state of Massachusetts Veterans' Services.

The subject of the email read "Discharge paperwork for Melvin B. Harris." I opened the email, waiting for the attachment to load. It was the honorable discharge for Melvin. *Perfect*, I thought, *this could provide some answers for us.* I opened the attachment and couldn't believe what I was reading.

Melvin B. Harris was a fraud!

While the discharge did state he had served in World War II, he was not a member of the 101st Airborne, nor did he attend any parachute schools! He did not jump into Normandy, nor was he ever in Bastogne. Lastly, he was *not* a member of the 326th Medical Company.

I was enraged. How could he do this to me? Here I was parading him around Normandy pretending to be a hotshot author and historian, yet I didn't even know the background of the veterans with me on the trip! His seat on the plane could have been filled with a legitimate claimant. I was mad as hell.

This was entirely humiliating. I was biting my nails on the bus knowing we had several museum appearances to go. They would be expecting Q and As with the veterans. This guy could be the end of me, I thought.

I was in too deep at this point. I had to roll with this secret while I was in Europe and pray the guy didn't get a microphone in his hands at any of the museums.

It turned out not to matter that much. Mel's lies were soon displaced by true stories of valor from the other veterans there with me. The sentimental and groundbreaking memories I was making with the other veterans began in part to wash away Mel's lies. On the tenth day, we were on the way home.

During the plane ride, I realized I hadn't said more than three words to Mel or his daughter since we'd left Normandy nine days before. The worry that he could have cost me my legitimacy as an author deeply troubled me. The years of hard work I'd put into my book could never be replaced.

When our plane landed I gave Mel a ride to his home. It was the first time I had ever visited. As I pulled up to the house, I was taken aback. Every window was boarded up with plywood. Vegetation had overtaken the place. It looked like it ought to be condemned.

"My wife had a severe hoarding issue. Things got so bad before she passed away, the fire department had to come and smash the windows open in order to remove all the stuff from our house. It was a fire hazard. You couldn't move inside my home."

I helped Mel into the decrepit-looking home. He lived there alone. Before I left, he turned around and hugged me tightly.

"You are like a grandson to me. I will never forget what you have done for me. I thought my life was over. You have given me a new reason to live," he said.

Suddenly I was teary-eyed. I started to think about Mel's life. Did he ever have a chance? He was a product of incest, a runaway, son of an alcoholic, husband to a hoarder, and now a lonely old man. What good would it do to expose him or embarrass his family? On the other hand, how much of *that* part of his story had been a lie, as well?

As I drove away from the house, I began to forgive Mel in my heart. But while I agreed to excuse him, I decided this would be the last time we would see one another. That turned out not to be the case. Mel died a year later, and I attended his funeral.

He was buried with a chestful of medals he hadn't earned. As I peered into the casket, I couldn't help but feel that while Mel may have been a liar, at least he was *my* liar.

CHAPTER EIGHT

Mobbed Up

Snowflakes covered the windshield of the 1957 white Cadillac Eldorado. The wipers were not moving. The snow was perfect for privacy. It was winter in Nashua, New Hampshire. Maurice Goldstein hunched over the steering wheel. He was beaten and bloodied. Tom Travesi gave him another whack across the back of the head from the back seat.

"You're gonna tell the fuckin' cops you wanna drop the charges. Right?!" Tom screamed.

Jay Raboin was sitting in the passenger seat. He held on to the grip of a silver .38 revolver inside his leather coat pocket. He watched his partner in crime further smack around Mr. Goldstein. Jay's temper had grown since the war. There was no middle ground. When he was pissed off, he saw only red. He was an angry man, meant business, and had zero remorse.

Jay watched as Mr. Goldstein refused to cave to the beating. Both thugs were not hearing what they wanted to hear. Their goal was to make Goldstein agree to drop charges against them and their crew members out of Providence, Rhode Island. Jay's fellow mobsters had burglarized Mr. Goldstein's home and vehicles just months before.

Jay was losing his temper. He was going to give Goldstein one more chance. As he leaned over to talk into his ear, Goldstein swatted him in the face. Goldstein, in fear that he was going to receive another blow to his head, was only trying to defend himself. But he didn't know that Jay's nose had been broken and was highly sensitive, the nerves having never fully healed from his war injury during World War II.

"I saw stars when he hit me. Then everything turned red. I pulled out the gun and shot him in the temple. The noise inside the car was deafening. When he went limp I was happy about it. I was safe again. I know that seems crazy, as we were the ones hurting him. But I developed such a protective behavior after the war, I would have hurt or killed anything in my way. I wasn't me anymore," Jay told me.

He had just finished a life sentence for the murder of Maurice Goldstein, a murder that he'd committed in 1959.

Jay initially wanted zero to do with me. He did not want to talk to a cop after being in and out of prison his whole life. I would have never heard of the old jailbird if it wasn't for his probation officer who approached me in a restaurant.

Just weeks before, I'd been sitting in the Winthrop Arms restaurant when a woman tapped me on the shoulder.

"Hi Andrew, you don't know me, but I loved your book. I am a probation officer and I feel compelled to tell you about the age of a parolee that just came under my supervision. He is ninety-eight and served in World War II. He is a lifer on parole since he was convicted of a homicide in the '50s. He was originally paroled in 1973 when New Hampshire got rid of the death penalty, but then he got caught with four kilos of cocaine in 2003, and went back to jail until now."

I couldn't believe what I was hearing. This man kills someone in 1959, slips the hangman's noose due to New Hampshire overturning the death penalty, and then gets caught with four kilos of coke in 2003? I mean, that puts him at the age of eighty or older when trafficking drugs!

I needed to know how this guy ended up in this lifestyle, and why he was continuing with it into his elderly years.

"Can you connect me with him?" I asked the probation officer.

The bar area was loud and the restaurant was packed. She looked around before answering me.

"Well see, I am kind of new at my job. The truth is, I'm not even supposed to share what I have already. It's against the rules. He is not living at a nursing home, he is in a halfway house," she replied. I told her that if I had a name I could take it from there.

After doing my own digging, I found the group home Jay Raboin was living in. It was just an hour south of Boston, so I hit the road with the rifle to go knock on his door. It was pouring rain on a Sunday, so I assumed he would be home.

It turned out this ninety-eight-year-old man was living in a group home with drug addicts, alcoholics, and other men fresh out of prison. As a police officer, I have made frequent calls to places like these, and they are far from comfortable retirement residences.

When I got to the place, it looked to be a standard Massachusetts multifamily house converted into a group home. It was a large ten-bedroom home serving as a halfway house for undesirables and those getting back on their feet again.

It was hard to figure out which door was the main entrance of the home. I saw a man smoking a cigarette on the porch, hiding from the rain.

"Can I help you?" he asked.

"Yes, is there a ninety-eight-year-old guy living in here?" I asked.

"Yeah, Jay," the man replied.

"Was he in World War II?"

"I believe he was," the man said.

I told this man my story and mission. I felt I might be wasting my time since I didn't know this guy's background. I could only assume he was not an outstanding citizen given his living situation. Halfway through the explanation of my book and the rifle journey, I could tell he was confused. It was as if he didn't believe me.

"Let me get the house manager," he said.

He disappeared for a moment and came back with another big oaf. The guy looked at me as if I had ten heads. I was forced to repeat myself again for the head moron.

As I explained who I was, the house manager tilted his eyeglasses downward and said, "Jay really isn't a sociable person."

"Okay, but I would like to get a chance to talk to him myself, and if he tells me to get lost, then so be it," I answered sharply.

"Ah. He is really not interested," the house manager countered.

"Well, he is his own man. He can make those decisions for himself," I shot back.

I was getting pissed off. I hadn't driven an hour in terrible conditions to have Tweedledee and Tweedledumber block me from entering the group house. But worse, they could now report to Jay and taint the waters before I could approach him.

The self-proclaimed "house manager" was still staring at me as if I were an alien. I turned and walked away. It wasn't going to be my day to meet Jay. I would have to come up with a plan B.

When I returned home I put pen to paper again. I wrote Jay a letter and put a copy of my book in for good measure. What with his being a prison lifer, I suspected he probably liked to read. I even slid a $100 bill in for his trouble.

I was honest in my letter. I let him know I was a police officer by trade and a historian by hobby. I told him I was not an ordinary cop. I valued his military service and wasn't looking to dig or pry into his life other than the time he'd spent in the service. Since I was unaware as to how he felt about the murder charge, or if he was even willing to discuss it, I made the letter strictly about his contribution to the Second World War. I asked earnestly for a reply, as I did not want to see other veterans take the wrong path in life or fall through the cracks, as I considered he may have.

For all I knew the guy he killed could have had sons or grandsons looking for revenge. I wanted Jay to trust me. I dropped the package at the post office and hoped for the best.

A few weeks went by, and, not having heard back, I figured Jay was not interested. The deadline for my second book to be completed was approaching. Yet the more I thought about Jay's story going to waste and those bums on the porch of the halfway house telling me to beat it, the more it got on my nerves. I jumped in my truck and headed back to the group home.

When I arrived my buddies were on the porch again doing what they did best, nothing. It had been a couple months since my last visit. I started over again as if they had never met me.

"Hi, I am here to see Jay. I have written him several letters," I said to the pair.

"He is not around," the house manager said.

I looked around to my left and right to make sure nobody was going to witness what I was about to say to these two scumbags, then whispered my next few words. Gradually my voice grew louder, however. It was the Italian in me, I guess.

"If you don't let me in this fucking house to see this grown-ass man who can make choices for himself, I am going to call all my buddies at the police department and tell them I need a welfare check on a ninety-eight-year-old man who is being taken advantage of. *Then once we are inside we are going to rip open every closet, pull open every drawer, and flip every fucking mattress until I find something illegal!*"

"Ok, ok, ok, he actually was sent to a nursing home a week ago. He ain't doing so good," the house manager said.

"Which nursing home?" I asked.

"Golden . . . Acres, or Golden Passages, or something," he replied.

"Okay, thank you."

I stormed off the porch and back to my truck. I googled around and found a Golden Harbors Health Care Facility just one mile away.

I drove the mile and parked my truck in the building's parking lot. Before I exited the truck I looked back at the rifle and decided to leave it there. I figured it probably wasn't a good idea to hand a convicted murderer a rifle the first time meeting him.

I walked towards the building and entered the motion-sensor doors. I told the receptionist I was there to visit Jay Raboin. She went down the list but couldn't find his name. I figured the adventure was finally over until she said, "Ah, here he is, room 412."

The receptionist had me follow her to his room, and there was Jay, sleeping. He was extremely skinny, hooked up to a urine bag, and clearly near the end of his life. The receptionist left me alone.

"Hi, Jay. My name is Andrew Biggio. I heard you served in World War II."

Jay woke up. He appeared unstartled. He didn't know me from a hole in the wall, yet he was immediately more receptive than his fellow roommates at the crack house had made him out to be.

"That's right. USS *Rinehart*," he replied.

It turns out Jay was a Navy man. He was a gunner's mate on the USS *Rinehart* (DE-196), which was a Cannon-class destroyer escort. The United States Navy in the mid-twentieth century designed 20-knot warships with the endurance necessary to escort mid-ocean convoys of merchant marine ships and troop carriers. Development of the "destroyer escort" was promoted by the need in World War II for anti-submarine ships that could operate in the open ocean at speeds of up to twenty-three miles per hour. Destroyer escorts needed to be able to defend against aircraft and to detect, pursue, and attack submarines. Most importantly, they needed to be able to outmaneuver U-boats.

Jay's job was assistant gunner on the 20 mm. His gun was positioned on the bow of the ship. During convoy escorts in the Atlantic he would scan the sky for enemy planes or boats. He spent his wartime experience dodging German wolfpacks and hunting the U.S. Navy's archnemesis, the U-boat.

"We escorted troop carriers and supply ships to England, North Africa, and France. We wouldn't know we lost any ships in the convoy until we got to port. There would be a list of ships that got sunk. The convoys were so large sometimes you didn't know," Jay told me.

During one convoy from New York to Britain, the USS *Rinehart* spotted an enemy sub.

"We didn't always drop depth charges. Depth charges could rattle the whole ship and mess with our sonar. It could take fifteen minutes for the sonar to get up and running again after a depth charge exploded. This time we fired the 'Hedgehog,'" Jay explained.

"What's a hedgehog?" I asked.

"The Hedgehog is an anti-submarine projector. It could shoot big mortar shells in the air and down into the ocean. It was a forward-throwing anti-submarine weapon. It fired up to twenty-four spigot mortars ahead of a ship. They were perfect when attacking a U-boat."

Although his body was rapidly failing, Jay's mind was fine for his age. He remembered pummeling the enemy submarine with bombs to the point paper documents written in German floated to the surface of the water.

"Our captain scooped the paperwork out of the water. We either sank the sub, or they played a trick on us by releasing the documents to make it look as if we destroyed them. U-boats did this from time to time to stop us from dropping depth charges," Jay added.

Jay completed his job with a satisfactory rating during combat. Time after time he manned the guns, conducted himself with discipline during general quarters, and was a good sailor under pressure. However, something was not right when it came to abiding by simple rules. He was written up time after time. He refused orders from senior petty officers, then went AWOL in the United States and England for six days at a time.

"I couldn't wait to get out of the Navy. I was glad to get out," Jay recalled.

The USS *Rinehart* continued to the Pacific without Jay. He'd become too much of a headache for his officers, and they'd transferred him off the ship while docked in Boston. He finished up his service with the U.S. Navy in Boston, which was the worst thing he could have done. Although he received an honorable discharge, Jay got involved with the wrong crowd while in Boston.

In Boston's North End, returning soldiers and sailors flooded the bars, cafes, and social clubs. Young men who had been indoctrinated in the military with rank structures and obedience to orders searched for work. It was a perfect recruitment opportunity for the mafia nationwide, but particularly for the Boston mob, whose future head don was also a Navy World War II veteran, Gennaro Angiulo.

Back in Pawtucket, Rhode Island, Jay's father had passed away when Jay was three. He'd grown up poor, and he'd looked up to those in the neighborhood who took care of his family. Sometimes those individuals were Providence wiseguys. Back in Boston, Jay figured he could become one of those men he had admired for helping him as a child. Plus, one of Jay's shipmates, Bobby Alamonti, was ready to introduce him to the right people. The two had served in the Navy together, and this was the perfect in.

"They had me doing small stuff. They paid me to go down to the docks and give out drink tickets to the different nightclubs to returning troops. At night I would walk around and promote the illegal card games we had. If the guys wanted girls I could do that for them too," Jay said.

After the majority of America's service members returned home, work dried up for Jay. There were, however, business opportunities back in Rhode Island for him. He moved to Pawtucket and did dirty work for the Providence mob.

"I wasn't full-blooded Italian, so I could never be a made man. I was an associate. They kept me busy, and I had plenty of money. I was treated good," he whispered from the hospital bed.

Jay and another associate, Tom Travesi, were ordered to burglarize the home of wealthy business owner Maury Goldstein in 1959. Maury owned several businesses in Providence and New Hampshire, including a roller-skating rink which brought in hundreds of thousands of dollars.

"Maury was holding out. Not kicking money up to the right people. We were sent to shake him down," Jay stated.

The meet-up with Maury turned bad. Jay and Tom thought they could intimidate Maury and send a message by burglarizing his house.

Maury in return went to the police and pressed charges, naming Jay and Tom. Charges could lead to a lengthy prison sentence back then.

The following months would shape Jay's life to the point of no return. The pair thought they could convince Maury to drop the charges, but this time they decided to send a stronger message. They kidnapped Maury the day before the trial. They forced him to drive his Cadillac to his business in Nashua—perhaps to burglarize the property he owned there, too. The three men wouldn't make it.

Jay shot Maury in the head in a fit of rage. Later, Jay and Tom ditched the car in a random parking lot. They continued to make phone calls back to Providence from a payphone in front of Nashua City Hall. Their getaway driver had to be sent, and he would take over an hour to pick them up. This pickup man turned out to be not the brightest bulb. He did not possess an active driver's license and could barely find Nashua on a map. Ultimately it was Jay's temper, and an unlicensed operator, that got all of them the death penalty.

"You know this isn't my life story," Jay told me. "There's more to my life than this."

"Well, do you regret anything?" I asked.

"*What is there to regret?! I am not sorry for anything!*" he yelled at me from the bed.

I was shocked at what I was hearing. While his body may have been failing, his mind was still sharp, as was his lack of remorse. He was aware of what he was saying. He simply didn't feel bad about murdering a seventy-year-old businessman.

Thanks to some motivated rookie cops who found this odd assortment of three men from Providence hanging out in downtown Nashua at 3:00 a.m. suspicious, all three men were detained. During an interview it was discovered two of the men had blood on them.

The next morning kids walking to school discovered the body of Maury hunched over in his car. The cops didn't know it yet, but they had already caught the culprits hours before. Further investigation showed firearm residue inside Jay's coat, and type-O blood, Maury's blood type, on his shoes and clothes. Both Tom and Jay were sentenced to hang.

As a twist of luck would have it, New Hampshire would get rid of the death penalty before that could happen. Jay was paroled in 1973. Even after he was given a second chance, he jumped back into the "life." This time he would help peddle the poison the mob always claimed they were too good to be involved in, drugs. By 1982 Jay had violated his parole by selling heroin and marijuana. He would do another twelve years in jail.

Clearly, this was the only life Jay knew. After several more stints in prison, he was locked up in 2003 for the last time—at age seventy-six. He'd been caught serving as a drug mule while working for the same connected guys in Providence he'd started out with. He was carrying five kilos of cocaine in his trunk when he was taken down by the feds. Jay ended up back in prison until 2012, when he was again released.

"Were you a part of organized crime because it felt like a brother-hood?" I asked.

He shook his head. "No. I didn't think it was a brotherhood. I just did my own thing," he said.

Jay reiterated that these kinds of things "weren't his story." He didn't rat, nor did he admit to being part of the mafia. He did not want to divulge more about his criminal activity, either.

While Jay claims these facts are *not* his story, I beg to differ. He spent most of his life in jail. He was eloquent; he was educated. He chose that life knowing full well what he was doing.

"I only ask about life after the military so we can prevent other veterans from going down the same road you did," I told him.

"I always found myself different than other veterans. Something was off. I was never on the same page as other guys when it came to being a veteran. At the hospitals, or the vets' clubs, I always felt I was cognitively a few steps ahead of them," Jay said.

I wasn't sure how to reply to this. As someone who had always been on the right side of the law, it was hard for me to grasp his mindset. In the end, I decided it wasn't my job to understand everyone, just to share this story. Perhaps a veteran somewhere out there would understand what Jay meant.

Jay was a felon, convict, and murderer, yet he still played his part in World War II. He was added to the rifle to show that sometimes the Greatest Generation wasn't always so great. A recent myth has grown in some quarters that only Vietnam veterans and Iraq veterans came home with PTSD and became criminals. Jay certainly proved that theory wrong.

I said goodbye to Jay and gave him a salute as he lay in his hospital bed. I had asked him some tough questions, but Someone else would soon be judging him, perhaps more harshly than I had. I bid him farewell.

CHAPTER NINE

Marty the One-Man Party

It had only been about fifteen years since Marty Schlocker returned from the Second World War. His new occupation kept his mind from brooding over being a former prisoner of war. What could be better than riding around in the beautiful California weather as a member of the Los Angeles Police motorcycle unit? His weight and health were back to full strength. It had been years since any bad dreams or triggers during his waking hours brought back memories of being overrun at the Battle of the Bulge. His outlet was working for the LAPD. He'd worked patrol at the academy, and now was cruising the freeways on a Harley Davidson with blue flashing lights.

"I got this call one time for a loud house party. The dispatch asked me to head over. I was the first officer to arrive. I parked my motorcycle on the street and walked up to the home. When I got to the front of the home, I saw there was a big, drunk house party on the front lawn. I asked the homeowner to quiet down, and figured it was an ordinary call," Marty told me.

Martin Schlocker, 17th Airborne Division

"How soon we learn that no call is ordinary," I replied with a smile as I sat at Marty's dinner table, some forty years after his police career had ended, and seventy-five years after World War II. We were bonding, cop to cop, veteran to veteran.

"After ordering the homeowner to control the noise of his party, a few drunk men came out of the house party screaming profanities at me. They weren't ready for me to shut down the fun," Marty said, rolling his eyes.

When normal communication failed with the drunk men, Marty put in a call for help using the radio attached to the back of his motorcycle. As soon as he made the call, the men jumped Marty. He was forced to square off with a particularly disorderly pair until backup arrived.

As he attempted to place one man in handcuffs, the other pushed him over. Marty went toppling over his motorcycle with only one hand cuffed on the other drunk man. Now on the ground, the perp tried wriggling away from Marty. He was able to swing his body around to a bear hug position across Marty's hips and torso.

"He was trying to mount me while we were on the ground. I knew if I let him get on top of me, it could be deadly, so I put him in a headlock."

Marty felt desperate. How long could he keep this man in a headlock before he ran out of stamina? The man was drunk, but Marty was winded. He couldn't reach for his radio, his pepper spray, or his gun. The rest of the partygoers, all of them belligerent, surrounded him. They offered no help. Marty realized he was doomed if backup did not arrive immediately.

"*You get any closer to me and I'll kill this son of a bitch!*" Marty screamed, while cranking the headlock more tightly.

Then the sounds of sirens could be heard in the distance. The cavalry was coming. Marty just had to hold on a little longer. Finally, there came a tap on his shoulder.

"Go ahead, I got 'em," an arriving officer said to Marty.

The two officers put the man into cuffs and threw him into the back of a paddy wagon. Dozens of officers showed up and rounded up the other disorderly partygoers. Marty brushed off his uniform. He gazed into the mirrors of his motorcycle and tended to his scrapes.

Later, he was not able to calm down during his shift, and that night he stared at the ceiling, unable to sleep. It had been a long time since he'd felt so vulnerable. Having to fear for his life brought back many memories of the war. His nerves were shot. His self-esteem and confidence were suffering. He had made up a lot of ground since being a prisoner of war, but now he felt like he was breaking down once again.

"That single incident triggered months of PTSD. My wife really didn't know how to deal with it. Everything had been going so well until that point," he recalled.

Holding on to the headlock for dear life as the crowd surrounded him brought back memories from some twenty years before of holding his arms around his wounded comrade as the Germans surrounded him in the vicinity of Flamierge, Belgium. The blow to his confidence after having to surrender to the Germans was similar to the effect of these unruly civilians ganging up on him while he was wearing the police uniform and doing his duty.

Marty would retire from the LAPD after thirty-two years of service. However, his experience with the 513th Parachute Infantry, 17th Airborne Division, in the Battle of the Bulge would forever shape his life. He'd been lucky to survive, considering his regiment had only half of its strength remaining after its three-day battle in the place called "Dead Man's Ridge."

"My start of the war was when my division was flown directly into Reims, France, on Christmas Eve. A few days later we were trucked into the town of Monty, Belgium. We thought we might jump into Belgium, being one of the only airborne units to not make a parachute jump yet, but that wasn't the case. Almost immediately after getting off the trucks we had to dig in, just like a straight-leg infantry soldier. Because I was a radio man, I had to dig a double foxhole for me and my company commander. He needed to be with me at all times so he could be close to the radio. Some sort of fighting had already ensued in this area before we arrived. I was on a ridge, and in the valley below there was a German tank on fire," said Marty, recalling his first day of combat.

Over the next few days, the valley became a death pit for Germans and American paratroopers. Marty's regiment, the 513th Parachute Infantry, would take the heaviest casualties of all the elements in the newly arriving 17th Airborne Division during the Battle of the Bulge. The men of the Scion Division would forever call this place "Dead Man's Ridge."

As Marty began to dig, sporadic artillery fire landed about the area. "The place was exactly what I thought a war zone would be. Smoke filled my lungs, and the smell of dead animals clogged my nostrils," Marty recalled. At the time, he was nineteen years old.

"The first casualty I remember was a Lieutenant Franklin Robertson. He was hit and wounded mortally by artillery. They dragged him by my foxhole and into a nearby home. He took his last breath on the kitchen table. The first things the guys did was take his boots off. He had brand new boots on. Nobody wanted to see those go to waste," Marty recalled, distaste in his expression.

The next morning, Marty's platoon emerged from their foxholes to probe the enemy. As Marty descended into the valley, he entered a disabled Tiger tank, pointing his M1 carbine into the turret first. The crew was dead. Marty reached into the holster of a dead German, removing a Walther P38. The man's body was shredded, most likely from bazooka fire. As temperatures dropped, snow fell on the patrolling paratroopers. Unable to make enemy contact, they headed back to their foxholes and prepared for a possible German counterattack.

"We were stationary in these foxholes for a few days. Then on January 5 or 6 we were tasked to advance on the town of Flamierge. The Germans were dug in all over the place. As we proceeded deeper into the valley we took small arms fire. When we hit the ground, I could feel it vibrating. I looked up and saw a row of Panzer tanks pouring into the valley," said Marty.

The fire from the enemy was so intense that his platoon needed to seek cover. All they could do was press their bodies against frozen soil. The men lay on their bellies, praying not to get hit. Nobody was going to charge into the valley to drag them to safety, that was for sure.

"Screaming Mimis began to rain down all around us, covering us with snow and dirt. My platoon commander, who often controlled the radio, wanted me to contact the company commander, but the radio was dead, and I had no batteries to replace it," Marty recalled.

Finally a frantic order was given to race into the outskirts of the town of Flamierge. Every man would be on his own. Marty and the rest of his platoon broke down the doors of several homes to take refuge in the basements. These seemed the safest places for the lightly equipped paratroopers. But a column of enemy tanks had observed the Americans dashing toward the homes to seek cover.

It wasn't German armor the men from the 17th Airborne had to worry about immediately, however. German infantry, witnessing the Americans entering the dwellings, gave chase. They took up posts near the American basement redoubts, and firefights began to erupt.

"We were in a fight for our lives. I dumped the radio, as it was now useless," Marty said.

He ran outside of the house he'd been holed up in and stationed himself at one of the corners. He emptied clip after clip from his carbine. German infantry dressed in all white lay in the roadways. Those who were hit had bright red blood seeping through their winter camo. The advancing Germans simply jumped over their dead counterparts and from all angles continued moving in on the American paratroopers. The rumble of approaching tanks was drowned out by gunfire. Then a bazooka team from HQ Company spotted the tanks.

"My dear friend Emmet ran out with his bazooka team and prepared their rocket. I watched as they kneeled down, and one man shouldered the weapon. I was rooting for them, but in a quick violent flash, they disappeared in a cloud of smoke. The German tank scored a direct hit on them," Marty recalled with a sob seventy-two years later.

Marty didn't have time to weep at the time. He needed to relocate himself. He was in danger from the tanks' continued onslaught. As he stepped away, an enemy mortar shell landed inside the home he'd been using for cover. A piece of shrapnel penetrated his boot and implanted itself in the meaty portion of his foot. Blood oozed out the side of his boot, but he was able to walk, and more importantly, to fight. He limped over to the doorway of another house where he'd seen Colonel Miller, one of his battalion colonels, exit moments before.

"The colonel grabbed me and told me to go operate a switchboard that had just been set up in the basement. I had never operated a switchboard before, but I understood the importance. As a radioman, it was key. That switchboard was the only way to communicate with the other battalions," Marty explained.

Around the switchboard in the basement wounded paratroopers lined the floor. They groaned and cried out in pain while Marty frantically tried to operate the switchboard. To his frustration, the radio unit was blown out, unable to function, and its operator was nowhere to be found. The explosions grew louder outside the home. Marty gave up on the broken system and threw the headset to the ground.

"I suddenly heard one of my sergeants, Sergeant Doyle Rush, yell to me from the top of the stairs. He said we were surrounded by the Germans and 'We gotta get out of here!'"

As Marty began to race up the stairs from the basement, a loud crash rattled the building. At the top of the stairs, Marty watched a wall of the home collapse as the barrel of a tank penetrated it. The German tank rammed through. It began to back its way out of the rubble, then moved forward, bulldozing over the pile of wreckage again.

Frightened to the point of panic, Marty ran back down the stairs and through the basement, jumping over several wounded paratroopers on the way. The basement extended under the home to an attached barn. There was a second stairway leading to an exit in the stable. He ascended the stairs to make his second attempt at escape. Then suddenly a German soldier appeared.

"We locked eyes with one another. I'll never forget it. He held a potato masher grenade in his hand. He threatened to pull the pin and throw it into the basement. He asked me how many of us were in the basement. I was so scared I couldn't speak. I held up three fingers and he ordered us to come up the stairs," Marty recalled.

Marty went back down the stairs and informed his fellow paratroopers there was no choice but to give up. The men stripped themselves of their gear and swung their rifles on their backs. Marty realized he still had the Walther P38 that he'd recovered from the dead German tanker in his waistband. He did not want to get caught with a war trophy. He threw the pistol behind him before ascending the stairs again. At the top, he gave himself up.

The Germans screamed at the captured paratroopers outside and stripped every remaining piece of equipment from their bodies except personal items. As Marty and the others were lined up outside, he observed one of his close friends from the platoon sitting against the wall of the house. It was his buddy Howard "Mac" McLaughlin, a friend since jump school.

"He was sitting with his back against the wall. Half his face was blown away. His jaw and cheekbone were gone. He couldn't talk. I'll never be able to get that image out of my head," Marty said, still tearful decades later.

"I asked the German officer to make sure Mac could get some help. He promised me he would. Last I heard he was transferred to a German hospital. That was the last I ever saw of him. He is listed as missing in action to this day. I was the last person to see him alive."

The memory got to Marty, and he began to cry at his kitchen table as we were sitting together. "I'm sorry. I have PTSD over this. I can still see his face," he added as he sobbed.

"You don't have to be sorry. There are so many younger veterans today who are going through the same torment. Your speaking about this event and showing your emotions allows younger veterans to see that they can live long lives with these hard memories. The next generation of veterans needs to know how to manage these thoughts as you have," I said.

I assured Marty that his story would do more good than harm. I was glad he could be so realistic in his description of his last memories of Mac McLaughlin.

Marty nodded his head, understanding my point. We returned to the winter of 1945. Things were about to get harder for Marty. Now he was a prisoner of war.

As Marty pleaded with the German officer to help Mac, he was pushed away into a moving line of prisoners. Marty was marched down the road and, to his surprise, forced into the driver's seat of an American Jeep. Another captured paratrooper was placed in the passenger's seat. A German soldier jumped in the back seat and pointed his MP 40 submachine gun at their backs.

Marty was instructed to keep his hands on the steering wheel as another German soldier chained the Jeep to a Panzer tank. The tank towed the captured Americans through a field, up an embankment, and onto the Bastogne highway.

"We passed what seemed like hundreds of German armored vehicles: Panzers, Tiger tanks, and half-tracks traveling in the opposite direction. The soldiers cheered and mocked me, and I was treated like a human trophy," said Marty.

Suddenly, a rapid barrage of artillery impacted the area around the German column. It was American. Marty and his German captors were forced out of the Jeep. They ran into a nearby wooded area for cover. In the chaos, Marty thought this would be a good time to rip off his dog tags and bury them in the snow. He did not want the Germans to know he was Jewish. His dog tags were marked "Hebrew," indicating his religious preference. When the artillery ceased, the convoy of prisoners was pushed back to the road at gunpoint. They continued the miserable trek.

Several miles later, Marty and the other POWs were dropped off at a checkpoint. They were briefly interrogated by a German officer who spoke perfect English. The U.S. Army was good at keeping young soldiers clueless as to their locations and what direction they were traveling in. Marty couldn't provide the German intelligence officer any real details even if he'd wanted to.

"That night we were given prunes and bread. That was the German infantry soldier's basic meal. We were gathered in a building and forced to sleep on the floor. We were freezing. All we had was our field jackets and jump boots, which were terrible in snow conditions."

The prunes and dark bread would be Marty's last decent meal for four months. The next morning, the captured men of the 17th Airborne joined the ranks of other American prisoners from different units captured all over Belgium during the Bulge offensive.

"We marched for a couple days and were put on a train. They were known as 'forty-and-eights,' because the boxcars could hold eight horses and forty cattle. But there was one hundred of us shoved in there. We were on the train for a week. We had to take turns sitting down because it was so tight. There was a hole in the floor for us to use the bathroom." Marty still remembered the trip with obvious disgust.

Similar to the experience of Clarence Cormier, veteran of the 106th Division, recounted in *The Rifle*, Marty's train came under attack by American fighter planes. Multiple P-47s dive-bombed the German train loaded with American prisoners. More men died as they frantically pressed together in the boxcars.

Finally the Germans let them out.

"We got on a little hillside, and with blankets spelled out the letters P-O-W in the snow. The planes flew so low on the next dive I could see the pilot waving at us!"

Hearing Marty's friendly fire story often makes me wonder if Clarence Cormier and Marty were on the same train. As far as I know, there's no way to tell.

Marty grew emotional once again as he recounted dragging out the dead bodies of soldiers who had been killed in the strafing of the boxcars. They had been tragically shot by friendly fire, but were fortunate to miss out on the torture of starvation and captivity that was soon to come.

"We never reboarded a train after that. The engine was destroyed by the P-47s. We had to march again. We marched for a few days before arriving at our first POW camp. The 101st Airborne soldiers captured in Bastogne were helping the Germans run it. They were helping process prisoners and take notes." Marty remembered seeing the Screaming Eagle patches on these men's shoulders.

"The food wasn't bad here, and there were places to sleep on floors. However, after a couple weeks there was an outbreak of meningitis. The Germans asked for 250 volunteers to march to another camp. I'd seen many soldiers who were not healthy enough to walk, so me and my buddy Robert Emmick volunteered. We wanted to stay together. So we figured it was a good idea." Emmick was also a New Yorker.

Marty, Emmick, and two hundred other prisoners marched for several days, eventually crossing the Rhine River. "We crossed the Rhine on a bombed-out bridge. The bridge had collapsed into the river, but we were able to cross on the beams and trestles still above water. Our feet got wet a little bit, but so did the Germans'."

While in the city of Bonn, the transferred prisoners made the best of what was supposed to be their new camp. The conditions were similar to that of the first stalag in which they'd been imprisoned. The decision to volunteer to go to the new camp seemed like it had been a smart move to Marty and Emmick, at least for the present.

"A week or so later British Halifax bombers filled the night sky. They dropped incendiaries on the city of Bonn, but hit our prison camp. Then came the five hundred pounders. We hid in a trench with our German captors as the camp got destroyed. Many guys got killed. It was not good."

After less than a week at the camp near Bonn, Marty and Emmick were without a home yet again. The bodies of American, British, and French POWs lay strewn about the camp. The living prisoners were ordered to bury the dead, and then it was off to another camp, marching once again.

This time the trip was far harsher. Sickly prisoners from the previous camp could not keep up. Many were malnourished and some too weak to make the 150 mile expedition to the new prison camp in Bad Orb, Germany.

During the journey, Marty and others stopped at a German hospital. Several men, including Marty, were assigned work detail. The duty consisted of holding down wounded German soldiers so surgeons could work on them.

"We would have one guy hold the legs and the other hold the arms and head. The German soldiers were having all kinds of surgeries done and there wasn't enough ether to put them to sleep. Guys had their limbs sawed off, while others needed their bodies sewn up. Some guys just died right there on the table. We would then bring the bodies outside and stack them up. Bodies were stacked about five feet high, like wood. I was surrounded by so much death at this point that dying doesn't become a thought anymore," he recalled.

After several days of work detail at the hospital, the group of American POWs were on the move again. The brutal march continued another hundred miles to their final destination in Bad Orb. Everyone had grown weaker. Food was scarce, and men were constantly falling out on the forced march.

"We did what we could to encourage guys to keep walking, but they just couldn't. The weather had gotten worse, and a lot of these guys had been living off a slice of bread a week at their last camp. They had no energy. We lost a lot of guys on that march. When we got to Bad Orb, Stalag IX-B was located on a mountain. We had to climb up. Some guys simply couldn't. It was hell," Marty said.

As for the men who died on the roadside or in ditches, their whereabouts will never be known. Perhaps they were the lucky ones. Stalag IX-B was one of the worst Allied POW camps in Europe. Its overcrowded situation alone caused disease and lice to run rampant in the enclosures. The Germans would strip down the American prisoners and steam their uniforms in an attempt to neutralize the lice, but this procedure only gave lice eggs more survivability. They hatched later on, and this doubled the lice population.

"The lice would keep you awake. They were more active at night. Every man sleeping on the wooden floors would be squirming, itching, and grabbing at themselves. Due to the overcrowding it was hard not to get stepped on by someone trying to go outside to use the bathroom," Marty said.

While at Bad Orb, Marty attended Catholic services. He was still doing his best to conceal the fact he was Jewish. Religious service was the only thing the men had to look forward to. Boredom was another brutal part of being a prisoner. There was nothing to do other than walk aimlessly around the camp day in and day out.

After a month of misery, Marty was now down to 130 pounds. There were times that giving up sounded good, but for Marty this was not an option. Distant gunfire and artillery grew nearer each day. The men tried to hold on to what life was left in them.

One morning the Nazi guards were gone. Tank tracks could be heard approaching.

Then there was the beautiful sight of Sherman and Stuart tanks crashing through the gates of Stalag IX-B. Their crews threw K-rations from the turrets to the prisoners. Marty cried at the sight of his liberators. The German guards were nowhere to be found. They had escaped into the night as the explosions grew closer.

"They put us in a group and DDT-ed us. It was insect spray that later was banned because it causes cancer. They covered my face, hair, and body in it. We were all naked and they gave us new uniforms. The next day a small airstrip had been set up. C-47s landed and we all jumped in. They flew us to Le Havre, France. It was the last time I saw my buddy Emmick. His frostbite was so bad he needed to be hospitalized elsewhere."

Marty and other prisoners were brought to Camp Lucky Strike, one of the biggest bases in France for American troops. There they had access to steak, ice cream, pie, and the food they'd dreamed of since being taken prisoner. However, this seeming horn of plenty was a death sentence for some, and almost for Marty himself.

"I ate so much, when I left the chow hall my heart started to flutter. My body couldn't handle it. My stomach had shrunk so much that my body didn't know how to process it. Last thing I remember was everything going black."

Marty passed out. He was rushed to a hospital, where he remained bedridden for two weeks. His heart was compromised, according to the doctors, and he was lucky to be alive. Other prisoners had died after such unsupervised eating. It was later a truism among returning POWs that the Army medical staff at Lucky Strike should have done a better job monitoring newly rescued men.

Marty returned to the United States as soon as he finished recuperating in France. His reunion with his family was emotional. But he still owed the Army time in his enlistment.

"They asked me to come back to Fort Benning and perform a jump for some military officers. I said, 'You've got to be kidding me. I'm still healing from being a POW.' I was too light, too weak. I was in no shape to perform a jump," Marty said.

He would finish his World War II service as an MP at Camp Mackall, in North Carolina. By 1946, he had finished his original commitment to the military. Soon after, he answered an ad in the newspaper to attend the LAPD academy. Marty would serve in the Army Reserve for twenty years and finish his stint with the LAPD after three decades.

In 1994 Marty received an interesting phone call. It was his buddy Mac's only son, wondering what had happened to his father, the man who went missing at the Battle of the Bulge. Marty was the first person who could give Mac's son an answer. He'd been the last person to see Mac alive and was able to answer many questions for this man who had grown up without a dad. Several weeks later the two met at Marty's home in California. They hugged and cried together. Mac's son had returned to Belgium multiple times to investigate what had happened to his father, but had never gotten closure until his meeting with Marty.

The two stay in touch to this day. Mac's remains may still be in Belgium, perhaps buried in a shallow grave. Perhaps one day he will be recovered, along with Marty's dog tags hidden somewhere in the snow.

As I concluded my talk with Marty, I saw beyond the older man to the teenager who'd had much of his young life robbed from him in this gruesome world war. But that scared young boy still inside had also helped him navigate his career as a good cop. He knew what it was like to be a prisoner. This kept him from being handcuff-happy and arresting people for no reason, as in my own experience I've known some power-hungry cops to do.

Marty the one-man party is an inspiration for young veterans and police officers who experience trauma in their lives. He is a prime example of why we should never glorify war. The costs are too high. Yet I consider myself fortunate to have been allowed to relive his experiences with him, and to share them with others.

CHAPTER TEN

Sinking Pride

"I wish you luck in your endeavor and good luck in the future of this country, wherever it's heading. I'm glad I won't be around to see it. Because this isn't the country I fought for anymore."

I stood on the front porch of Mr. Bill Allen and felt dismay. I held the rifle in its case in one hand, and with the other shook Bill's hand as his screen door closed behind us. While we had had a great interview, the man, now age ninety-seven, was saddened by the current state of affairs in the United States. Bill was a Tennessee boy who grew up playing basketball, football, and baseball. These days, it nearly killed him inside to see professional athletes kneel during the national anthem.

Bill wasn't just a proud World War II veteran. He was one of the only survivors remaining of naval ship LST (Landing Ship Tank) 523, which struck an underwater mine and sank not far from Omaha Beach after D-Day. He watched his ship break into pieces and his crew drown. The national anthem, and pride for his fallen service members, had been important to him for nearly eighty years. I couldn't blame him for feeling the way he did.

Bill Allen, LST 523

I wanted my visit to give him hope for the future of America's youth, but when I left he was still angry. Before the door closed all the way, I got in a last word. "I promise I will help turn this country in the right direction. There are more people out there like me than you know."

"I hope so," Bill said. The door shut and the interview was done.

I sat inside my rental car in Murfreesboro, Tennessee, wondering what had just happened. Most of my visits with World War II veterans were jovial. They enjoyed seeing a young man interested in World War II and the men who fought in it. But Bill Allen felt terribly let down. He had been an athlete his whole life and viewed athletes as role models. For so many athletes to use the American flag as a means of taking out their social frustrations made him cringe. The flag meant much more to him than a piece of cloth; it was a symbol. It represented the lives of every sailor on LST 523 who went down with his ship. That's what those who target the American flag forget. Both white and black veterans died with that flag on their shoulder.

The United States as a country has not been perfect. No country is without a dark history or a past full of hateful baggage. But the United States has come a long way in Bill Allen's nearly one hundred years. The Second World War itself was a prime example of the progress the country made. The war couldn't have been won without our buffalo soldiers, Navajo code talkers, Japanese Americans in uniform, and the women's Nurse Corps. People of every color and creed united to end Nazism, genocide, and oppression. The sacrifice of our melting pot of a U.S. military united us all. This is what Bill Allen recalled the American flag representing.

But Bill was now an old man. Many of those who remembered World War II were gone, and it must have seemed to him as if it was Bill versus the world. The best way for me to honor Bill was to share his story. I wanted to let him know that his fellow sailors did not die in vain, but paved the way for grateful Americans like me.

In May of 1943 Bill rushed to join the U.S. Navy right out of high school. He was shipped off to Bainbridge, Maryland, for boot camp. "It was mostly boys from Delaware in my class and we were there for about six to seven weeks," Bill recalled.

"The Navy taught you how to be disciplined, be on time, and be physically fit. I had no trouble physically because I was always active playing sports growing up. My photo hangs in the Murfreesboro hall of fame for being an amazing athlete during high school," he added.

I could tell sports was an important topic to Bill, which was why the professional athletes had upset him so much when they protested the national anthem.

"What did you do after boot camp?" I asked Bill.

In perhaps a hat tip to his athleticism, he had been assigned one of the most physically demanding jobs of the Navy, that of a hospital corpsman.

"As a corpsman you are a medic. You could be assigned to the Marines and not necessarily on a ship. They could send you anywhere. You would have to carry the wounded and treat multiple patients at a time. During another seven weeks of hospital corpsman school we learned first aid, basic medicine, and minor surgery," Bill recalled.

Having been a Marine myself, I was aware of the strenuous job being a Navy corpsman could be.

"During hospital corpsman school a group of us became really close with one another. Five of us were from Tennessee, one guy from Georgia, another from North Carolina. We all were sent to New York together," Bill recalled.

While in New York, Bill and the rest of the southern hospital corpsmen waited to be assigned a ship in Lido Beach, Long Island. The boys were desperate to stay together. They were all similar, came from the same backgrounds, and shared the same values. Bill said of his friends, "If you met one of us, you met us all."

"While we awaited orders, we found out that if we ended up on an LST it would require forty hospital corpsmen. This made us all hopeful we would remain together. The men pushed to be assigned to an LST, and got their wishes answered," Bill said.

The group of inspiring young corpsmen were shipped down to New Jersey to meet their new ship. LST 523 awaited them on the dock. She was painted with a camouflage pattern on the hull and was 50 feet wide and 325 feet long.

"She wasn't a big ship. She wasn't a fighting ship, no large guns, just enough to defend with. The point of an LST was to deliver vehicles, equipment, and soldiers on a beach landing. Amphibious operations was its main purpose. The front of the ship would open up and drop a large ramp."

LSTs proved to be essential in the invasions of North Africa, Sicily, Italy, and throughout the Pacific. Now Bill and the rest of his crew would be put to the test in France. Waves of LSTs could dump whole divisions on enemy soil within minutes. They had been successful enough to justify Operation Overlord and the attempt to liberate France.

LST 523 would set sail from Boston and head to England for training maneuvers. The largest invasion yet for Allied forces needed practice. Bill and his crew would take part in numerous exercises to prepare themselves for the invasion of France. Their role would be important in dropping supplies for ground troops in need of reinforcements, but the main task was loading wounded soldiers and keeping them alive on the ship so they could be evacuated back to England. This mission had to be orchestrated among hundreds of ships.

"Our first stop was Plymouth, England. We were carrying a heavy load of logistics that we'd brought from Boston. We off-loaded all the equipment, then all the medics attended chemical warfare school. We had to be prepared for a possible chemical attack by the Germans upon a beach landing. There was also the possibility that the corpsmen may need to care for patients who have been exposed to chemical agents," Bill explained.

Once the corpsmen had finished their training, LST 523 was loaded for the final time. "We had loaded the ship to the max with trucks, ammo, and soldiers. We went out at night and anchored off the coast of England. We knew this was it," Bill recalled.

LST 523 waited overnight as other ships began to debark with their logistics and join her at sea. Anchored around her was just a fraction of the invasion fleet that had set sail on the night of June 5 and into the morning of June 6, 1944. "As the sun rose, I went on the deck and saw there were more ships than God to the left and right of us heading for Normandy. It felt powerful being part of something like that. Pictures do not do any justice."

"There were so many ships taking part in the invasion. When we got the signal for our turn to drop our load on Omaha Beach it was around noon time. The men were still fighting to take the beach and surrounding areas. We dropped our ramp in about three to four feet of water and took our first casualties right there. The soldiers' packs were so heavy that if they lost footing they would drown. I watched others make it to the beach, but others stepped on land mines, causing an eruption of sand and smoke," Bill said. The carnage in his sector of Omaha Beach was massive.

As soon as LST 523 unloaded, the men began to bring aboard the wounded. Stretcher after stretcher was brought up the ramp. Corpsmen assisted one another by marking the foreheads or head bandages of the wounded. These markings indicated that the wounded man was to receive morphine. By the time the tide came back in, the LST was ready to pull out to sea again, this time with nearly two hundred casualties on board.

"We treated those with severe wounds and those with minor injuries. Those who died on board we cleaned up as best we could and laid them down in a certain area of the ship. There were surgeons aboard doing minor operations. By the time we got back to England there was a pile of amputations stacked up in the rear of the ship." Bill recollected the trip with a distant stare. He seemed to still be looking at that stack of body parts from so long ago.

LST 523 delivered its wounded back to England, then reloaded with a fresh stockpile of troops, trucks, and tanks.

"We made three trips to Omaha Beach. I had seen so many bloody, filthy soldiers in agony. Some were so dirty we cleaned them up as best we could while knowing they weren't going to make it. By our fourth trip in, ground troops had made good progress gaining significant territory in Normandy. We were feeling safe and confident about our landings on the beach from here on."

On June 19, LST 523 prepared for its fourth delivery to the shores of Normandy. Waiting for the tide to come in on Omaha Beach, she anchored about five miles away from her regular landing zone. Eager fresh troops crowded the deck of the ship checking their vehicle's gas, oil, and tire pressure. Men went over their equipment, inspected their gear, and looked over maps of Normandy.

"Around 11:30 a.m. I ate some lunch and went topside. There was a terrible storm coming. The waves were rough and a couple soldiers invited me to sit in the cab of their truck," Bill remembered.

A few short minutes after Bill had moved inside the truck, a tremendous explosion erupted from the center of the ship. Debris crashed down on the truck's hood and roof, and the windshield shattered. The three men inside had been shielded. Bill and the others were not hurt, but were in shock. They flung the doors open to exit the truck.

The LST, a flat-bottomed ship, which would normally float above underwater mines, had been lifted up by the swells of the storm and then quickly forced down low in a wave's trough. This caused the ship's hull to strike a mine placed in the channel by the Germans. The detonation had occurred upon contact and struck at the center of the vessel.

"The ship broke almost in half immediately. As I jumped out of the truck I soon realized we had struck a mine. On my half of the ship, men lay around the deck missing limbs and screaming for help. Soldiers and sailors began to abandon ship, jumping over the sides. Everyone knew there was no hope for the ship; it was cut in half."

"As each portion of the ship sank lower and lower, large waves would sweep the wounded sailors off the decks, never to be seen again," Bill recalled.

It was never an easy decision for hospital corpsmen to ignore a wounded brother in arms. However, Bill knew he must decide whether to go down with the ship or jump off and swim for his life.

"Either way, I thought I was going to drown. It was either drown with the ship or swim away and drown. So I made the call to bail," said Bill.

As Bill prepared to jump off the portside of the ship, he saw someone he knew with a life raft one hundred feet away.

"It was my friend Jack Hamlin. He'd managed to get ahold of a life raft. He called out for me to not attempt to swim out to him, as the water was too rough. He said he will come to me. That was a brave action for him to attempt. As the ship sank, it could create a massive suction on everything around it. It could have pulled him and the raft under the ocean as the ship continued to sink," Bill noted.

As Jack got closer with the raft, Bill left LST 523 for the final time, leaping off just a foot away from the life raft. In a few strokes, Bill grabbed hold of the raft and pulled himself on. Both men then paddled away as what remained of LST 523 sank to the bottom of the sea.

"Injured soldiers and sailors floated in the water. We attempted to pull several of them onto our raft. We got four of them out. Two of them were hurt really bad, but this was as many as we could hold for now."

The men on the life raft paddled away from the fateful scene, until a motorized LCVP approached them. The men transferred themselves onto the small landing craft. The skipper of the boat figured it was the best decision to get the severely wounded to shore. There was a field hospital on Omaha Beach that could treat them quickly. The coxswain steered the boat toward shore.

"The storm now was at its peak. The waves were as high as I had ever seen in the Navy. The coxswain tried relentlessly to get us to the beach. He couldn't do it. To his credit, if he wasn't as good a coxswain as he was, we might have sunk in the LCVP as well."

Mother Nature denied the chance to deliver the wounded to the beach. The skipper muscled the steering wheel of the LCVP and headed back out to sea. Bill and the other wounded soldiers and sailors kept their eyes out for a larger ship that might take them. Luckily, the first ship they spotted threw a net down. It was a Liberty ship manned by Merchant Marines.

"Will you take our survivors?" the coxswain yelled to the Merchant Marine hanging over the railing of the Liberty ship.

A voice aboard the ship shouted back, "We will take all you bring us!"

While Bill and those who were able climbed the net, a basket had to be lowered for others who, though still clinging to life, were so seriously injured they couldn't climb. As Bill reached the top of the net he was greeted by the captain of the Liberty ship.

"You boys get some dry clothes on. Go down below and get some hot food," the captain told them.

Bill and his buddy Jack went below. They were given food and coffee, but something was wrong. Their bodies wouldn't allow them to swallow. They were in shock. They had no thirst or appetite.

"The food looked great. I took one bite but couldn't chew or swallow. I took a sip of my coffee. Same thing, I couldn't get it down. I looked at Jack and he was dealing with the same issue. The captain came back over to us. He saw our plates were still full and put his hand on my shoulder," Bill recalled.

"Looks like you guys had a rough day. Why don't you get some rest?" the captain said.

Bill and Jack made their way to a couple of warm beds. They tried to sleep. The Liberty ship rocked back and forth on the ocean, and as soon as the two closed their eyes, a sudden movement of the ship would cause them to jump up with anxiety.

"We just kept reliving what had happened. I was wide awake and couldn't sleep. I called to Jack, who was in the bunk below me."

"'Jack, you awake?'"

"'Yes. I can't sleep.'"

"'I don't think I'll ever sleep again,'" Bill replied sadly.

The two went topside. Both Jack and Bill, now in baggy, nameless Merchant Marine uniforms, sat on the bulkhead of the ship. They stared off into the distance, watching battleships fire their guns into the country-side of Normandy. The Navy was still supporting infantry units as the offensive continued. While day turned to night, Bill and Jack watched tracer rounds soar into the sky.

"The names and faces of our crew began to run through my head. Why was I spared, I began to ask myself." Bill thought while watching the tracer rounds. "So many fatherless children, husbandless wives. Why me?"

The suffering, crying, and drowning men filled his head. LST 523's final moments replayed again and again.

"Why did the life raft appear? Why did I sit in that truck? I should have been crushed by falling debris."

Thoughts that a nineteen-year-old boy should not have to ask himself raced through Bill's mind as he gripped the railing of the Liberty ship. Ten hours after the sinking, Bill began to weep. He'd been a religious man who attended Sunday school; now it was hard for him to believe what he'd been taught for his whole life until then. After seeing the suffering, death, and misery, it was hard for Bill to believe God was good.

"I could have became an atheist very easily that day," Bill told me.

Of the 145 Navy personnel on LST 523, 117 perished on June 19. Twenty-eight sailors survived, including Bill. While Bill questioned his faith in God, he realized something that changed his perspective. All twenty-eight of the men who survived had attended church services with him on June 5 before the invasion.

Spotting the life raft, finding shelter inside the truck, and being rescued by the LCVP were signs to Bill that God had played a hand in sparing his life. He continued to practice his religion and devotion to God thereafter, and kept the legacy of LST 523 alive for eight decades. He wanted, for the sake of the killed, to live a life which the fallen soldiers and sailors would have approved of.

"I got to go back for the seventieth anniversary of D-Day," Bill told me proudly.

Seventy years after the invasion, PBS was doing a special documentary on sunken ships from D-Day. They paid for Bill, his wife, and daughters to return to the English Channel and float directly over the location where LST 523 sank to the bottom of the ocean on that fateful day in June 1944.

The documentary producer showed sonar imaging to Bill of what was believed to be LST 523. There was an obvious blast hole in the center of the ship, and this was the only LST sunk in that precise location. The computer imaging was impressive technology. However, the crew took a step further. To Bill's surprise, they walked him across the deck and showed him a small two-person mini submarine.

"Want to take a closer look at your ship?" the crew member asked.

Bill hopped into the mini sub with only enough room to lie on his stomach, the operator lying next to him. The submarine descended to the bottom of the channel, and there she was. Bill was viewing LST 523 for the first time in seventy years. She was dark and murky-looking at this depth. Tanks and other vehicles were still strapped by chains to her deck. Other tanks lay next to the ship, flipped upside down on the sand, probably thrown out by the detonation itself.

"We circled the wreckage a few times. She was just how I left her. Although we couldn't see a number painted on the side, it was definitely LST 523. I even located the spot I jumped off. It was the final resting ground for so many of her crew," Bill said.

Returning to see LST 523 at her sandy place of repose was another checkmark at the end of Bill's life. He could finally say a proper goodbye to his crew members. The guilt of surviving eased.

Yet, upon returning home from his trip from France in 2014, Bill saw that more and more social unrest featured on the news every night. By 2020, Bill's patriotic accomplishment and his farewell to his crew seemed buried underneath protests, flag-burning, and national anthem boycotts. He felt disappointed and let down by the country for which he'd sacrificed so much.

As he expressed his views to me in his driveway, I wanted to assure him that this country could unify again, just as it had on December 8, 1941—the day after Pearl Harbor. Just like it did on September 12, 2001, the day after 9/11.

I stressed to him that there were many more young men and women like me, but Bill seemed to take this with a grain of salt. I sensed he felt this wasn't enough. I felt disheartened to know we had drifted so far as a nation that one of the members of the Greatest Generation, one who built this country through sacrifice, had been so let down.

"It is easy to attack the flag. It can't defend itself unless worn on the shoulders of men who died for this country in a moment's notice. Regardless of their skin color, the bravest men have had their caskets draped with that flag," Bill told me.

As I put the rifle inside my rental car, I made one last promise to Bill. I said that I would do what I could to get this country back on the right track with my book.

"Well good luck to ya," Bill sharply told me. I understood where Bill was coming from. Yes, there were injustices taking place in our country, but it certainly wasn't the American flag's fault.

Now, of the twenty-eight sailors who survived his ship's sinking, he was the last one left. That flag represented too many white crosses in the Normandy cemetery for Bill to see things any other way. And some of those crosses represented the soldiers and sailors of LST 523.

CHAPTER ELEVEN

The Pacifist

"**Y**ou can pick it up if you want," I suggested.

Photos of World War II veterans in their late nineties holding up an M1 Garand always made for badass content on my website.

Charles Ketcham finished writing his signature on the rifle. He took one step back and looked at it. The rifle was in the bed of my truck, still flat in the case. He'd agreed to meet with me outdoors since the COVID pandemic was still in full swing.

"Go ahead, lift it up," I said again, preparing my camera.

"No, I'd rather not," he said firmly.

I was surprised, and perhaps a bit irritated.

"I vowed I would never pick up a gun again," Charles added.

My dissatisfaction turned into a solemn understanding, even though I had met so many other veterans who had proudly scooped up the rifle and slapped it against their palms like it was nothing.

Charlie stood next to the rifle as it lay in the open case. I figured that was the closest photo I was going to get. Charlie was now ninety-five

Charles Ketcham, 10th Armored Division

years old and living in Lexington, Massachusetts. I wanted to understand what had made the elderly man a pacifist.

I locked the rifle in its case and placed it in my truck, and the two of us went for a walk around his neighborhood. The weather was fairly warm, and we sat on a park bench next to a jogging trail.

It wasn't a shock to learn that Charlie had been drafted. He was a little younger than most veterans I was meeting, born in 1926. This year of birth was certainly destined to make him a replacement in the Army war machine.

"I completed my basic training at Fort Stewart. My basic training was quick. I can't say I learned a lot, it was intense. I could tell the big Army was rushing this. We dug holes and let tanks drive over us to get the feel of real combat," Charlie recalled.

As a member of the high school class of 1945, Charlie was in basic during the Battle of the Bulge. The country had been at war for three years, and there was an urgent need to get new recruits overseas. Those born in 1926 would be some of the last Americans to see combat, some of them barely eighteen toward the end of the war.

"I served with the 10th Armored Division, 54th Armored Infantry, Company A. It was also known as the Tiger Division. I was a replacement for the casualties they took during the Bulge. I joined them just outside Trier, Germany," Charlie explained.

In a field somewhere in Germany, Charlie met Company A of the 54th AIB. Their armored halftracks formed a semicircle around their sleeping area, guns pointing towards the city of Trier. These men were battle-hardened. They had been fighting since October in places like Metz, Alsace-Lorraine, Luxembourg, and Belgium. To Charlie's relief, they were not unkind to him.

"They treated me like a little brother. I knew I was going to learn more from them than I had in basic training, and I did. They taught me more in just a few days outside Trier than I learned at infantry school," said Charlie.

Being in an armored infantry unit, Charlie and the others had half-tracks at their disposal. These tracked armored vehicles were mounted with a .50 cal turret, with two .30 cals on each side, and could fit a squad of twelve soldiers inside. The men could dismount during an assault at a moment's notice, each with his own rifle.

"At nighttime we put all the halftracks in a full circle. We slept inside and had one man per halftrack awake. If anything moved outside our circle I was told to shoot it. All this firepower with all those halftracks was like a 360 degree death blossom," Charlie recalled.

The next morning Charlie's squad leader walked up to the bridge. Across the bridge, the once beautiful ancient city of Trier had been transformed into a zone of destruction. Through a pair of binoculars, Charlie witnessed for the first time what war looked like.

During the Battle of the Bulge there were three heavy air raids on Trier. On December 19, thirty British bombers let loose 136 tons of high-explosive bombs, and two days later American bombers dropped 427 tons of bombs, including incendiaries. Soon after that, another 700 tons of bombs plastered the city. Four hundred and twenty people were killed. Fortunately, many civilians had already fled, but regular German troops still had command posts operating there.

During the bombing, 1,600 houses were completely destroyed, and numerous ancient buildings were obliterated. Between December 16, 1944, and January 2, 1945, the U.S.A.F. and the R.A.F. dropped an astounding 1,467 metric tons of bombs. The only undamaged structures left in ancient Trier were the Roman ruins. The bombers had hit the ancient cathedral, the oldest Romanesque church in Germany, and, during one direct hit, its bell had shaken loose and fallen through the tower.

"The Romans had been in Trier in AD 170. They built the Porta Nigra, which was like a large gate to the city. It looked like part of the Colosseum in Italy. It was the only building that wasn't destroyed by the bombing that I could see with binoculars."

The men of the 10th Armored Division readied themselves for the ground assault on Trier. As they gathered around their circle of half-tracks, an armored field artillery unit swarmed in nearby. This unit set up its artillery pieces and began to soften up Trier even more before the men of the 10th Armored were set to go in.

"Throughout my war experience I noticed our field artillery would come in, set up fast, shell the hell out of a place, then pack up and leave. When the Germans began to fire counter artillery the only people in the area was us! I learned to hate both friendly and enemy artillery," Charlie said.

"Mount up!" screamed the first sergeant, and halftrack engines fired to life with a roar. Charlie's squad jumped into the back of their own halftrack, rifles between their legs. Two of the men manned the machine guns mounted to the sides, another manned the .50. The platoon of halftracks patrolled towards Trier in a dispersed arrangement, in case of mines or rocket attacks. One by one they raced over a bridge, inexplicably not destroyed, and into the outskirts of the city.

The company began its assault, guns blazing. The speedier halftracks blitzed ahead with tanks following behind to reinforce their advance. Shells from the machine guns rattled onto the floor of the halftrack as the armored vehicles raced around obstacles and buildings. The machine guns intensified their fire at German positions, and even more hot shell casings fell into the collars of the soldiers' field jackets, burning their necks until they could reach in and pull them out.

Then it was time to dismount. Charlie jumped out of the halftrack and raised his M1 Garand to his shoulder. To his surprise, German troops were coming towards him with white flags in hand. They were surrendering.

"Being in the armored infantry allowed you to fight a different style of war than just being a foot soldier. We could lay down so much firepower with all those machine guns and keep charging forward. I engaged visible targets, German soldiers, but am unable to say if I hit anyone. I was scared to death, but glad my first combat experience had the enemy giving up easily," Charlie recalled.

Although pockets of resistance held out, the defense of Trier fell apart. The fighting was not as heavy as previous battles, and the 10th Armored was able to swoop in with minimal casualties. The Supreme Headquarters Allied Expeditionary Force, General Dwight Eisenhower's HQ, radioed General Patton's army to halt outside of Trier because it "would take four divisions to seize the city." Unbeknownst to Eisenhower, Trier was already in American hands. The 10th Armored Division had pushed through with the infantry. Patton then sent his now-famous message, "Have taken Trier with two divisions. . . . What do you want me to do, give it back?"

Charlie walked by the Roman Porta Nigra structure. Dead Germans lay strewn about the area. They had been shot by members of the 10th Armored Division. It was his first time observing enemy dead. The Tiger Division meant business. By this point in the war, they had little sympathy for the Germans.

The 10th Armored Division continued to move at lightning speed across Germany, often getting so far ahead that their resupply couldn't keep up. The armored divisions paid a brutal price for this near the city of Crailsheim. There, the 10th Armored had pushed nearly twenty miles behind enemy lines and gotten themselves surrounded.

Charlie may have missed Bastogne, but Crailsheim would turn into the worst battle of the war for the 10th Armored Division since the siege of Bastogne. It was the strongest defensive turn of the German army since the Battle of the Bulge.

After dark on April 5, as Charlie recalled, two tanks led the way with halftracks behind them, all making for the city. The rest of the attack column consisted of another four dispersed tanks, and four halftracks following behind them. The 10th Armored Tigers were ready to rumble.

The Germans were ready as well. Multiple ambushes broke out against the advancing Americans. The lead element was slowed by this enemy resistance. Roadblocks, anti-tank fire, and a dense tree line on both sides of the roads limited maneuvering capabilities. This was also the perfect cover for snipers and ambushes.

The 10th Armored Division had penetrated a hornet's nest. Four German divisions, including an SS Panzer division, encircled the town of Crailsheim and cut off the first column of the 10th Armored troops.

More columns of friendly armored vehicles were bogged down along the roads approaching Crailsheim. They were caught in a murderous crossfire from hidden assailants on both sides of the byways. Those soldiers in open-top Jeeps were cut in half by machine guns. The armored infantry at least had the chance to hide behind the armored plating of their halftracks. Tank drivers battened down their hatches. The attack stalled.

"Our lieutenant called the squad leaders together saying that 1,000 Krauts had attacked Crailsheim in early morning, cutting us off. Radio reports claimed enemy planes were active, and their airfield was only twenty kilometers away as well," Charlie recalled.

The Tigers found themselves in a major shit storm. Just as the briefing finished, a jet-propelled German plane soared overhead. It was one of the first of its kind. It was traveling so fast the men could not keep their binoculars on it. Charlie's platoon, distracted by witnessing this German jet fighter, then heard the terrifying sound of a Messerschmitt homing in on them. The Messerschmitt came in guns blazing, strafing Charlie's platoon.

"We ran into the woods as the planes dived in on us. It was bad. We hadn't had to worry about the Luftwaffe for a while, but now it seemed they had plenty of planes to attack us with," Charlie recalled.

The order was given to dig in. Some 325 enemy planes are estimated to have defended Crailsheim, more than the Allied forces had seen in months.

The Luftwaffe continue to swoop in with Me 109s, Me 110s, and the new Me 262 jet as the 54th Armored Infantry took cover as well as they could outside the city. Elements of the 10th Armored were cut off from one another, and all were running low on ammunition. Anti-aircraft batteries were able to shoot down fifty of the attack planes while soldiers hugged the ground in their foxholes. Clumps of dirt and grass continually rained down on Charlie.

They could only sit in their holes for so long. Fearful that they'd be killed either sitting still or while on the move, they knew the only hope lay in an advance into the city. The men remounted their halftrack and pushed forward, with multiple Jeeps leading the way.

"As we came up on an intersection our convoy was fired upon by a volley of Panzerfausts from alongside the road. The Germans popped out of a drainage ditch shooting their bazookas. The first shot hit the Jeep right in front of us square on the left side. Both of the driver's arms were blown off and still gripping the steering wheel. The next warhead went over the hood of our track into the field on the right of us."

Charlie's squad opened fire on the Germans from their halftrack. The enemy troops hunkered down but were exposed, unable to crawl back to the drainage ditch they had emerged from. Machine gun fire and the volley of fire from M1 Garands blew their uniforms right off their backs as they tried to crawl away from the onslaught.

After two days of fighting, Charlie's squad was left with limited to no ammunition as they occupied the edge of Crailsheim.

"My squad leader asked me to run back to some halftracks stationed in the rear that were carrying ammo. I sprinted a few hundred meters back to the rear column. Snipers had been taking shots and killed a few officers, so all the tanks and halftracks were buttoned up. Some of the tracks were out of supplies. I banged on hatch after hatch of tanks and asked if they were carrying ammo. They thought I was crazy exposing myself to sniper fire, but I had no choice. I was able to carry eight bandoleers, four on each arm, back to my squad," Charlie remembered.

As he jogged with the ammo belts around his arms, he reached the location where he'd left his squad. They were nowhere to be found. Desperate to seek cover, Charlie dove into the woods to his right. With eight bandoleers on his arms and carrying his rifle, he'd lost his breath. He knelt in the trees gasping. In front of him was an opening. A beautiful meadow gleamed in the sun just through the woods.

Suddenly a voice yelled out, "Here! Here!"

"I thought it was a G.I. yelling for help. As I followed the voice, I soon was standing over a catastrophically wounded teenaged German soldier. He couldn't have been older then eighteen or nineteen, my age at the time. His stomach was blown open entirely. He looked like he was shot with a high caliber round of some sort. I found it shocking he could still be alive. He continued to speak to me in German. While I didn't speak German, I knew exactly what he wanted. He kept pointing at my rifle. He wanted me to shoot him. He wanted me to put him out of his misery. We stared into each other's eyes. I pretended like I didn't understand what he wanted. Perhaps if I was older, I would have pulled the trigger . . . instead I just cried with him," Charlie recalled.

The nightmare in Crailsheim came to an end when a fleet of C-47s dropped much-needed food, ammunition, and fuel to the 10th Armored Division. This operation provided the Americans with more supplies than the German defenders. The resupply mission proved a classic example of how America was able to win the war in Europe: logistical superiority. Next, American fighter planes were directed by radio to bomb and strafe fortified enemy positions.

By April 9, 1945, an escorted convoy of supply trucks broke through to elements of the 10th Armored Division as well. The Tigers were now supplied by air and ground. Nevertheless, the road into downtown Crailsheim remained a task for the fearless and resilient. Americans and Germans battled in the rubble of the smoldering city. A *Stars and Stripes* reporter wrote, "The fighting at the outskirts of Crailsheim was some of the worst along the Western Front."

Hitler Youth, civilians, and SS troops all played a hand in the fight against the 10th Armored. It was a bloodbath.

After three days, higher headquarters decided that Crailsheim, once regarded as "vital," was not worth any more bloodshed. On April 11, the division was ordered to pull out of what was now deemed an "unimportant" city.

"The withdrawal was a hard pill for the men to swallow. Even though the city had been left to the Germans and 10th Armored losses were extravagant, we had managed to capture two thousand German soldiers, kill more than a thousand, shoot down fifty valuable German aircraft, and divert large numbers of German troops. Keeping those bastards on us allowed many other Allied divisions to press further into Germany," Charlie stated.

It was Crailsheim that would change Charlie's outlook on life.

"That day with the young German soldier begging me to end him was a day that has haunted me forever. Here was another blue-eyed kid, just like me, dying with his guts hanging out," Charlie recollected, shaking his head.

This was the experience that had turned Charlie into a pacifist. He'd never wanted to pick up a rifle again. The mortally wounded German boy, forced into military service, was asking to be put down like a dog. That's what real war was.

Charlie's experience was another example of the lack of unalloyed glory in war. When the teen German soldier died that day, both he and Charlie lost something. Both of those soldiers, American and German, were robbed of their youths.

As I ended my meeting, I couldn't blame Charlie for not wanting to pick up a rifle again. And, while Charlie didn't grasp it in his arms like the other old warriors did, the rifle had still served its purpose. It provided the lesson that combat wasn't what it appears to be in movies, where one side wins, the other loses, and the heroes live long and prosperously. There were no heroes that day in Crailsheim.

CHAPTER TWELVE

The Natives

A t a conference in 2018 in Washington, D.C., that announced the Code Talkers Museum in honor of the Native Americans who fought in World War II, President Trump presented three surviving Navajo code talkers. First introduced was a frail old man who was president of the Navajo Code Talker Association. His name was Peter MacDonald.

MacDonald, who served with the 6th Marine Division in China, talked about sacrifices made by Native Americans during the war. It was a moving speech, and afterward he introduced two other code talkers. MacDonald repeated multiple times how he considered the United States a great country. There was no "woe is me" tone in his voice. These were men who had come from nothing yet had made their mark on history for a country that hadn't been particularly fair to Native Americans since its birth as a nation.

The Japanese broke every secret code American forces employed in the Pacific—that is, until the United States began to use Native Americans on its radio frequencies. The enemy simply could not decipher these messages. It wasn't a language known in that region of the world.

Louis Levi Oakes, Mohawk tribe

The Navajo sacrifice for our country during World War II resulted in many, many battles won, and victory in the Pacific theater. However, what people often are not aware of is that the Navajo were not the only Native Americans who used their language to win the war. There were almost a dozen different tribes in all, including Comanche, Choctaw, Seminole, and Mohawk. All used their native languages to throw off the enemy.

I was ignorant of this myself until the 2018 Marine Corps League Convention in Buffalo, New York. A special guest by the name of Mr. Levi Oakes, a Native American code talker, attended. Levi was not just any code talker, but the last of the Mohawk code talkers. He was *not* Navajo. I obtained his contact information, and a week later I was driving with the rifle from Boston to the New York–Canada border. Levi's daughter Dora told me to meet her at the local casino, and from there she would escort me onto the Akwesasne Mohawk Nation Territory Reservation.

I had imagined rolling hills, mountains, and streams, but the Mohawk reservation was nothing more than a scattered trailer park. This is not an insult to the Mohawk people, but more of a clear revelation of where America pushed these people two centuries ago.

When I entered the small home, I was swarmed by grandkids and great grandkids. The children flocked around, wondering what was in my plastic case. There were bedframes and mattresses all about the home. It looked as if there were three or four generations living under one roof.

As a proud Italian American, I was taken aback. I had always defended Christopher Columbus and Columbus Day. I had to admit that this experience allowed me to glimpse the other side of things.

Peter MacDonald with the author

Meanwhile, the children continued to pelt me with questions about the rifle. "What's that? What is that?"

"Well, this is what your grandpa used in the war a long time ago," I explained.

"He did?" exclaimed one little girl. She looked to be around seven years old. I propped the case up and the whole family gathered around the rifle. As the kids looked on, Levi entered the dining room slowly, wheelchair-bound, pushing with his feet. At age ninety-eight, he looked as one would expect a Native American his age to look: he had silver hair and golden-brown skin creased from years of hard work.

Thomas Begay, Navajo tribe

I brought the rifle up to the kitchen table, and Levi wheeled himself closer.

"That's where I was!" He pointed to the words "Luzon and Leyte" already written on the rifle by other veterans.

Levi had served in New Guinea and the Philippines during the Battles of Leyte and Luzon. In the 442nd Signal Battalion, Company B, he'd carried the unbreakable code in his head, along with a radio on his back. He'd used the Mohawk language to help liberate the Philippines.

"I want you to sign your name right next to those words, Luzon and Leyte," I told him.

Without any help or assistance, the old Native American wrote his name. My own sense of accomplishment was exhilarating. I had checked off an important piece of World War II history with Levi's signature. Afterward, his daughter wheeled him outside, where we ate lunch.

"I came all the way up from Boston," I told him.

"I've made that trip a few times," he shot back. "I was an iron worker and helped put up Prudential Tower." The Prudential Building was one of the key skyscrapers in Boston's skyline. I knew the building well. As a police officer, I'd had monthly meetings on the nineteenth floor to discuss security in the Back Bay Area.

Levi talked more about the skyscraper, then he and his grandkids taught me a few Mohawk words. Levi mentioned words he'd used in combat, like "enemy tank," which had been converted to the code "kettle pot" in his language for radio chatter.

"Did you lose any fellow Mohawks during the war?" I asked.

"Oh, yeah." He looked off into the field next to his home. "One minute you would be talking to them on the radio; the next minute, silence."

This had occurred several times during transmissions in combat.

"The Mohawk language is called Kanien'keha," Levi said. "Only seventeen of us Mohawks, who all fought in the same theater, spoke it during the war. I am the last one."

Mohawk was one of thirty-three indigenous languages used to send encoded messages between Allied forces fighting against Japan. Levi truly was the last Mohawk.

Our meeting was short. It was apparent Levi was battling mild dementia.

"I'll make my way back to Boston someday," he said. "I would like to see the Prudential Tower again."

"When this book is finished, you'll have to come to the book signing," I told him. "I'll take you by the tower myself."

I said goodbye to Levi and to the adorable Native American children who had encircled me during the visit. As I drove home I could already see myself notifying every iron worker in Boston that a Native American code talker was coming to see the building he'd helped construct in the 1960s. The members of the iron workers' union were rough, patriotic, and many of them veterans themselves. They would probably show up in the thousands.

My journey to the Mohawk reservation made me hungry for more rare stories, especially from those of unusual ethnic backgrounds. A few weeks later, I was driving though northern Arizona—Navajo Nation. The roads were desolate, and the sky seemed almost to touch the ground. I was on my way to Tuba City, home of Peter MacDonald, president of what was left of the Navajo Code Talker Association.

There was nothing that informed me I was on a Navajo Indian reservation. Once again, expecting to see bald eagles soaring overhead, wild horses, and lakes, instead I was met with rusted cars, rundown trailer parts, and packs of stray dogs running about. It reminded me of the Mohawk territory, but on steroids. I couldn't help but wonder again if we as a country were responsible for these living conditions. Engine blocks of cars sat on people's front lawns like ornaments. Not a blade of grass was in sight, and tumbleweeds rolled down the streets.

I walked up to the trailer and Peter's daughter answered the door. She was beautiful, and the first Navajo woman I had ever met.

"Come in," she said. "Dad just gave a speech at the high school. He will be right out."

I sat on the couch and stared at a painting of Peter on the wall. Suddenly the curtains to his bedroom opened and in he came, dressed in full Marine Corps League uniform, ribbons and all.

We talked for an hour.

"There were over three hundred of us when we went to the premiere of *Wind Talkers* in Washington, D.C. I didn't care for the movie, but now there are only thirteen of us left."

I'll never forget his disappointment as we talked about the movie.

"The code talkers all agreed the film could have done better describing the birth of the Navajo language within the U.S. military, and not made it solely an action movie where Nicolas Cage ran around screaming with a tommy gun." His disappointment carried over to the way the media incorrectly portrayed code talkers from every nation.

"Whether they were Navajo, Mohawk, or Cherokee, a lot of books and documentaries failed to explain how the code talker top secret program was started by twenty-nine Navajo in 1942," he said.

I asked Peter, who had been involved in the association for so long, who his favorite code talker was. Without hesitation, he replied, "Tommy Begay."

Thomas Begay had been a Marine Navajo code talker on Iwo Jima, and then, six years later, found himself trapped in the brutal Battle of the Chosin Reservoir during the Korean War. "He survived two of the U.S. Marine Corps' toughest engagements in history."

I figured Thomas was one of the Navajo code talkers from the past, but I was wrong.

"He is still alive in New Mexico."

Peter grabbed my rifle and peered over it.

"You'll be the first Navajo code talker on that rifle," I said.

"You hear that, Dad?" his daughter asked. "You're the only Navajo on the rifle."

Peter was proud to sign the rifle.

Even though he was the first Navajo to add his name to the rifle, I knew I needed to find a way to meet Thomas Begay.

Leaving the dusty reservation, I stumbled upon a gas station quick-stop store. There, an arrow pointed to the back. It read: "Code Talker Museum." The small building held Navajo code talker paraphernalia. There was Thomas's name on a list of original code talkers. His current home was listed as New Mexico.

Unable to locate an address for Thomas through further research, I considered the meeting with Peter MacDonald probably the best I could do in that regard. Then that very day I received an Instagram message from a Navajo man in his thirties who had seen the photo with Peter posted on my website. He introduced himself as having been a caretaker for a code talker who had passed away.

The young man thanked me for my dedication in remembering World War II veterans. He sent a picture of a business card that read: "Thomas Begay, WWII and Korean War Survivor," and asked if I had ever met this particular code talker.

I couldn't believe it. It contained Thomas's email and phone number. A few weeks later, I was on my way to New Mexico.

Thomas's son answered the door, then called out in Navajo to his dad, who was in a separate room.

Around the corner came Thomas, dressed in full Marine Corps regalia, just as Peter had been. He wore a Navajo necklace and a full set of ribbons, Army jump wings, and combat action badges.

"Okay, I gotta head back to work—he's all yours!" his son said, then left me alone in the home with his legend of a father.

Thomas and I sat at the kitchen table. The first point he wanted to make was that he hadn't joined the military to be a code talker. "I was already trying to join before I knew there was a top secret code talker project. I just wanted to join the Marines and kill Japs."

When he first went to join at the local recruiters in Flagstaff, he was told he was too young to sign up without a parent's permission.

"My mother could not read or write English. She used her thumb-print to allow the government to enlist me into the military."

A young Thomas was on his way to becoming a Marine when his Native American background flagged him for special opportunity. "Many Navajo were failing the code talker school. They couldn't understand how to adopt the code into our language and decipher it back to English. It wasn't easy."

Thomas mastered the skill and eventually graduated basic training and code talker school. He then joined the 5th Marine Division—a division that was soon thrust into the meat grinder of Iwo Jima. For thirty-six days Thomas deciphered messages in the Navajo language. He gave coordinates, enemy locations, and fire missions for his brother Marines.

He served a month and a half, then contracted malaria and needed to be medically evacuated. After the Marines, Thomas went back to the reservation.

"I went home for two years and I missed it. So I joined the Army in 1948 and went to jump school. I became a paratrooper just before the breakout of the Korean War. I was assigned to the 11th Airborne Division as a Morse code operator."

Thomas's communications assignment didn't place him in the rear, however. He was transferred to the 7th Infantry Division while in Korea. In five years, Thomas had gone from Iwo Jima to the deadly Battle of the Chosin Reservoir in North Korea. There he was surrounded by one million Chinese soldiers.

"I can still hear them screaming as they charged at us, one after another."

"What was worse, Iwo Jima or the Chosin Reservoir?" Both are considered the worst battles in American military history.

"The Chosin!" Thomas answered definitely. "At least if you got shot on Iwo Jima, you had a chance to survive. In the Chosin Reservoir, if you got shot, you would freeze to death."

The terrain was challenging on all fronts. "It was so cold that sometimes we would go to pick up a body and their arms would snap right off!"

This man had certainly seen hell, yet he was able to keep it together and lead a long life. Thomas was now ninety-five years old. He had been married for seventy years, had kids, fought in two wars, completed college, and worked for over forty years for the federal government.

"I was a Native American Indian relocator. I helped many Navajo move off the reservation to new places and obtain new jobs. I made my way up from a GS-11, -12, and then retired as a GS-14."

Thomas was proud of this accomplishment. For one thing, it proved that there was more to his story than just blood and guts. He never used his minority status as a crutch, and never held a grudge. He, like Peter MacDonald, loved his country. He had made a name for himself against all odds and turned tragedy into energy. His was a story every veteran could learn from.

Within a month I had three Native American code talkers on the rifle. Knowing they were thrown back to reservation life after the war made me often wonder if, as a country, we did enough for them. Thomas Begay, however, had gone from being the son of a mother who could neither read nor write English to retiring from one of the government's highest-level occupations as a GS-14. This fact illustrates proudly the ideal of America as a land of opportunity for all.

CHAPTER THIRTEEN

Vive la France

From late November to early December 1944 members of the 82nd Airborne were catching up on rest after nearly two months of front-line action in Holland. Men were given passes to Reims, Paris, and other locations in France. In the opera district of Paris, trucks roared up and down the streets as soldiers crowded the walkways. One paratrooper stood on the sidewalk staring at an old apartment building. Soldiers on leave moved around him like schools of fish around a submerged rock.

Most men were thinking about getting home for the holidays, but not Rob Heurgue. He *was* home. He was out of his dirty field jacket and into a clean dress uniform. He repositioned his hat on his head, broke from the crowded sidewalk, and crossed the street. It had been four years since he'd seen his mother and father. Two bronze stars now protruded from his jump wings, marking his parachute landings in Normandy and Market Garden. It had been hell to get this far.

He straightened out his uniform one more time and rang the doorbell. The door was flung open. It was Mom . . .

Robert Heurgue, 82nd Airborne Division

Robert, now ninety-seven, halted in this moment of recounting his story. His lips began to quiver. He was still viscerally affected by that emotional reunion seventy-eight years ago. It felt to him as if it had been yesterday, that moment when he reunited with his family in war-torn France.

"Did you sleep in your old bed?" I asked to break the silence.

"Mm-hmm," he murmured, nodding.

Robert was not a big talker and could barely hear either. The rifle lay across his kitchen table alongside his battery-operated listening device, which connected to a pair of headphones that helped Robert hear better.

"What was it like to sleep in your bed again four years later?" I yelled into his listening device.

"It was good. Nothing much had changed. My dad came home from work, and I got to see him, too," he replied.

Robert hadn't been in his own bed in Paris since 1939. Four years ago, his mother had put him on a boat to the United States. They were unaware he would be stuck there once war broke out in Europe.

"Why did your parents send you to the U.S. to begin with?" I asked.

"I had a sister living in Winthrop, Massachusetts. She was married and doing well for herself. My parents figured I could spend six months there. Little did we know it would be four years and a world war for us to reunite," Rob explained.

In early 1939 Robert boarded a ship in Le Havre, France, destined for New York. The ship was filled with Polish and French immigrants looking for a new life. After several days the old coal-powered ship pulled into New York Harbor.

Robert couldn't believe his eyes. "There I saw the tallest buildings I had ever seen. I had never seen skyscrapers before. It also happened to be the World's Fair," he recalled with a smile on his face. If it wasn't for the Second World War, coming to the United States for the first time might have been the most memorable event of his life.

"I spent only a day or two in New York before taking another boat to Boston. There I moved in with my sister in Winthrop, Massachusetts."

Robert was able to attend Winthrop High School. Although his English was not perfect, he was able to participate well enough. But this dream trip to America became an exile once Germany invaded France.

His father worked as a jeweler in Paris and was a veteran of World War I. "I knew my family would be okay. Yet, there was a period of time that we did not get any mail from them, and we could only read the headlines in the newspapers," Rob recalled.

With no ability to return, Rob attended school in Winthrop from fifteen to eighteen years of age. He went to work for his brother-in-law, who was also a jeweler, but in Boston. Mail from his parents in France was frequent, but life was not easy under Nazi rule.

Robert lived the life of any teen boy in the United States, which included being on the government's radar to be drafted once war came. The situation in Europe grew worse. By 1942, the boy who had come to America for a vacation had been drafted into the U.S. Army.

"I was told to report to my local recruiting station. I personally didn't mind. Life had been so tough trying to survive as an immigrant during those days, I was better off in the Army," Rob said.

His first duty station to report to was Fort Dix, New Jersey. "From there I was sent to Georgia for infantry school. I never experienced summer heat like that—not in Boston, or France, or any place," he recalled.

During his basic infantry school, a paratrooper addressed his platoon. The man with the bloused boots and fancy hat told the new recruits they could jump behind enemy lines and earn more money. This was an easy sell for Rob.

"We all knew we would be going to war soon. The idea of jumping in behind enemy lines seemed a lot better than going first on a beach."

Rob and three others from his platoon were sent to Fort Benning, Georgia. It was here they completed the Army's parachutist school. "It was hard, a lot of running, some didn't make it. You had to complete five jumps, four during the day, and one at night," Rob said.

Rob became a paratrooper and earned his silver jump wings in the relatively new program. While at Fort Benning, a new opportunity arose.

"I always loved fireworks. One of my favorite days in America was the 4th of July. I loved to light firecrackers, so I applied for demolition school. Now this way I could play with the big fireworks. My instructor was the actor who later played in the movie *The Best Years of Our Lives* [Harold Russell]. He lost both of his hands in a training accident after I had left the program," Rob recalled.

During demolition school, Rob learned how to make, plant, and set plastic explosives. He and his fellow students also practiced how to use TNT to their advantage. Rob became an infantryman cross-trained with explosives.

After demolition school, Rob was Europe-bound. His first stop upon leaving New York in March of 1944 was Belfast, Ireland, then finally he was off to England. He was assigned to division headquarters of the 82nd Airborne Division, located at Braunstone Park in Leicester. This assignment was most likely due to Robert's ability to speak and read French.

"I was placed into the defense platoon. Our responsibility was to protect division headquarters no matter where they went," he said. The division was already well known for its actions in North Africa, its jumps into Sicily, and its fighting in Italy. He was excited to join such men.

While in England, Rob and his division trained for what was to come. He used his explosive skills to blow holes in wire fences and practiced night jumps. Training never ceased. On their last night jump, Rob's C-47 troop carrier got a flat tire during takeoff. The plane skidded off the runway and into a ditch.

"Just like that, our jump was cancelled. But an eager lieutenant refused to let it be. He found us a replacement aircraft and we took off." They soared into the pitch-black English countryside, but because of the late takeoff they found themselves in the wrong place at the wrong time—and totally directionless. While the practice jump was a failure, it was good to see how fast things might go wrong in a fast-changing combat situation.

"Our lieutenant refused to admit we were lost. I lost some faith in Army leadership after this," said Rob.

"One day in late May we were told to collect all our belongings and we would be moving locations in England. We boarded trucks and were transported several miles away. When we arrived to the new location, it was an airfield with barbed wire protected by armed guards. We were tossed into airplane hangars with cots. After several days here they told us we would be jumping into France," Rob said.

Once briefed on this top-secret mission, the men could not leave the guarded airfield. They had to study their drop zones. The paratroopers practiced with sand tables and model terrains of their objectives. Each man had a mission once on the ground in France. There was no sugarcoating it; they were to lead the spearhead of the invasion. Their job was to clear the way for ground forces arriving by boat. The U.S. Army was still concealing the exact area of France where they would be dropped with code words like "Carrot Town" and "Murder River" on the model terrains.

"I guess they didn't want the whole English countryside finding out," Rob said and laughed. Soon, the fake town names were erased, and the real cities were labelled. Places like Carentan, Sainte-Mère-Église, and the Merderet River were revealed to the paratroopers. The jump would be into the Normandy region of France.

"They showed us the latest aerial photos on June 3," Rob recalled. "The photos showed telephone poles placed in open fields, and marshes that were flooded intentionally to prevent an airborne invasion."

On June 4 the invasion was supposed to be underway, but due to high winds and rain it was postponed.

"Now we were all on edge," said Rob. "We knew it could be any moment. Guys cleaned their weapons and rearranged their equipment. I carried an M1 Garand with twenty-one rounds of armor-piercing ammunition. I also had two fragmentation grenades and an anti-tank Gammon grenade. It was my job as the platoon demolitionist to prepare all these kinds of grenades for the platoon. I checked each grenade to verify the safety pin under the screw cap was securely in place before adding the plastic explosive. Gammon grenades could explode on impact and were useful against German armor."

It was an immense responsibility for the nineteen-year-old. One false move or one unchecked grenade could lead to an early detonation, especially from the jolt of a parachute opening during a jump. Heavier weapons like bazookas, mortars, and machine guns were rolled into a bundle which was then loaded under the belly of the C-47 transport planes. These bundles would be released as the paratroopers exited the aircraft.

"June 5 the weather still wasn't great, but it was better; we knew the invasion couldn't be held off forever," Rob continued. "Finally that afternoon we were told 'This is it!'"

Rob and the other members of the 82nd Airborne crowded the chow line for their last meal. Thick slices of ham and bread were served. "I ate once, went back in line and loaded some ham into my mess kit. I knew this would taste better than a K-ration. I don't understand why more guys didn't do the same," he laughed.

Rob put another thick ham sandwich into his pack. Once his personal gear was prepped, he helped load supply bundles under his C-47. Each paratrooper had to enter the plane with the aid of one or two others. The amount of gear with which each man was equipped was astonishing. "We needed to be pushed up the ladder climbing into the aircraft," Rob recalled.

Once seated inside the C-47, paratroopers on each side of the plane were facing one another. Some troopers had their faces painted; others fiddled with their helmet straps and reserve chutes. Everyone seemed to have the coming drop on his mind. Rob looked to the front of the plane to see his jump master, Sergeant Burke, boarding last. He sat in the number one position next to the open door. Rob was not far away, occupying the number two position across from the open door.

Finally the engines of the C-47 sputtered and then began to roar. The men of the 82nd Airborne were ready for their 2200 hours takeoff.

"It was still daylight when our plane lifted off the runway," Rob said. His expression was faraway, that June 5, 1944, sunset still fully present for him.

"What was going through your mind as the plane took off?" I asked. I assumed Rob was going to give me the "Nothing, I was young and dumb" response I'd often heard before, but Rob caught me off guard.

"At that moment, I could not help thinking that it was to be the beginning of the most important battles of the war. The outcome had to be successful. Defeat was unthinkable. For some of us it may be the last time we would see England, or anything else for that matter."

These were powerful thoughts for a nineteen-year-old boy stuck inside a C-47 as it climbed upward. The plane began to circle the airfield, waiting for all the other C-47s to take off. Once every plane was in the air and the formation complete, it was 2300 hours. Darkness covered the earth as the armada of planes headed for France.

Robert described how uncomfortable it was being stuffed into a C-47 like sardines. "It hadn't been an hour in the air and guys already had to piss. We were sweating, and we stunk. The army had 'gas-proofed' our uniforms, a process that rendered the fabric airtight on our jump suits. If the Germans couldn't see us, they were certainly going to smell us."

Paratroopers with nervous bladders began to relieve themselves in the tail section of the plane. A bucket full of urine rattled in the rear of the fuselage. As the journey continued some men fell asleep, others drifted back to their personal thoughts. Robert felt he was going home after all this time, returning to France with a rifle and parachute, not a suitcase and passport. May 1939 was the last time he'd been there. Now his feet were going to touch French soil again. It would be on June 6, 1944, the day of days.

"Looking out the door of the plane I could notice we were leaving the English coast. From my vantage point I could see the white crests of the waves below. I soon fell asleep, too."

Rob gazed for a long while at the rifle on his kitchen table.

I waited. Memories seemed to race within him. Finally he was ready to continue.

When Rob awoke, enemy tracers were zipping past the plane's open door.

"I lost track of time and was suddenly aroused by bright streaks of tracers shooting into the sky. It was anti-aircraft fire coming from the Channel Islands. It was greenish and would curve right past our door. It filled the sky between planes." This was no longer a game. The enemies were real and were trying to kill the paratroopers. Some paratroopers in other planes would not make it, their aircrafts exploding over the French countryside.

The show of firepower woke everyone on the plane.

"*Stand up and hook up!*" called Sergeant Burke, giving the order to his stick to prepare for the jump.

"All the men struggled to stand. We grabbed the cable running down the center of the plane. We attached our static line. It must have been very crowded at the front where I was, because there wasn't enough space for everyone to stand in a single file with all the equipment we had on," Rob recalled.

The paratroopers raced through the gear-check procedure. They depended on one another to ensure that everyone was properly hooked up and ready to go.

"The jumpmaster was the last man in the stick. He called out that his equipment check was ok, and every man from him out would repeat the same all the way down the plane," Rob said.

At last the French coastline appeared. Rob estimated his aircraft was now at one thousand feet. At that moment the pilot turned on a red light by the door. The jumpmaster gave the order: "Stand in the door!" Sergeant Burke moved forward into the open doorway, hands on each side, ready to lunge out. Rob placed one hand on the door and the other on his static line, prepping to be the second man out.

The plane's engines changed tone, slowing down. It was clear they were over their drop zone. Without warning, tracer rounds began to tear into the C-47. The doorway exit became an inferno. The plane lurched, then dove down, picking up speed. Sergeant Burke lost his balance, falling backwards and rolling down the floor and into the tail section of the plane. A large aerial photo of the drop zone was sucked out the plane's door.

Men were thrown around the plane and became tangled in their static lines. Much commotion ensued as the injured and wounded para- troopers struggled to stand up. Rob helped Sergeant Burke regain his footing. The C-47 was now at treetop level, the countryside unwinding rapidly below them. This continued for several minutes, until suddenly the plane was over water again.

"That's when I realized we'd missed our drop zone. We flew right over the whole peninsula and back towards the Channel again."

For a moment Rob thought they were going to head back to England. Then the plane made another 180 degree turn and headed again for the French coast.

"I looked at my watch. We had been standing in this position with all our equipment for forty-five minutes, since the red light came on," Rob said. The men were sore from their heavy loads.

With no other plane in sight, Rob's C-47 found land again at around seven hundred feet, Rob estimates. The warning light turned green, someone yelled "*Let's go!*", and out the boys went.

One by one, those who were not injured or wounded felt the shock of their parachutes opening at 130 miles per hour. "In less than three seconds my parachute jerked open. With the plane going at that speed it snaps you back to reality, violently!" Rob recalled.

Rob remembers a full moon during his initial descent, but then a cloud passed over it. Suddenly the well-illuminated countryside became dark. He was unable to see ground. For the moment, all seemed calm, no tracers, no gunfire, no other parachutes nearby. Then *wham*, Rob hit the ground like a "sack of flour."

"It really was a clumsy landing," he said with distaste. "But I was alive, so what else could I ask for? Other paratroopers landed in the ocean or flooded fields and drowned. My harness and leg straps were so tight that I would have had the same fate if I'd landed in water."

Now on the ground, Rob removed his gear with a sense of urgency. He unbuckled his parachute harness, removed his reserve chute, slid his rifle out of its case, and aimed it. For now, he hadn't been spotted. He unshouldered his rifle and began to remove more equipment. He took off his musette bag, gas mask, and ditched an old World War I seventeen-inch bayonet he had recently been issued.

"I had spent precious time, but I was now ready to find the rest of my squad. I wanted to collect our heavy weapons that were scattered around the drop zones," said Rob. "It became evident there was no way to tell which way the plane was flying when we jumped. Therefore, it was impossible to locate the other men or bundles of supplies that floated down."

Rob started walking with no destination in mind. He crept carefully over hedgerows, listening to any suspicious noises. In the dark ahead of him he could see the outline of a figure. The outline of the helmet did not appear to be German, and a clicking noise could be heard coming from this person. Rob crouched low and raised his rifle just in case. With his finger on the trigger he called out the password, "Flash!" The reply from friendly forces was supposed to be "Thunder."

When Rob got no response, his finger closed in further on his trigger. More clicking could be heard emanating from the unknown individual. Rob yelled "*Flash!*" even louder a second time. The person responded with, "Where's your cricket?" It was an American. With much relief Rob lowered his rifle.

"The 101st Airborne were given these little metal clickers called 'crickets.' We did not have them," Rob recalled.

The 101st Airborne paratrooper was also looking for his squad. Rob reset the safety back on his rifle. The encounter could have been a deadly mistake. The two U.S. soldiers had been on separate protocols. Rob was the one who was out of place, however, having been mis-dropped into the 101st Airborne sector.

After their brief encounter, the pair stayed together, figuring two were better than one. Rob ran into the hedgerows, climbing over one side and down the other. To his surprise, he was immediately able to locate members of his platoon. The men of the 82nd had been busy locating equipment bundles and heavy weapons. Sergeant Burke, the first man out of Rob's plane, now had a half dozen soldiers gathered to start his patrol. He took the lead and used his map to try to get the platoon on the right track.

Robert found himself in the rear of the squad with two medics and a paratrooper by the name of Corporal Blackwell. "I was now carrying an additional 250 rounds of machine gun ammunition. It started to become a real burden, as we were climbing up and down hedgerows constantly. I looked at the two medics who had only small backpacks, and asked if they would help me carry the ammo. They told me they could not carry weapons or ammo as medics. Boy, did this set me off!"

Rob's first patrol in Normandy did not turn out to be pleasant. He viewed the chaplain, medics, and others in his stick as liabilities since they did not possess weapons. They were also from division headquarters and were not fully trained.

They could not read maps or navigate in a patrol properly, for instance. As the squad hurdled another hedgerow, Rob waited for the chaplain ahead of him to pop up and give the signal it was safe to follow. The hand signal never came, and when Rob climbed over his squad was nowhere in sight. They had continued without him.

Rob dropped the cans of ammo in frustration. "We are better off without them. I speak French and have a map," he said to the remaining three men who were also left behind. He talked over the situation with Corporal Blackwell, who agreed to lead this small patrol toward the rendezvous point. The two medics were not sold on the idea and decided to try to catch up with the squad. Rob said nothing, but he was relieved. He viewed them as a hindrance at this point.

Rob and Corporal Blackwell huddled over the map, using what moonlight there was to see. They proceeded in the opposite direction from the medics, who were going the wrong way. The pair made their way through several small fields and eventually arrived at a home. "There was no sign of life, nor any German vehicles or equipment," Rob recalled.

The two paratroopers waited. They listened carefully, as alert as hound dogs. Noisy insects and farm animals were all they could hear. Rob went to the front of the home and tried the door. It was locked.

"I went to a window, shined my flashlight inside, and could not see anything out of the ordinary. So I punched out a window panel with the butt stock of my rifle."

The sound of breaking glass seemed to be amplified by the quiet night. Rob retreated a dozen yards and waited for a response. Nothing. Rob crept back, reached his hand through the window, and unlocked it. He opened the window and climbed through into the home. "As soon as I was in, I opened the front door and waved for Corporal Blackwell to come in."

Blackwell stood guard in the doorway while Rob searched the rest of the home. He rummaged through drawers and cabinets. "I found a stack of letters with the return address of 'Turqueville' on it. I pulled out my map and located a small village two miles east of Sainte-Mère-Église with that name. I knew that this must be where we were."

Happy for the map and thankful for his ability to read French, Rob was ready to tell Corporal Blackwell what he'd discovered when screaming erupted from the doorway of the home. Rob rushed back to see Corporal Blackwell bear-hugging a French woman. The woman was struggling to free herself. Rob spoke to her in French.

"I told her to calm down and that we were American paratroopers. I said we were not there to harm her, but we only broke into the home to find out information of where we were." The woman ceased struggling and Corporal Blackwell released her from his grip.

The woman and Rob conversed in French, and she confirmed that they were indeed in the hamlet of Turqueville. The woman told Rob she and her child had been sleeping when they were wakened by the hundreds of planes overhead. She grabbed her child and ran to a nearby farmhouse, fearing an Allied bombing raid.

Halfway through the discussion, the woman grew anxious and pleaded to go back to be with her child, who was still hiding in a barn. As Rob prepared to dismiss the woman she made one final comment. She told Rob that a German patrol had just passed through the area looking for Americans in hiding.

This remark sent chills up Rob's spine. He had originally thought this home could be a good place to bed down for the night. Would this woman alert the Germans to their whereabouts while they were sleeping? Could they trust her to keep quiet? Perhaps she feared she might be killed for letting them hide in her home. Tying her up was not an option. She wouldn't be able to tend to her child.

Questions raced through the nineteen-year-old paratrooper's brain. Rob reached into his pocket and gave her money for the broken window, and the woman went running into the night. Rob looked at Blackwell and said, "We can't stay here."

Sleeping in the house might be suicide. They would have to remain alert all night if they did so. The pair moved a few hundred yards from the home and kept watch. There was zero point in aimlessly walking around in the dark, especially knowing that Germans were around. As soon as the first rays of sunlight touched the ground, Rob and Blackwell were on the move again.

"As the sun rose we met other paratroopers rising from the fields. One lieutenant was trying to assemble a platoon after losing track of all his men during the drop. It was clear we were not the only ones to be dropped in the wrong area," Rob recalled.

The paratroopers assembled a patrol and headed in the direction of Sainte-Mère-Église. "We stopped to eat a quick breakfast. Most men pulled out their K-rations, but I still had that delicious king-sized ham sandwich I made back in England." Rob chuckled. Seventy-eight years later, and he was still proud of his quick thinking.

As Rob and the others marched into Sainte-Mère-Église, it was evident a battle had raged there the night before. Not all the other paratroopers from the 82nd Airborne had had a peaceful landing. "There were trees that bordered the town square. I saw two parachutes hanging in the trees. Two dead troopers hung there, about ten feet off the ground. They never had a chance to get out of their harnesses. They were riddled with bullets." Rob shook his head mournfully all these decades later.

While in the town of Sainte-Mère-Église, Rob finally was able to locate men from his original platoon. Division headquarters put Rob to work right away.

"Intelligence officers brought me to the town officials and numerous French civilians. Our commanding officers wanted to know the strength and location of the German units in the vicinity."

As the day grew old, more men from Division HQ and the 82nd Airborne began to filter into the town. Everyone was catching up after being mis-dropped all over the peninsula. By the end of the day on June 6, a camp had been set up outside the town perimeter in an open field. Rob's platoon provided security for the Division HQ with the newly arriving automatic weapons. They created a guard-duty roster, and by nightfall, the men had a chance to rest.

"It had been almost forty hours since I last slept," Rob recalled. "I found a depression in the ground, set my backpack as a pillow, and lay down. That might have been the fastest I ever fell asleep."

For the next thirty-three days Robert was glued to Division HQ, where his French skills were utilized.

"Myself and three others would take a Jeep out and gather what information we could from the civilian populace," Rob remembered. "On my third day in Normandy I was almost killed." He chuckled in the present, but he was not chuckling when he came under enemy MG 42 fire that day. "That gun can shoot 1,200 rounds per minute. When you get hit by it, you aren't gonna just get hit with one bullet either."

During a ten-man foot patrol, Rob's squad pushed farther outside Sainte-Mère-Église. Rob was lead man when the MG 42 machine gun rounds zipped by his head. "I dove for the ground. The bullets could have made my head disappear. When I rolled into a bush I found a German hiding there. He was scared out of his wits and wanted to give up immediately. He must have been in a forward observation post, but he wanted nothing to do with fighting and just kept his hands raised."

Rob's squad was calling for him to fall back. Little did they know he would be emerging from the bush with a prisoner. Rob and the German scurried back to the rest of the squad. This was a good grab for Division Headquarters, a chance to find out what remaining German forces occupied the area.

The rest of Rob's time in Normandy was uneventful. Division HQ did not have the sexiest of missions, but the role Rob played for the 82nd Airborne's success in France was important. After a month and three days, Rob was on his way back to England. His next journey as a paratrooper awaited.

Rob's next combat jump was made as part of Operation Market Garden. "It was on a Sunday. It was around noon when I jumped into Holland." He gazed at the wall behind me in his kitchen, envisioning the jump again. This clear visualization was a common occurrence among

World War II paratroopers. When recollecting their jumps, it was as if they were physically watching the parachutes fall to the earth once again.

"The weather was good, broad daylight on September 17." Rob floated to the earth again. This time he landed in an open field near Groesbeek in the Netherlands, known as "Drop Zone Whiskey." It was a perfect jump. Rob broke free of his harness, sorted out his equipment, and made a dash for the tree line a few hundred meters away.

"We set up division headquarters in the woods next to the drop zone. We dug foxholes, and had branches to cover them to stop any rain." However, it wasn't the rain Rob and his platoon had to worry about. One mile away, the British and Canadian paratroopers had also set up camp.

"The Canadians loved their tea. They would often start a fire to boil their water. The Germans could see the flame and smoke and begin shelling us." Often the German artillery would fall short of its target, landing on the Americans instead of the Canadians.

Rob lay in the fetal position in his foxhole. Shells exploded all around him. "It was the tree bursts that made things worse. If a high-explosive shell detonated amongst the trees it would send thousands of deadly splinters and chunks of wood into the men below. We had several men injured from this." This easily preventable shelling of September 1944 still upset Rob.

The tea-making mistake which drew the German artillery would be one of a series of errors for the Allied forces during the campaign. By late October, the 82nd Airborne withdrew from Holland and back to France for rest. Operation Market Garden would ultimately fail for a variety of reasons that historians debate to this day.

The strategic outcome of the operation didn't mean much to Robert. He was slated to go back to his home country of France again. His next mission was to finally see his mom. When the men of the 82nd were given liberty in November to visit Paris, Rob reunited with his family. For two days he forgot about Normandy and Holland. He ate his favorite meals, hugged his mom and dad, and slept in his old bed. It had been four years since he'd heard his mom's voice. But in just two days this must come to an end.

Leaving home to rejoin his unit again was emotional. The fact that he'd been able to reunite with them at all seemed miraculous.

Rob would survive the Battle of the Bulge and would push into Germany. He would live through the war and enter that apartment again in Paris to see his parents on the way back to the United States. So many others would never return to America, having given their all for the liberation of Europe.

When the war ended, Rob left the Army and headed over to France to live. He spent much more time in the home he had grown up in. Soon he needed a job, and the U.S. government was hiring.

"I took a job working in graves registration as a civilian." Rob traveled all over Europe helping excavate remains of U.S. soldiers buried during the war, of which there were plenty. The bodies or remaining bones would either be placed in permanent cemeteries in Europe or sent back to the United States for local burial. It depended on the family's request.

"I had to open the graves of guys killed in combat. Sometimes it would be a whole body or at times just a single bone. Sometimes a soldier would be completely unidentifiable. Some bodies still had rotting flesh. It all depended how the body was preserved," Rob recalled.

Rob had to inspect each soldier's body for proper identification. It was imperative that the right remains were sent to families when they wanted their loved one buried in the United States. In the span of months Rob inspected hundreds of his fellow servicemen who had made the ultimate sacrifice.

"It was something you became numb to. I saw many from my own division, but there was one that will always stand out to me," he said.

While opening the casket of an Army officer in Belgium, Rob was taken aback. It was the remains of one of his lieutenants, killed in Germany. After nearly three years, Rob gritted his teeth and positively identified the young man.

"This is where it all hit me. The war finally caught up with me. I grew emotional, grateful I survived," Rob recollected.

After seeing that America's war dead made their final voyage home, he assisted with the repatriation of fallen service members in Belgium, Germany, and North Africa. He served thirty years working for the Department of Defense as a civilian contractor. Rob eventually returned to the United States. He became an avid motorcycle rider. He raised a son, James.

In 2021, Robert returned with me to Normandy once again. We entered the town of Turqueville seventy-eight years later, on the morning of June 6. The commanding general of the 82nd Airborne was there this time to meet PFC Robert Heurgue. The two walked the streets of Turqueville together. I stayed in the background. This day was about the All-American Division, a historical moment for the division and its legacy.

I watched Robert converse with a woman who had survived the battle as a teenage girl. She stood behind a chest-high wall in front of her home as she spoke to him. The two were now in their nineties.

She described what she remembered of D-Day. Her home was used to collect wounded German soldiers during the battle. She told Robert in French that the Germans screamed and moaned all night from their injuries, and that it was nothing short of hell. She figured she and her family would die in the ongoing battle taking place in her very own backyard. The next morning when she'd looked out the window, she witnessed what she described as "a blanket of white" everywhere. These were the parachutes of the hundreds of paratroopers that had landed the night before.

Parachutes filled the trees and covered the yards of her neighbors. She knew this was the beginning of freedom. Decades later, the French woman kissed Robert on his cheek, thanking him personally for France's liberation.

Watching Rob speak in his native tongue to his own people on the anniversary of D-Day was a sight I'll never forget. Rob had experienced both sides of the war. He and his family were victims of the Nazi occupation. He was subsequently made use of by the U.S. Army to take his country back. Rob seemed to have more familial skin in the game than most veterans.

We attempted to locate the house he had broken into during the night of the invasion, but we could not. Many of the homes had collapsed after the war or been unrecognizably renovated. Nevertheless, to be with Rob again in his authentic drop zone is something I'll never forget.

Vive la France.

CHAPTER FOURTEEN

Fever Pitch

C link!

A baseball went soaring through the air towards second baseman Jack Hamlin. He was fiddling with his three-fingered glove, and his delayed reaction caused him to miss the line drive. There was now a man on first. His team, the Joplin Miners, was a minor league baseball team out of Missouri that provided backup players for the New York Yankees. Jack reflected that stupid plays like that would not help him make a trip to the majors one day.

Jack was distracted. He would soon have to decided what branch of service to join. If he hesitated even one more day, the government would decide for him through a draft notice. The nation was at war. Jack was twenty-one years old. His age group was due to be drafted.

"I had read enough books about World War I to know I did not want to be in the trenches. I certainly did not want to be in a submarine a mile underwater either. Most guys wanted to go see action, but that just wasn't me. I was completely okay without seeing combat," Jack said. He fiddled with that same three-fingered baseball glove seventy-nine years later at his home in Springfield, Missouri. At the age of 101, Jack had no reason to be anything but brutally honest.

It was during that baseball game seventy-nine years earlier that Jack had decided he would join the U.S. Coast Guard. To him, joining the Coast Guard would keep him in the United States and away from the fighting in Europe or Japan. He was an exceptional ball player. Maybe he could manage to play baseball during the war. Then, if he stayed in shape and survived the war without injuries, he might still possibly make it to the Major League.

Such thoughts raced through his head as the inning ended and his team jogged back to their dugout.

"What's wrong with you? Snap out of it!" the team manager said to Jack. Jack's distracted mind was not the only thing causing his errors on the ballfield. He'd spent several days with a sore throat. He hadn't been feeling well in general. His body ached and he felt great fatigue—something was not right.

"I went to the doctors, and they diagnosed me with rheumatic fever. My weight dropped to eighty pounds. I was in the hospital with a couple other boys who had it too. They didn't make it. It was a serious illness back then," Jack said. "As far as I was concerned, I was lucky. But the side effects of rheumatic fever damaged my heart. It took me a year to recover."

By 1943, all of Jack's friends, along with most of the young men of Springfield, had enlisted in the service. Delayed by his sickness, Jack finally made a quick decision to join the Navy's flight program.

"I failed the physical," Jack recalled. "My heart was damaged from the illness. I had an irregular heartbeat now that the doctors picked up on. They denied me entry into the Navy."

Jack now felt unmotivated by the prospect, but his friends suggested he try the Coast Guard as he'd originally intended. Jack wasn't optimistic. He figured he'd be booted again for his heart. Nevertheless, he decided to give it a shot.

Jack and his buddy went to the Coast Guard recruiter. Surprisingly, he passed the physical and entered service in the U.S. Coast Guard.

"I was sent to New Orleans for basic training. I didn't find it that physically demanding. Although I had made a recovery from a serious illness, I was always in good shape playing baseball and football back in Springfield. After completing basic training I went to boatswain's mate course in Rockaway Beach, New York."

Upon his completion of boatswain's mate school, he was permitted to wear the crossed anchors insignia on his shoulder along with his rank.

"If you wear the crossed anchors on your shoulder it means you're part of one of the oldest and proudest communities of all. Boatswain's mates are the heart of every ship. As one of them, you'll perform a wide range of duties, making you the jack-of-all-trades on ships, whether you're standing watch as a lookout, tying knots, assisting as a search-and-rescue swimmer, or handling weaponry. It's a job that came with adventure and pride. At the end of the day you are the top deck hand," said Jack.

The Coast Guard's boatswain's mate school also trained participants to fire the ship's mounted automatic weapons. Jack learned how to break down and clean various machine guns and small arms. However, the weapon Jack became most familiar with was the 20 mm anti-aircraft gun. The ship to which he would be assigned would have one mounted on its bow.

"While in New York City, I was assigned to my first ship, eighty-three-foot Coast Guard Cutter 23 (83408). It had a thirteen-man crew and was made out of wood. Only 220 of these kinds of boats were made during World War II. We had bunks down below. Our primary mission was to sail the Atlantic Coast from Long Island, New York, to Block Island, Rhode Island, and hunt for enemy subs," Jack recalled.

For now his original plan seemed to be working. He wouldn't have to leave the United States to fight overseas. The men of USCG 23 were living the life. They were on sub-hunting duty near the best cities on the East Coast, from New York to Boston to Newport, Rhode Island. They would tie up in every city, drink, and invite girls back to the boat. For these twenty-year-old men, it was living the dream. Plus there had been no submarines in sight.

"My favorite city to stop in and have a drink was Newport, Rhode Island. There was a bar there right on the dock. I had a cute little cocktail waitress there. My, oh my."

But these good old days were short-lived. Coast Guard Cutter 23 was called back to Staten Island and received new orders. This time, it wouldn't be hunting submarines along America's hopping East Coast. Jack's crew was kept in the dark on where they would be going, but they knew it would be somewhere far away when they saw their boat hoisted to the deck of a Liberty ship by a crane.

"This large Liberty ship used its cables and hoisted four of our cutters out of the harbor and onto its deck. I knew were going somewhere. I just hoped it wasn't going to be the Pacific," Jack recalled.

More Coast Guard crews of the different cutters boarded the Liberty ship. At night they slept in their own cutters, which were mounted on the deck of the ship. The boredom intensified over several weeks. Finally they discovered they were bound for England.

"Our cutter was hoisted off the deck and lowered back into the water as the Liberty ship approached the harbor of a town called Poole. In the coming days, more Liberty ships dropped off other cutters. We ended up with six cutters all together, docked next to each other. There was a fire station not far from the docks. This is where we would take our showers. Local families in the area would always invite us to their homes for dinner. Poole became our home. The people were wonderful to us," Jack recalled.

While in England, Jack's crew continued their partyng habits. The young men of his cutter drank with the soldiers and sailors around Poole. However, two men didn't join them. The ship's captain and master chief were instead attending nightly top-secret meetings. As Jack learned later, these briefings were part of the planning stage for Operation Overlord, the invasion of France.

On the morning of June 5, the men were ordered to stay aboard ship. The captain called a meeting on the deck. There would be no liberty tonight. The men must prepare the cutter for the sea.

"They didn't tell us where we would be going exactly, just to prepare for action out at sea. We were told we would have to be light and maneuverable. We removed the depth charges from the boat. We got rid of any useless equipment that wouldn't be mission essential, even though we didn't know the mission, just that we would need to be quick, and have plenty of room on the cutter," Jack said.

"When we left in the early morning of June 6, it was still pitch-black out. We were told we were rendezvousing with a Navy convoy outside the Isle of Wight in the English Channel. When we got there, there were LSTs, LCIs, and other Navy craft waiting. It was then we were told we were heading to Utah Beach in Normandy, France. Our mission was to serve as a rescue float only. My captain pointed to all the other ships, and said none of these skippers are allowed to stop to rescue or pick anyone up during the invasion. That would be our job! If those boats changed course, or tried to pick soldiers or sailors out of the water, it could jeopardize the whole momentum of delivering troops to shore. Big Navy vessels as such could cause traffic jams, and worse, hold up reinforcements from getting to the beach. That's why our job as a cutter rescue was paramount," Jack explained.

The young seamen aboard the eighty-foot boat acknowledged their captain's order. The water was rough. Their little wooden cutter was tossed around violently, especially compared to the larger Navy ships of the fleet. Though thousands of miles from home and surrounded by hundreds of boats, Jack glanced over at the ship next to his and saw that it was Landing Ship, Tank (LST) number 50. It was the same LST he believed Ralph Carter, one of his buddies from Springfield, was aboard, at least according to a recent letter from his mom.

"So my skipper pulled alongside it, and I started yelling, 'Do you happen to have a Ralph Carter on board?' It was pretty dark, but there was one sailor smoking a cigarette on the deck who heard me. He yelled back, 'Absolutely we do—he's our commander. Who is this?' I said, 'Just tell him Jack Hamlin from back home!'"

"A few minutes later, I heard a voice in the dark call back to me. 'Hamlin, what the hell are you doing in that little rowboat?' I said, 'Let

me tell you something, Lieutenant Carter, if your LST is sunk or torpedoed, you'll be the last son of a bitch I pick out of the water.'" Jack
chuckled at the memory.

After this warm moment, the two ships soon drifted away. As the
sun came up, Jack knew the convoy was nearing its destination. The
sound of battleships firing their guns grew closer and louder.

"The sea was rough, getting across the Channel. Our wooden
ship was only five feet from the sea, and the swells were high. We
broke off from the convoy and headed for what my commander told
us was Utah Beach. We stayed there for a few hours, then we were
redirected to Omaha Beach. We were told the boys were having a
hard time there and it was a worse situation. We had sixty cutters in
support of the Normandy beach landings, and Omaha Beach needed
all hands."

Omaha Beach was a totally different scene. Ships weren't coming
and going after dropping off their soldiers as they had on Utah Beach.
There were landing crafts beached on sandbars, LCVPs tipped upside
down, and a major traffic jam of ships waiting to get in to shore.

"We were a mile from the actual beach landings. However, some of
these LCIs or LCVPs had inexperienced coxswains. They were dropping
guys off in water over their heads. When the landing craft would hit a
sandbar, the coxswain would think that meant they were close enough
to the beach to release the ramps. Yet in all actuality the water was seven
to ten feet deep at that distance. We lost so many men from just drowning," Jack recalled.

Coast Guard Cutter 23 spotted the first soldiers who needed help.
The men were lucky enough to have life preservers. They were survivors
of a landing craft that had been swamped and sunk due to the rough sea.
Jack's crew used long poles with hooks on the end to grab the desperate
soldiers and pull them from the water.

"Our first couple of stragglers that needed to be scooped out of the
water were not wounded. Their ships had sunk, or got swamped during
the first wave. But more bodies began to float in our direction. They were

not wearing life preservers and you could see they were in much different shape then the first group of men."

As the current pulled more bodies in the direction of Cutter 23, it was evident these were men who had combat injuries. Some had no arms, no heads, or were floating facedown. The only way to know if someone was alive was to get in the water and check directly.

"Being one of the lightest men on the boat, myself and the gunner's mate, Jack Turk, tied ropes around our waists, held on to a lifesaver, and were dumped off the side of the boat. We floated along the ship, swimming from body to body and checking if there was any life in some of the men who drifted in our direction. We were told only to rescue the wounded. Under no circumstances could we fill our boat with dead corpses and not men who had a chance to survive," Jack recalled.

Finally Jack came across a man somehow still holding his rifle. He was calling out for help. Jack swam over to the soldier. Part of his face was hanging off. The saltwater had washed the blood from his face, exposing this shocking wound to Jack. Jack had one arm on the lifesaver and the other around the exhausted soldier as his crew reeled them in. Both men were pulled to the deck. Jack took a second to catch his breath. His shipmates laid the wounded man next to other injured soldiers.

While Jack sat on the bow, Gunner's Mate Jack Turk took his turn floating in the ocean with the lifesaver, leaving the 20 mm gun unmanned. A fighter plane appeared in the sky. Every ship in the vicinity opened fire on the enemy aircraft. Bullets and tracers zipped into the air. Jack sprang up and got behind the ship's 20 mm gun. He swung it around and contributed to the wall of lead being pumped into the sky.

"I saw the German plane begin to smoke. It flew over us and out of sight. Everyone aboard our cutter was sure I landed hits on that aircraft, but who knows. The whole beachhead opened on that plane!" Jack remembered.

Now that enemy planes had been spotted in the area, Jack switched places with his gunner's mate and went back into the water. With a rope around his waist and lifesaver in hand, Jack jumped in the water and shoved away from the cutter in the direction of objects he'd seen floating his way.

"Missing arms, missing heads, body after body of boys I could do nothing for. Finally I grabbed another soldier. He must have been eighteen, looked like he was right out of high school. He was burned badly but still breathing. I lunged to grab him just before his head went underwater. Our boys pulled us back in and lifted us aboard. We had about seven injured on board and we needed to get them back to a hospital ship if we wanted them to live!"

Jack's cutter started its engines and spun around. They had to travel ten miles out to deliver the wounded to another ship. Their orders were to drop the wounded men off to an LST with hospital corpsmen and doctors aboard. The ten-mile route took a while. When they arrived, the sailors of the LST lowered a basket stretcher over the side to hoist the wounded aboard. The injured were too weak or otherwise unable to climb a net. Each was pulled up by a stretcher on cables.

"We headed back to Omaha Beach after dropping off the wounded. We could only travel eleven knots, so it took a while. I'm sad to report that on this round we found fewer survivors. We pulled maybe another four or five out of the water. I credit our cutter for maybe saving fourteen or so lives total on D-Day. The Coast Guard itself saved 1,400 men that day, and one nurse who fell overboard. One cutter saved 150 men. We all did our job that day," Jack said proudly.

By the second day on the Normandy coastline, Jack's cutter was nearly out of fuel. The cutter consumed 100 gallons of fuel per hour at cruising speed. They needed to head back to England. Jack was still wearing the same salt-covered dungarees he had been when jumping in and out of the water. A change of clothing would be nice.

"While on the way back we passed by the port of Le Havre, France. Le Havre still hadn't been liberated yet, and we could see with our binoculars German PT boats docked in the harbor. We wanted to avoid them at all costs, but suddenly just ahead of us a parachute appeared to be coming down into the ocean from the clouds. We radioed for permission to rescue this airman who bailed from his plane, and we got the green light," Jack said.

Jack's cutter sped towards the descending airman. As the airman plunged into the ocean, the crew of Cutter 23 was there to pluck him up with their pole hooks. After they brought the airman aboard, they discovered he had a deep wound in his left leg.

"We soon learned he was a Canadian fighter pilot. His plane was shot down and he bailed out over the sea. Luckily we were there to grab him before the German patrol boats did. We applied bandages to his leg and transferred him to the next British ship we saw while crossing the Channel," Jack recalled.

The crew of Cutter 23 returned to Poole, England. They had served their purpose during D-Day and would be refitted with depth charges again. The mission was to protect the English ports from German U-boats until October of 1944.

"Come October, we got reassigned to Cherbourg, France. We traveled over the English Channel again and docked at what would be our new home for the rest of the war. We continued to conduct sub patrols off the Cherbourg Peninsula and escort ships coming into the area."

The men of Cutter 23 were comfortable while stationed in France. While fulfilling their duties, they were able to partake of social life in the French towns. The boys chased women, drank, and explored the countryside. On Christmas Eve, however, disaster struck five miles off the coast.

"We got a distress call that the SS *Léopoldville* was torpedoed and sinking. It was a Belgian troop transport ship carrying an American division aboard. The radio call asked for all Allied ships possible to respond. I had just told most of our crew to go out and enjoy themselves on Christmas Eve, and I would keep watch. I had a few girls on the boat with me. I kicked them off and grabbed a random soldier on the dock to come help. Only three of us were on board when we left the port to go help."

Léopoldville was fully loaded for the Battle of the Bulge with 2,223 reinforcements from the 262nd and 264th Regiments, of the 66th Infantry Division. There was an insufficient number of life jackets, and few troops had participated in the poorly supervised lifeboat drill as *Léopoldville* had sailed from Southampton.

At approximately 6:00 p.m., one of two torpedoes launched by a U-boat struck the starboard side and exploded. The direct hit killed 300 men and flooded three of the ship's compartments. Most of the Americans aboard did not understand the "abandon ship" instructions, which were given in Flemish. While some soldiers joined the crew in departing lifeboats, many did not realize the ship was slowly sinking. They stayed aboard anticipating the ship would be towed ashore by tugboats. While the other escorts searched for the U-boat, British destroyer HMS *Brilliant* came alongside. Soldiers on *Léopoldville* jumped down onto the smaller HMS *Brilliant*. The destroyer could take only 500 men and headed for the shore, leaving some 1,200 additional soldiers still aboard.

"When we arrived there was a destroyer next to the *Léopoldville*. Many of the Belgian Congolese sailors who were crew members departed the ships on lifeboats, leaving the Americans to fend for themselves. They did not help or form a good evacuation plan. I remember pulling along the other side of the ship, and their deck was so high up. The soldiers were not panicking at that time. They were all waiting in line with their long, wool winter coats, helmets, and rifles on their back. I guess they thought they would get a chance to de-board properly, so no one was willing to jump in the water for us to rescue them at that point," Jack remembered.

That night there was a rise-and-fall sea swell between eight and twelve feet. When the U.S. soldiers realized the ship was sinking faster, they began to jump down onto neighboring ships. Some men leaped from forty feet up or higher, and their limbs broke when they landed on torpedo tubes and other fixed equipment on the deck of the British destroyer. Some men fell between the two vessels and were crushed as the two ships brushed into each other.

Due to poor communication between the Belgian crew and the Americans, it took nearly an hour for those stationed in Cherbourg Harbor to realize the *Léopoldville* was sinking. Then several hundred

Allied vessels were sent toward the distressed ship, Jack's cutter included. Men on the *Léopoldville* had been left with no choice but to jump overboard.

"Men were drowning wearing those wool coats. They were designed for the winter conditions of the Battle of the Bulge. We hooked a few men, but I was left with no choice but to get back in the water. All I had on were my dungarees, top and bottom," Jack remembered.

Jack had little time before he would fall victim to hypothermia himself. He submerged himself into the water off the side of his cutter and headed towards the men jumping overboard. *Léopoldville* was nearly impossible to see at this point.

"I heard a man yelling for help. I could see his face in the dark, above the water. I tried swimming over to him, but the current was sucking him further away from me."

"*Help, please! Oh God help!*" the soldier cried.

"I did not have enough slack in my rope. He kept drifting away from me. I couldn't get to him. It haunts me till this day," Jack said. These years later, safe in his living room, Jack began to cry.

Jack, at age 101, was the oldest man I had ever witnessed crying. He had carried the wrenching pain for nearly eighty years. I gave him a moment to collect himself before I pulled my rife from its case.

"Jack, I am proud to announce you will be the first Coast Guard veteran to sign my rifle," I told him.

"You're kidding me! Wow, look at all those names. . . . Am I really the first one? The first Coast Guard veteran?"

"Sure are, not many of you around, not even back then," I replied.

He proudly added his name to the rifle. Now I finally had someone to represent the hard work and sacrifice of America's Coast Guard veterans during World War II. I was one step closer to representing the whole war on the M1 Garand.

On that Christmas Eve of 1944, most of the men from the *Léopoldville* pulled from the water had already frozen to death by the time American rescue boats arrived. It had been hours since the attack. Of the 2,235 U.S. servicemen aboard the *Léopoldville*, about 515 are presumed to have gone down with the ship. Another 248 died from injuries, drowning, or hypothermia.

This was the final intense experience of the war for Jack. When the war was over he returned home and continued his baseball career in Springfield, Missouri. Unfortunately, making it to the majors was not in the cards. He became an insurance salesman, local state representative, and an advocate for veterans in Springfield. He led a noble life, returning to Normandy some seven times for annual commemorations.

As he walked me out of the apartment building of his assisted living community, three resident women were shooting pool in the recreation room near the elevator.

"This is the man who is going to be writing my story," Jack said to the women. He was clearly still a ladies' man.

"Really? You're Andrew? We all were fighting over your first book. We loved it," one elderly woman said to me. Jack had lent my book around after I'd mailed him a copy.

"Is that the rifle in that case?" another woman asked.

"Go ahead, take it out," Jack insisted.

I popped open the case and the women swarmed me. Jack picked up the rifle and said, "Look, you see that, there's me right there." He pointed to his signature.

He handed the rifle to one of the women. As she lifted it up, he helped her shoulder it. The two aimed in together, with Jack behind her.

As I left, I told Jack he'd better make it to 102 so he could see his story printed. I was certain he would. Then I bid a fond farewell to this Coast Guard playboy, and off I went in search of others.

CHAPTER FIFTEEN

"We Collect White Bodies First."

I t was a warm, sunny day in the town of Wereth, Belgium. It's a town few from outside the region would have heard of. It was the site of a war crime seventy-eight years before. Now Virginia Tech ROTC cadets had stopped in town as part of a field trip related to their curriculum to view a somber reminder.

In the town stands a monument dedicated to eleven African American soldiers who were assigned to the 333rd Field Artillery Battalion. These eleven soldiers were beaten and subsequently executed by the 1st SS Panzer Division during the second day of the Battle of the Bulge. The monument was erected not only to the black men murdered that day, but for all black soldiers who served in World War II.

The ROTC students stood near the stone monument as their instructor gave a speech. The students appeared to be a bit bored. It had probably been a long day. They were in the middle of a cow pasture, deep in the heart of rural Belgium. It was enough to send anyone drifting to la-la land, especially dealing with a six-hour time zone difference.

Marvin Gilmore, 458th AAA Battalion

I watched the group from my bus window just before we interrupted their teacher. What was about to happen to these students was a once-in-a-lifetime experience. And it all unfolded by mere coincidence. Their field trip happened to coincide with my trip to Belgium along with four veterans. One of those veterans happened to be a ninety-seven-year-old proud black man by the name of Marvin Gilmore.

For these students to meet a World War II veteran in the United States was rare. For them to meet a World War II veteran on a battlefield in Belgium in the year 2022 was extraordinary. For these students to be at one of the only monuments dedicated to black soldiers who fought in Europe and to be able to converse with a living black soldier seemed almost a miracle. Yet that's what they were about to experience.

Our bus pulled up to the monument, and one or two students peered over at us. The hydraulic door opened and out came Marvin Gilmore, cane in hand. Marvin was a black World War II veteran who had served in a segregated unit. He landed on Utah Beach in June of 1944 and fought his way through Belgium and Germany.

His thick gray hair was slicked back, similar to that of Frederick Douglass. Several gold rings gleamed on his hand as he gripped the handle of his cane. He carefully took his first step off the bus. The gravel path that led to the monument could be a death sentence for someone his age should he happen to trip and fall. The ROTC instructor stopped his speech. Marvin's footsteps on the gravel became audible. You could hear a pin drop.

The students seemed captivated. When Marvin began to speak, their eyes were glued to him. The cadets' attention remained riveted for the next thirty minutes.

"These are future military officers from Virginia Tech. Is there any advice you can give them?" the instructor asked as he introduced the group to Marvin.

The students' eyes began to water even before they heard Marvin begin his speech. This monument was dedicated to eleven black soldiers who had been tortured, beaten, and killed because of the color of their skin. The SS assassins had even cut a finger off one of the bodies as a souvenir.

Every one of those students saw those brutally murdered young black soldiers in Marvin. The tears began to flow as Marvin spoke. There were no words of resentment. He did not ask this younger generation to feel bad about segregation. He drove home one message to the future military leaders: "Always tell the truth, and always stand up for yourself."

I could see more tears forming in the eyes of some of these muscle-bound, eager college students' eyes. Each of us felt the sting of how the Wereth 11 were killed, and some were probably aware of how these soldiers had been treated in the segregated Army in the '40s. As the students asked for a picture with Marvin, I stepped back and took a few photos of my own. This was historic. Marvin would likely be the last African American World War II veteran ever to visit this monument.

As the students left, Marvin moved closer to the stone memorial. It read, "On 17 Dec. 1944 11 African-American Soldiers of the 333rd FAB were captured and massacred here by the SS. This site is dedicated to all black soldiers of WWII. In honor of Pvt. Curtis Adams, Cpl. Mager Bradley, Pvt. 1st Class George Davis, Staff Sgt. Thomas J. Forte, Pvt. Robert L. Green, Pvt. 1st Class Jimmie L. Leatherwood, Tech 5th Grade Nathaniel Moss, Pvt. 1st Class George W. Moten, Tech 4th Grade William E. Pritchett, Tech 4th Grade James A. Stewart, and Pvt. 1st Class Due W. Turner."

Marvin shook his head and closed his eyes. "Mmm, mmm," he murmured. He could have easily been one of these men during the war. Marvin was originally assigned to the all-black 458th Anti-Aircraft Battalion.

"I was trained in the 40 mm AAA gun. When we loaded onto our LST during the invasion my eyes were glued to the sky. It was part of my training, to spot enemy planes. However, my unit did not act as an AAA battalion during Normandy. After the landings we were assigned to all types of jobs. We drove trucks for the Red Ball Express, and participated in graves registration."

The time when he was most vulnerable and exposed to capture was when he was a personal Jeep driver for a British officer in Caen, France.

"I had to drive them all over the countryside looking for enemy gun emplacements. One wrong turn, or if we got lost, we could have been captured just like these men here. We were in enemy territory all the time in Normandy," Marvin said.

Marvin's enemy was not just the Germans during the war. He also had to watch his back against racist whites and jealous black soldiers from the South.

"The fellas from the South always envied me, or others from the North. Most of us were more educated and were not so submissive to the white officers. This really irritated the guys from the South, who were raised dirt-poor and to fear the white man."

Marvin had a few close friends in his unit that he trusted. The men did their job collecting the dead and wounded from the countryside of Normandy. "The trick to was to never look at the faces of the dead. Just look at the body, wrap them up, and load them on the truck. Their faces could stick with you forever."

Hundreds of the bodies collected by Marvin and his fellow black soldiers still rest in France at Normandy American Cemetery.

As the 458th AAA Battalion pushed farther into northern France, they were equipped with anti-aircraft guns again. Enemy plane attacks became more frequent, and Marvin was assigned to Battery A.

"We were dive-bombed by Messerschmitts. A lot of guys got hurt, including me," Marvin recalled.

Suddenly the *moo* of a cow interrupted our conversation at the Wereth Memorial site. Our tour guide, Reg Jans, a local battlefield historian, interjected, "The home the eleven soldiers were taken prisoner from is just up the road. We can drive there and take a look."

Moments later, we arrived at the home in which the Germans had rounded up the eleven black soldiers. In the front yard we met a lovely woman by the name of Solange DeKeyser. She was the president of the Wereth 11 Memorial Association. She guided us into the home. I stood behind Marvin as she explained what happened here seventy-eight years ago.

"By the morning of December 17, 1944, the Germans had entered the town of Schönberg, where the 333rd Field Artillery Battalion were dug in. The German blitz into the Ardennes region of Belgium caused them to overrun many American units supporting the strategic city of St. Vith. Two batteries of the 333rd Field Artillery tried to displace to St. Vith, where the 106th Division held out, but they were brought under heavy fire. Those not killed were forced to surrender. However, eleven men from the two batteries managed to evade capture. They darted into the woods in the hope of reaching American lines. At about 3:00 p.m., they approached the first house in the nine-house hamlet of Wereth, Belgium, owned by Mathias Langer.

"The black soldiers were cold, hungry, and winded after having to high-knee through the deep snow. The men only had two rifles between them, due to their hectic retreat. The Belgian family welcomed them and gave them food, siting them at a wooden dining-room table. But this small part of Belgium did not necessarily welcome Americans as liberators. The area had been part of Germany before the First World War, and many of its citizens still aligned themselves with Germany and not Belgium. The people spoke German but had been forced to become Belgian citizens when their towns were awarded to Belgium as part of the First World War repatriations.

"Unlike the rest of Belgium, many people in this area welcomed the Germans in 1944. Mathias Langer, the homeowner, was not one of these people, however. At the time he took the black Americans in he was hiding two Belgian deserters from the German army and had sent his oldest son into hiding so the Nazis would not conscript him.

"Around the wooden table, the eleven black soldiers sat down. Mathias Langer and his twelve-year-old son Hermann served them bread and butter. It would be their last meal. An hour later, there was a knock at the door.

"A four-man German patrol of the 1st SS Division, belonging to Kampfgruppe Knittel, stood in their doorway with guns at the ready. A Nazi sympathizer had tipped off the SS patrol that there were Americans hiding in the home. The Americans surrendered quickly so as to not get their hosts killed. The soldiers were made to sit on the road in the cold until dark. The Germans then marched them down the road. Gunfire erupted, and the soldiers were left in a ditch," said Solange, finishing her story.

"I can't believe some bastard ratted these guys out," I stated.

"Believe it. The family of the man who did still resides in the town," she added.

The bodies of the eleven soldiers were not recovered until a month later, when American forces began to retake the area. The twelve-year-old boy who had served the poor soldiers bread stopped an American truck on the road to inform them where the bodies were. The driver replied, "We collect white bodies first."

There was something remarkable about the home we were now in. The wooden table at which the doomed soldiers had sat down for their last meal was still standing in the dining room. It was worn and old. Marvin wasted no time walking over to the table and pulling out a chair.

The 130-year-old table squeaked as Marvin sat down. He placed his arms on the table. He closed his eyes and held to the sides. He could feel all eleven of his segregated brothers. There was complete silence. Marvin would be the last black veteran to visit this home, sit at this table, and be reminded of what his race went through during World War II.

Watching Marvin sit at that table helped all of us comprehend just a little more of what black Americans faced in the 1940s. The dining room was dedicated to all eleven soldiers. The soldiers' photographs were framed and hanging on the wall. Some did not have any known photographs, however, as they came from extremely poor backgrounds with no access to cameras.

Marvin with the rifle

Marvin held the framed photos. He was quiet. He didn't ask any more questions. In this moment, he knew he was representing the black population that served in World War II. It was one of the proudest moments I had put together. But soon it was time to go.

On the bus ride back to our hotel, I asked Marvin what it was like to serve a nation that didn't treat him as equal. He stated, "I loved my country, and Joe Louis, the famous boxer who enlisted in the Army in 1942, said it best to his critics. He said, 'There's lots of things wrong with America, but Hitler ain't going to fix them.'"

Serving as a police officer in recent years made me self-conscious about the image my profession had, especially with its history of negative run-ins with black citizens. On the bus ride home, I hoped Marvin was proud of me for taking him to the monument.

CHAPTER SIXTEEN

Battle Buddies

"**C**'mon, we are taking you to dinner!"

Morrie Bishaf jumped into the driver's seat of his car and Len Messineo hopped in the passenger side. The car was newer, perhaps a 2020. The ages of the two men combined added up to 194 years. But here I was, sitting in the back seat and holding on for dear life. Morrie really wanted to buy me a meal, and we were going there fast. I had just interviewed him and his best friend of seventy years, Len.

The two met their freshman year of college. The aspiring engineers bonded quickly after finding that each had fought in World War II. Morrie served with the 104th Infantry Division, while Len served with the 20th Armored Division. These two boys from Chicago never spoke about the war again after the day they met—that was, until I pointed a camera at them and started asking questions.

Morrie and Len went on to work with each other for thirty years. When they retired from their original employer, they started their own business. The two went from designing flak jackets and helmets as defense contractors to spending their golden years together creating

Len Messineo (left), 20th Armored Division, and Morrie Bishaf, 104th Infantry Division

bicycle parts with their company. They were inseparable. This was why it didn't surprise me that when Morrie told me he would not return to Germany, Len also declined the offer.

I survived the drive to dinner. As I surveyed my plate of ribs, I realized the following day would be Morrie's "Alive Day." Military veterans who were wounded in war often refer to the anniversary of that day as their "alive day." For Morrie, that day was February 28, 1945. This was the day nearly his whole squad was wiped out near Cologne, Germany.

The 104th Timberwolves were known as the "night fighters." "I supposed they called us wolves because they used us for a lot of night missions. Honestly, I preferred to fight at night as opposed to the day.

During the day we slept, and it was harder for the Germans to see us at night," Morrie said.

Morrie served with the 414th Regiment, Company A. He carried an M1 Garand, was nineteen years old, and spoke Yiddish. "I tried not to speak Yiddish all the time. I was paranoid of the Germans finding out I was Jewish. When I absolutely needed to speak it, I did, mostly to civilians," he added.

At that time, some eleven million people spoke Yiddish worldwide. It had a strong Germanic influence, and the language was used across Europe. The vowels and dialect were a bit different than modern German, but Morrie made it work when speaking with Germans.

Morrie was a replacement for the 414th Regiment, joining the unit in its defensive position outside of Aachen. "My grandkids always ask me if I ever slept in a foxhole, and quite honestly, I never did. Because my division was always on the move at night, that gave us the ability to sleep in bombed-out buildings in every town we came across in the day, which there were plenty of. I spent two months advancing through the Roer area of Germany. It was a major industrial area, so destroyed buildings there were enough of," Morrie said.

The Timberwolves were one of the only divisions that conducted their maneuvers at night. Morrie joined his regiment as the division left their sector near Aachen and headed into Eschweiler. This would become Morrie's baptism by fire.

"It seemed as though the Germans were not used to fighting at night. We were advancing at lightning speed. The other fellas I was serving with said the Germans were no longer fighting like they had earlier in the war. They seemed as if they were on the run." This assessment proved overly optimistic.

"Although you couldn't see through the sights of your M1 at night, none of that mattered. The Germans would flee, and tracer rounds would zip through the battle space, causing a frightening display. We had overwhelming firepower."

In Eschweiler, Morrie aided his platoon commander in speaking to German civilians. "I was told to ask how many German soldiers were in the area, what direction they fled in, and how long they had been in the town for," Morrie remembered.

The Timberwolves moved into Düren. Artillery kept Morrie awake during the day as the division drew closer to Cologne. His company was running low on sleep, capturing town after town and taking hundreds of prisoners.

"On February 28, we were about eight miles outside the city of Cologne. My platoon was advancing at a moderate pace. Keep in mind, we were exhausted. But some major in the rear was not satisfied with the speed of our patrol. He had some Jeep taking him to the front so he could see what was going on," Morrie recalled.

As the officer and his Jeep driver passed through the middle of Morrie's squad, the Jeep struck an anti-tank mine. Morrie's squad had been in a staggered column, five men on each side of the road, when the Jeep hit the mine.

"All I recalled was a flash, and the Jeep went into the air. Next I was facedown on the ground. I don't even remember hearing an explosion. The mine annihilated the Jeep. It was in pieces, with a large portion still working as a flaming ball. Whoever was in the Jeep was killed instantly. My whole squad was wiped out," Morrie recounted.

As Morrie rolled over, he realized the left side of his body had been peppered deeply with shrapnel. He peered over at what was left of his squad. Some men were facedown and not moving; others screamed for help. It was a devastating sight.

"One fellow was asking me for help. He was in far worse shape than I was. I double-checked myself before I went to assist him. I was hit in my leg, thigh, my arm, and back. My helmet had a huge dent in it. I was a bit dazed, and it took me a few minutes to collect myself," he recalled.

Morrie began to treat himself. He swallowed penicillin pills. Then a medic came and helped him sit up. It was then he witnessed other medics working feverishly to save the lives of his squad.

"Some of the guys were in complete agony. I had to hop up and help. I hobbled over and helped the medics lift a few guys off the ground. There were about fourteen of us wounded or dead. One guy had just got out of the hospital from injuries he sustained in Belgium, and he was hit yet again. I helped him to the aid station, then I collapsed too."

At the aid station, Morrie had pieces of shrapnel removed from his body. His wounds were very deep and could become infected if not treated properly. The decision was made to evacuate him to France for further recuperation.

"I was put on a medical train back to Liège, Belgium. It was a horrible experience. There were beds three or four high on each side of the train. Everyone was groaning and moaning. Blood was trickling all over the floors. Everywhere you stepped there were bloody bandages and guts. Nurses and doctors rushed up and down the corridors tending to patients. It was hell."

After his arrival in Liège, Morrie was transported by ambulance to the 197th Medical Evacuation Hospital in France. There he spent five weeks recovering, eating ice cream, and enjoying music. The rear echelon was a different world compared to the front lines.

"I couldn't believe where I was just two days before, compared to what I was experiencing now. Food brought to my bed, pie, live music. It was a little disheartening to know that some of these soldiers in the rear only knew this kind of war. I felt guilty not being with the guys on the front instantly, after my first bite of ice cream."

In early April, Morrie returned to the 104th Division. His unit was in Halle, Germany. They were holding that position and waiting for the Russians to link up with them.

"By this time the war was over for me. They had us scheduled to take a boat home in May. The division was being told to be ready to deploy to Japan, but as history would suggest otherwise, it never happened," Morrie concluded.

While Morrie wound down the war waiting for the Russians, Len was in Austria overlooking a fleet of Mercedes-Benzes belonging to

Hitler's generals, and possibly to Hitler himself. His 20th Armored Division had been in theater less than a month.

With one of the shortest combat chronicles of the war in Europe, the 20th Armored Division saw only ten days of active combat before Germany's surrender. Yet Len's unit, Task Force 20, was responsible for capturing Munich, a stronghold and powerful symbol of German strength.

"There was a military academy and training ground for the SS in Linhof, Germany. Hitler's most elite troops would train here. We couldn't get through to Munich because this facility was holding us up. The SS were in dugouts, tunnels, and in the windows of the school."

Len was part of a heavy mortar platoon in the 20th Tank Battalion. They set up their 81 mm mortar and began to drop a smoke screen on the SS school. This temporarily blinded their fanatical enemy so that Task Force 20 could assault.

In a manner similar to the Japanese in the Pacific, the SS troopers had constructed underground tunnels. The cadets were radicalized by their SS instructors, who also defended the training facility alongside them. The enemy did not want to surrender, and planned to fight to the death—which they did.

"I don't remember anyone surrendering at all," Len said. "Once we finished laying down smoke, we switched to high explosives and helped level the whole area. The mortar barrel became too hot to handle, so we dismounted from the halftrack. We ran from hole to hole and threw grenades into their tunnels. None of them surrendered. They were not just students either. I saw full SS officers lying dead around the compound."

From April 29 to 30, the SS cadets were entrenched in elaborately prepared dugouts and behind the thick walls of their training facility. The academy also served as an anti-tank school. The remainder of its defenders used small arms, machine guns, and hundreds of Panzerfausts against Task Force 20. In all, they killed almost fifty men from the 20th Armored Division.

"We killed seven hundred SS troops, who fought stubbornly and without valuing their own lives. This victory destroyed the defenses of Munich, Germany, and we hauled in our halftrack towards the city," Len related.

Around the same time, elements of the 20th Armored Division assisted with the liberation of the Dachau concentration camp. They were joined by the 42nd "Rainbow" Division and the 45th "Thunderbird" Division. These were units that had experienced extensive combat, were battle-hardened, and had endured thousands of casualties since the start of the war. But what these soldiers had faced during their combat expedition across Europe did not compare to what they found in Dachau. This exceeded their worst nightmares.

There was a 20th Armored Division memorial plaque placed at the gates of Dachau in 1996. I wish I could have shown Len personally, but I knew he wouldn't go without Morrie. I also wished I could show Morrie where he had been wounded in Cologne and bring him to where the other men from his squad were buried. But I knew he wouldn't go without Len. They had been the longest consistent friends who were veterans that I had met on the rifle journey.

Their choice not to go back to Europe wasn't based solely on the brutal reminders of war but also on health reasons. I respected their decisions and was grateful the two had allowed me to hear their stories of World War II.

While we sat at dinner, Len and I spoke about the current war in Ukraine. "You know, I always hear people saying that the world has gone to hell, that things are crazy. I think I have finally come to terms in my life that things have always been crazy. I don't remember a time where there wasn't a war, or life wasn't crazy. It's always been that way. We just have more ways to view the craziness on TV and on our phones."

Hearing Morrie talk about today's current affairs reassured me things were probably going to be okay. His was a voice I could trust. I looked over at Len, who was enjoying his glass of wine. I was glad to be in the company of these two men. It's not every day that two World War II veterans take you out to dinner. I just hoped I would survive the car ride home.

Len and Morrie are more than friends. They had become family to one another. They had been there for each other through the loss of a spouse and health scares—and they even raised their kids to be friends. When Len lost his vision, he was no longer allowed to drive, so Morrie began to pick him up. I often walk away from my talks with veterans pondering how to be a better husband, father, or family man myself. That day I learned about everlasting friendship—because that is what battle buddies are for.

CHAPTER SEVENTEEN

A World of Hurt

Jake Ruser was a twenty-year-old medic with the 4th Infantry Division. His 12th Regiment was assigned to assist the 28th Infantry Division in the Hürtgen Forest in November of 1944. While he had already seen the dead and dying on the Normandy front, he was stunned as he reached the top of a hill in Hürtgen Forest. Four piles of American bodies, frozen solid, were stacked as if ready to be placed on a pallet and moved with a forklift.

"It was an odd thing to see on a battlefield. Usually guys are in a pile, maybe laid out next to one another, but these bodies were stacked perfectly like cordwood. There were four neatly stacked piles about six feet high. Longer bodies were used to create a more stable structure than shorter ones. One layer of bodies was laid the long way, then the second-row bodies were laid across. I never saw anything like it," Jake said.

"Well, who did that?" I asked, sitting on his sofa seventy-eight years later.

"It was the first time the Americans and Germans had a truce. The fighting was so brutal, casualties littered the forest. Both sides allowed

Jake Ruser, 4th Infantry Division

their medics to enter the battlefield and retrieve the dead and wounded," Jake explained. He figured the Germans were the ones who had stacked the dead GIs in that fashion.

Jake had arrived in the Hürtgen Forest just after the truce ended and the battle started up again. As a medic from the 12th Infantry Regiment, he was temporarily assigned to the 28th Division, a unit that had lost many medics.

"I had never been so miserable as I was in the Hürtgen Forest." Jake shook his head as he showed me his Purple Heart and Bronze Star with a "V" for valor. The Hürtgen Forest, and the thirty days he spent there, nearly broke him. He had been a combat medic with the 4th Infantry Division since Normandy. There was something about the Hürtgen Forest that made it seem a meat grinder compared to the rest of the war.

Jake fought in the frigid weather of the Battle of the Bulge, and before that through the murderous hedgerows of Normandy. He crossed the Rhine and, as a medic, treated both civilians and German soldiers in the push to take Central Europe. He was the first man I met who had enough points to go home before the war was over.

He hung his uniform back up on a hook. His medals clanked together, making a noise similar to wine glasses clinking together in a dishwasher. He remembered everything about his wartime service. It wasn't his choice to be a medic, it was the Army's. He did his job to the best of his ability. He was one of the proudest men I'd met, and the son of a World War I veteran.

As he stepped back, his eyes were still glued to the medals. They brought back intense memories, it was easy to see. "My dad and I both put on our uniforms together one time. His World War I uniform still fit him, and he wore it on Veterans Day in 1950. I put mine on, and we took a photo together. I have it somewhere," Jake said.

His dad was also a Purple Heart recipient. He was wounded in November of 1918, just a few days before the war ended, while fighting with the 79th Infantry Division during the Meuse-Argonne campaign.

"Even when I returned home, my father never spoke about his war experiences. His best friend was killed right in front of him during an artillery barrage. I knew it bothered him, but he never took it out on his family or was an angry man," Jake recalled.

His father's traumatic war experience would serve as a lesson for Jake. When he returned home with similar experiences, Jake learned how to handle it like a gentleman, just as his father had. His dad served as living proof that Jake could also live a long, peaceful life after war.

The spirit of Jake's father had also followed him to the hedgerows of Normandy.

"During our push through the Cherbourg Peninsula, the first Army unit I came across other than my own was the 79th Division on our flank. It was even my father's same regiment, the 314th. It felt good seeing the Cross of Lorraine on their shoulder. It was the same patch my father had worn during World War I," Jake said.

Seeing his father's former division adjacent to his own division felt to Jake almost as if his dad were looking after him. As the combat intensified during the Normandy Campaign, the young medic became a seasoned aidman himself.

"It wasn't my choice to become a medic. It all came down to what train I hopped on after my Army physical back in the States. Some guys' trains headed to artillery basic training, others infantry, some communications, mine went to a medic camp. I had no interest in the medical field or passion for being a doctor or anything like that. The Army said I had to be a medic and that was it. A lot of guys who got stuck being a medic didn't like the fact we were not supposed to carry guns. However, those were the rules. We had to stick by the Geneva Convention as much as possible," Jake explained.

On June 13, Jake, along with other replacement medics, landed on Utah Beach. The new medics' original orders were to establish the first evacuation hospital in the Utah Beach sector. Their job would be to help with the evacuation of wounded soldiers from France back to England.

However, on June 14, just two hours before Jake was supposed to meet the doctors and surgeons for the new evacuation hospital, the 4th Infantry Division sent out an emergency request for medics to help fill their ranks.

"On June 18, I joined the 4th Infantry Division outside the town of Montebourg. We walked all day and all night to catch up to them. When I joined them, I reported to the medical officer. He pointed me in the direction of a company that was now using a German pillbox as a shelter. It was nighttime when I became the newest member of the 2nd Battalion 12th Regiment's Medical Detachment," Jake recalled.

The medical officer introduced Jake to the company. There was no warm and fuzzy time to get to know one another. The medical officer quickly broke away from the introductions and hurried to a night meeting to discuss the next day's mission. The Normandy offensive was continuous.

"At 4:30 a.m., we began our march. We had to catch up to the rest of the regiment, which had headed into the forest. This is where I saw my first German. He was dead, but the sight of him still startled me, because he didn't look dead. He was kneeling perfectly on both knees with rifle in hand. The rest of the men assured me he was dead. He was shot clean through the front of his head. The rifle barrel was lodged in the dirt with the buttstock pressed up against his chest, keeping him from falling over."

As he walked by the German Jake glanced at him, shocked that a corpse could maintain such a position. Soon his attention was taken from the macabre scene. The rendezvous area was near. They were preparing for an attack, and Jake would serve as a litter-bearer.

"I remember my first patient. We were supporting E, F, and G Companies during their assault. Whichever company was on the line, we had to help. It was 11:00 p.m. at night. I ran out to no-man's-land to reach him. We loaded him up on the stretcher and ran back to the rear. The fella was wounded during a withdrawal. I don't remember his exact injuries, but he had to have a wound that inhibited being able to walk for us to go out there and get him," Jake said.

The 4th Infantry Division made its way toward Cherbourg in late June. Jake would distinguish himself on June 22, earning a Bronze Star for valor when the Germans countered the 2nd Battalion's attack with white phosphorus mortar shells.

"On the way to Cherbourg there was an open field with plenty of wounded in it. The sky began to rain white phosphorus. I ran out anyway, dodging the falling chemicals. If it hit you it continued to burn under your skin. It was torture, and the men who lay on the field were being burned alive by it." It took some prying from me to get Jake to recall the many rescues he'd made, but he remembered them all.

During the shelling, Jake evacuated a half dozen casualties. Not only did he drag the wounded off the battlefield, but he had to remove the burning metal from their wounds. The soldiers were screaming in agony, the only relief being surgery or cold compresses. A few months later, Jake was pinned with his first Bronze Star for his actions that day.

On June 25 Jake's company helped liberate the city of Cherbourg. There, they set up an aid station in what was considered an "open hospital."

"An open hospital was a medical facility where both Germans and Americans could treat their wounded. We allowed the German surgeons to continue to tend to their patients until we had enough American medical personnel to take over. There were times we had to drive a German colonel to get more medical supplies in town, and bring them back to the hospital," Jake recalled.

While running on and off the battlefields in June, all Jake possessed to identify himself as a medic was a small red cross armband. On July 22 the Army took the further step of collecting the helmets from the medics in the battalion and painting red crosses on them. It turned out that medics from other divisions were being shot and killed. It was not clear if this was on purpose or if the Germans simply could not recognize American medics during combat.

"When you were in Normandy, did you have harder wounds to treat than others?" I asked.

"Believe it or not, if a guy stepped on a mine it was easy to treat. There was not much blood. If the mine exploded up in their bottom from the ground, it lodged dirt and rock in their wounds. This clogged their wounds and blood vessels. We would put tourniquets on them and they would have a chance to live. But if they were driving a vehicle and hit a mine, then they would bleed profusely. The explosion would impact the undercarriage, and the shrapnel from the mine and steel from the vehicle could injure them worse."

In August of 1944, Jake's company drove to Paris. It was the official liberation from occupation by the Nazis.

"You wouldn't have known a war was going on! People came out with bottles of champagne and climbed all over our vehicles. You had to be careful not to run people over. Some of their bottles of champagne had dirt all over them. These people buried these bottles for the day this celebration would come!" Jake exclaimed.

Jake's memory of the liberation of Paris seemed a major highlight of his life. It was a memory not just for him, but one of historical importance. I felt lucky he shared it with me.

The next pivotal moment in Jake's military experience was November 6, 1944. The 12th Regiment was rushed to reinforce the 109th Regiment, 28th Division, in the Hürtgen Forest. The 109th Regiment had nearly become combat ineffective due to its heavy losses.

"When we got to the forest, it was still a beautiful forest. The trees had pine needles on them and were in one piece. After a month, it wouldn't be so pretty. I saw a Jeep stuck in a tree when I left, also a body or two, too high to reach. As far as I am concerned, this became the bloodiest battle of World War II!" Jake stated. It was a bold claim, but one he was certainly in a position to make.

His aid station was set up 1,300 meters from the front line. He had to climb down a ravine, over a creek, and up a hill to the front. This is when he encountered the neatly piled bodies of dead GIs stacked four abreast.

"The bodies were only a hundred feet from the front lines. The soldiers were from the 9th Division on the bottom and the 28th Division on top. I could tell by the patches on their shoulders. These were gathered up during the truce," Jake explained.

Pretty soon Jake had his first casualty to deal with. This man wasn't physically wounded but was having a mental breakdown. He was suffering from what was known then as "combat fatigue."

"This guy finally cracked up. He had already been wounded three or four times since the war started. This time he couldn't handle it anymore. He had been through a lot and just couldn't take any more shelling. We had to tie him down to the stretcher, he was that mentally out of it!" This was one of Jake's first cases of shell shock.

"We didn't call it PTSD then. This became more and more common as the war went on. These guys needed breaks, but sometimes the Army didn't have enough replacements to fill the ranks, so guys were forced to stay on the front lines."

As elements of Jake's 12th Infantry Regiment became known as the 12th Regimental Combat Team, they began to relieve those of the 28th Division. The mission of the 12th Regimental Combat Team was to clear the woods south of the town of Hürtgen. After five days on the ground, and scores of attacks and counterattacks, the 12th Regimental Combat Team had incurred more than five hundred casualties. They were unable to penetrate enemy lines or the enveloping landscape. At this time, Jake became a casualty himself.

"We jumped off on one of our attacks on the tenth of November. We were stopped cold. We got one squad across this highway and then were pinned down. American artillery laid a barrage down for one hour, then the Germans countered it with their own artillery for an hour and a half. During the enemy barrage, the Germans infiltrated the minefield behind us and cut us off from the rear. We were basically surrounded.

"Later in the day we took over a German bunker. We moved the wounded inside. As the day grew long, their wounds really began to bother them. We knew if we didn't get them evacuated infection would set in. One soldier stepped outside to see if there was an escape route he could formulate. He was shot through the head instantly. And this tracer round set his head on fire. His hair smoked from under his helmet."

As the desperate medics huddled over their wounded in the German bunker, it was evident they were surrounded. While rummaging through the bunker, and to Jake's astonishment, they found a large white flag with a red cross on it.

"The coincidence was surreal. Here we were, a bunch of medics, trying to make a break for it, and we found a German medic's flag. One medic got a tree branch just outside the bunker and tied the flag to it. The other seven of us each took a wounded soldier on a litter and left the bunker."

As the medics dragged their wounded, the lead soldier held the red cross flag up high. Miraculously, the Germans allowed them to pass through the lines without being massacred. They carried the wounded 1,500 meters across the lines, down a ravine, up a hill, and another 1,300 meters to the rear echelon aid station.

"I will always ask myself, to this day, how we did it. It was difficult to travel that kind of distance with that form of terrain individually, never mind carrying patients. Anyhow, we managed," Jake said proudly.

"As I was making my way back an artillery shell exploded in the tree above me. I was holding my helmet tight to my head and tree-burst hit my hand. Debris collided with my helmet. My head was okay, but my hand was bleeding," Jake recalled.

"Who bandaged you up?" I asked.

"No one. I began to run and administered the bandage to my own hand. It wasn't that bad. The fighting in the Hürtgen was so extreme no one walked away without a scratch. It rained shrapnel every day. The only time you utilized a medic was if you couldn't walk. Everything else was considered walking wounded or self-treatable."

Jake had become friendly with a supply sergeant who made frequent trips to his field hospital. The supply sergeant would travel back and forth by Jeep from division headquarters resupplying Jake's field hospital with much needed plasma, bandages, and morphine. Jake tended the wounds on his hands as the supply sergeant jumped in his Jeep to make another supply run.

"Shortly after he left, we got word a Jeep had hit a mine down the road. We went to the scene and it was my friend, the supply sergeant. His leg was hanging off by a tendon. We applied tourniquets and bandages to the leg. To his misfortune we had to get rid of what was left of it. I had to cut my own friend's leg off. That's when it becomes personal. When you're close with someone you're treating, and have to amputate part of his body. We took scissors and cut the remaining tendon." Jake shook his head as he described the grisly operation on his friend.

By the time the 4th Division moved out of the Hürtgen Forest, Jake had been there a month. "It looked like a tornado had hit the area before we left. If an infantryman survived three days during the battle you were considered a veteran. They moved us to Luxembourg during the Battle of the Bulge. Even though the Germans were not attacking from that direction, we had to hold the line there. It was considered a break, I suppose," Jake said.

"Was there ever someone that you regretted not being able to save?" It was a question I felt compelled to ask, given his extensive combat experience.

Without hesitation, Jake brought up a terrible incident on the Siegfried Line during March of 1945. While the 4th Division prepared to go on an offensive they were given tank support. Jake and the other medics staged behind one of the tanks as they waited for orders to push forward.

"One of the tankers unbuttoned his hatch and jumped out of the tank. Had to take a piss pretty bad I suppose. He was standing next to the tank and an air burst of artillery went off just above him. He fell to the ground and was convulsing."

As Jake and the other aidmen ran out to rescue the tanker, they carried him on a litter back to the aid station. They got him in the tent and analyzed his wounds.

"The tanker was still breathing. He had a pulse. His chest was rising up and down. His body was fighting, but nobody was home upstairs. We had two different surgeons look at him. The doctors said he was brain-dead, but it was tragic to watch his body still thrash around. He was struggling to stay alive. We had to leave him in the corner of a tent on a stretcher. It didn't feel right, but there was nothing we could do for him. It took a while for him to finally die. We tried not to watch."

There was a crack in Jake's voice as he told me the sorrowful story. Jake shed a tear and had to clear his throat to continue his story.

Not long after the Siegfried Line offensive, Jake had enough points to return home. The United States Army used the Adjusted Service

Rating (ASR) score during the World War II demobilization effort. It was designed to return troops back to the United States based on the length of time served, family status, and honors received in battle. Jake was the first veteran I met who had accrued enough points due to medals and combat experience to be allowed to return to the States before the war was over.

Though Jake's combat time had ended, his service in the Army continued. While stateside, the Army made him a nurse. He was assigned to Thomas England General Hospital in Atlantic City, New Jersey. Thomas England General Hospital also became the largest amputation center in the nation, with 1,625 patients. It became the job of this hospital to perform re-amputations necessary for fitting artificial prostheses properly.

"I was assigned to the paraplegic unit. All my patients were paralyzed from the waist, mid-chest, or the neck down. I had two guys I spent a lot of time with. One that I admired and tried to help was only eighteen. He was only in the war a month or two and got paralyzed from the shoulders down. I tried my best to motivate him. I often wonder how long he made it after the war."

"The second patient I remember was a pilot. He was a brand-new 2nd Lieutenant. He had crashed practicing taking off in the U.S. He never made it to the war. He was paralyzed from the waist down."

The hospital assignment in Atlantic City proved a tough job, if not so physically dangerous. If there was anyone who witnessed sacrifice up close and personal, it was certainly Jake.

After the war Jake remained involved. He attended various 4th Division reunions and took after his father by becoming active in the Veterans of Foreign Wars. He got married and had two children, raising them in Philadelphia.

While he stayed active, I knew he didn't enjoy talking about his wartime experience. I asked if I could pass along his information to several museums wanting to conduct interviews, but Jake declined. I was grateful he had chosen to speak with me. In return I offered him a trip to the Hürtgen Forest again, seventy-eight years later. Jake agreed, and it was off to Germany we went.

Before we left, I designed a bronze plaque and brought it along.

Once we were inside the Hürtgen Forest, I was awestruck at the steepness of the hills he had carried the wounded up and down by stretcher. Even for a twenty-year-old medic, this must have been exhausting. The Hürtgen Forest is a dark place still. The trees block out the sun. It had to have been an extremely depressing place to fight. World War II foxholes still covered the sides of some of the hills, and Jake examined these. It was his first time back, and memories flooded him.

After a while, we left the forest and made for the Hürtgen Forest Museum. There we came upon that bronze plaque I had deposited before with the administrators. This was the first memorial of its kind in the area.

I asked Jake to pull the protective sheet from this plaque. He was unaware of the plaque's purpose and was surprised at my request. He pulled away the sheet.

Then Jake read the plaque I had created. "In honor of the soldiers and medics of the 4th Infantry Division who gave their lives in the Hürtgen Forest from November 1944–December 1944. May their sacrifices never be forgotten. Dedicated by Jake Ruser, a 12th Regiment Medic who returned to this location 78 years later."

"Andy, I'm speechless," Jake said.

"You deserve it," I replied.

Jake was blown away. I was glad he'd made the trip back with me. His war had been epic. He'd traveled from Normandy to Germany as a medic. It was appropriate to honor the 4th Division in the Hürtgen Forest.

A tear fell from his eye onto the plaque. In a way, I wish the tear could have stained it permanently. God bless the medics of World War II.

CHAPTER EIGHTEEN

The Bloody Acorn

In 1947, Jack Moran sat in a college class doodling on a piece of paper, like many a college student trying to fend off boredom. But Jack wasn't etching stick figures or practicing his signature. He was drawing scenes of combat. He found himself recreating an entire scenario from memory—the memory of being pinned down on Hill 360 in Obergailbach, Germany, just three years before.

On this day, Jack didn't pay attention to the class. Once he started outlining the rock pile where he'd taken cover for hours, he couldn't stop. He drew the hill littered with bodies, incoming artillery, tanks, and light machine gun nests.

By the time he finished, he had a full college-ruled notebook filled with such carnage. The scene would stick with him forever. Seventy-eight years later he showed me the same notepad. He'd saved it all this time.

The division with the most veterans who have signed my rifle is the 87th Infantry Division, "The Golden Acorns." This was not something I did on purpose. For one reason or another, they happened to be the largest group of survivors I encountered, totaling fifteen. Meeting fifteen

Jack Moran, 87th Infantry Division

veterans from the same unit in the year 2023 was astonishing. Even better, I was able to collect interviews from many of them.

It was during a trip to the American Veterans Center (AVC) in Washington, D.C., when I first met ninety-seven-year-old Jack Moran. The AVC had asked me to host a World War II veteran panel. Jack and I met there and hit it off. Later, in the hospitality suite of the hotel, Jack had a beer in one hand and the M1 Garand in the other.

He might as well have been twenty years old again. His wealth of knowledge about his unit, the 347th Regiment, 87th Division, was vast. Jack served in Company K from France all the way to the end. I couldn't stop talking to him. Jack was a "no B.S." kind of guy. For instance, he had no problem telling me what he thought was fabricated or wrong in my first book. I enjoyed this immensely.

Before Jack could reel off another critique, I said, "Then why don't you come to Belgium with me and show me yourself?"

Jack thought about it and replied, "Challenge accepted!"

A few months later Jack and I were destined for Belgium and Germany.

Jack's combat experience hadn't started in either of those countries, however. His trial by combat started in France—rare for a unit like his, arriving in Europe relatively late in the war. However, the German army was not entirely flushed from some French territories. The 347th Regiment served as new boots on the ground and much needed relief to some units that had been fighting since the beginning of summer.

As Jack and I waited for our plane, he whipped out that sketch from his college class seventy-five years before. He remembered "Hill 360" in France in minute detail. He pointed to stick figures representing bodies of fallen soldiers.

"Before we ended up in this situation, our regiment landed in Le Havre, France. Every one of us was green, and the war was raging. We were trucked to Metz, France. The Northern France Campaign was still in effect. We were taken by truck from Metz to within ten or twelve miles of the front. We met boys of the 26th Division in every little village we went through, and they were very glad to see us, as they had only gained sixty-four miles in the past seventy-three days. They had really taken a beating.

"We reached a large open field by dusk. There was a woods at the other end of the field and we thought the front line was just on the other side of the woods. We didn't find out till later that the woods was about two miles deep. We lay in the field for about two hours and finally moved just into the woods where we were told to dig in. But the ground was too hard and full of roots. We took a chance that the trees would protect us if we were shelled, and we lucked out because we found out the next day that that area received a terrible shelling about three hours after we left."

Jack's memory was one of the best I have encountered for his age. Many men had recalled combat to me, but none so completely as he did. He remembered nearly every day of his World War II experience. He remembered names, locations, and events as if they were from last week. His was truly one of the best firsthand accounts of combat I ever got.

As we got closer to talking about Hill 360, I could tell it was still difficult for Jack, no matter how cavalierly he spoke of it. The paper he was holding with the sketch on it began to shake. He began to recollect what it had been like as his new unit got closer to the front lines.

"As we moved deeper into the woods from our previous positions, shells started bursting up ahead and we could see the big flashes they made. We eventually met the guys from the 26th Division, who we were relieving. They told us as much as they could about the situation in front of us. We found out we were about to engage the 1st Panzer Division, and usually the Panzer divisions were somewhat staffed by SS troopers. There were 28 men left in their company we were about to relieve. Out of the original 156 they lost 51 men just the previous afternoon. We snuck across a small field and crept up to the holes we were to occupy. My buddies Edgar, Torres, and I were the BAR team. We were together in a fairly large foxhole with a good field of fire for our automatic weapon," Jack recalled.

Our plane was about to board, and I was captivated by Jack's story. While on the plane I sat next to him to hear more. Typically I tried to sleep on the overnight flight to Germany, but I knew in this case that once we got overseas I would be distracted by all the other veterans and *their* incredible stories. I asked Jack to continue his account as the plane's landing gear went up.

"It was dark when we first got into position. It seemed like the sun was coming up seconds later. Time flies in combat sometimes. We thought we could see movement out in front of our positions, but we did not fire because we weren't sure what was out there. In dim light at a few hundred yards, our chance of hitting anything was not very good, and we would give away our positions. Suddenly a firefight started on our left around 6:30 a.m., but we couldn't see what was happening because a small rise of ground was in the way. We could hear tanks trying to move up to support us, but the Germans were obviously trying to stop them. The 1st and 2nd Platoons crawled up to our positions to join us in a daylight advance. I Company was in a patch of woods a little ways to our left. They bumped into several machine gun nests as soon as they started to move out. I learned later that Hughie Gorman, one of my basic training friends, was in the I Company advance and had been hit in the face in the very first moments of that fight. I never did learn how seriously he was wounded or if he survived at all," Jack recalled.

"At a signal, we climbed out of our foxholes, lined up in a spread formation, and started to advance over an open field. We could have just as easily gone down along the hedgerows and avoided some exposure, and I mentioned that but we were told that orders were orders, so we started out. We hadn't gone fifty feet when the first 88 barrage hit. Their spotters could obviously see us coming. It was our first exposure to enemy fire, and it was really something. They were high velocity shells and the noise they made as they came in was very scary. One of the first shells landed about a hundred feet to my right and I immediately heard several screams. I looked over and saw that guys from my squad—Shadle, Phillips, and Valesco—were all down. They were wounded or dead. Tommy Langston, my squad leader, was lying in the mud about twenty feet in front of me and he looked back and gave me a big grin.

"Why was he grinning?" I asked.

"I'm not sure, but I grinned back. I'm sure those grins were trying to cover up our true feelings at the moment. He threw me a K-ration, which was going to be my breakfast when I would get time to eat it, and shortly we got up and advanced another two hundred yards with more 88s coming in, but fortunately causing very few casualties. We made it to a road in the middle of a large area of open farmland and dug in beside the road. Ahead of us the land sloped down and we could see the spires and rooftops of a little town called Obergailbach. Near where I was lying was a small stone marker about two feet high that had the word 'France' on one side and 'Germany' on the other, so we knew that we were right on the border between the two countries."

The tales I'd heard of the men from the 26th Infantry Division taking extreme casualties became a reality to me. Jack and his buddies surveyed the battlefield where the fighting had been going on the last couple days before their regiment arrived.

"Late in the afternoon my buddy Bill Hundley and I crept up to check the scene of battle in which it was reported that fifty-one of the 26th Division boys were killed. It was shocking to find bodies everywhere we looked in a large radius. Heads, arms, and legs had been ripped from many of the bodies, and in a number of cases their intestines were strung out five or ten feet from their bodies. It was our first glimpse of the horrors of war, and it shook us deeply. They had been blasted by terrible firepower. It's hard to imagine how a battle could be so intense and violent. One young lieutenant was sprawled facedown in front of a small grotto of the Blessed Virgin. There was a big hole in his right side, and someone had stuffed rags into it to try to stop the bleeding. I doubt if a medic could have saved any of them. It was a real disaster."

Jack and his buddy began to pick up belts of ammunition and two light machine guns to bring back to their own foxholes. It was evident someone was watching them. Out of nowhere, a German 88 came screaming in, landing just ahead of the men. Jack began to run, but it seemed the shells were following him. This is how deadly accurate the 88 was. He dropped the belts of ammo and machine guns to pick up speed. He dove behind a hedgerow as the last shell impacted on the other side, covering him with dirt and clumps of grass. Luckily the hedgerow absorbed the shrapnel.

"In the morning we received orders to attack Obergailbach. We hurried across another open field under heavy artillery fire and curved down to high ground above the town. The first few homes we came across, we hit the rooftops with bazookas to keep the Germans nervous and moving if possible. The Germans controlled Hill 360 on the other side of the town and had very good artillery observation, plus tanks up there firing their 88s at anything that moved. A shell exploded about twenty-five yards from me, wounding more of my squad mates. My pal Moser was wounded, and shrapnel killed Private First Class Reingold and Private Rappaport. As Rappaport was dying he said, 'I wish my brother was here to help me.' His brother was a doctor back in the States. Reingold was hit in the spine by a very large piece of shrapnel and died immediately. We tried to stop Moser's bleeding as much as possible and bundle him up with whatever clothing and tarps we could spare. It was quite cold. Shock would set in fast if he was not kept warm. He lay there in the mud for a number of hours before the medics could get him out. Others from my platoon who helped evacuate Moser ended up getting wounded by a mortar. From my memory, it was Private Ralph Mistrot who was wounded, and a nice young kid named Heideman was killed just moments later. It was becoming a bloodbath," Jack recalled.

As Jack and what was left of his platoon reached the left end of the town, they were told to dig in. Several 88s whistled right over the men's freshly dug foxholes. Then one screaming shell scored a direct hit on Jack's platoon. Sergeant Castles and two others disintegrated upon the high-explosive shell's impact.

The 88s were coming from the German Tiger tanks on top of Hill 360.

As Jack and the others pressed against the walls of their foxholes, an anti-tank crew wheeled up a 105 Howitzer. The crew of the 105 blasted a single shot at one of the Tiger tanks. The Tiger tank backed into the woods, the shell apparently not destroying the tank but most likely ringing the bells of its crew.

At 4:00 p.m. that day, word was passed down to K Company to bypass Obergailbach, rush across a 300-yard valley, and attack Hill 360 without artillery preparation. Only seven men of Jack's squad were available for the attack. When they reached the bottom of the hill, these few men entered a kind of berserk mode and charged up the hill firing from the hip.

"I was carrying the BAR and a lot of ammunition this time. We flushed out Germans as we went up the hill. They fired at us from their foxholes and other positions. Private First Class Harbaugh got three Germans with his rifle and Corporal McKeever got five with grenades, and hit a German captain in the back of the head as the captain was running away," Jack said.

"My friend PFC Teddy Novakowski ran out in front of us firing a light machine gun from the hip and killed several German riflemen. Enemy shells were coming in, and that plus the mines our men were setting off made for a deadly situation. Tommy Langston got hit and as I was running past him I could see a huge bloody hole in the left side of his chest. Tommy had borrowed my little folding shovel a little earlier in the day, but I didn't want it bad enough to roll him over and take it off his belt. Private Olson and Private Canopy and PFC Noble were also killed at the base of the hill. Sergeant Cafasso was also hit bad, and several cooks came up to carry him down the hill. But a shell exploded near them, killing and wounding some of the cooks and wounding Cafasso a second time.

"I somehow got to the crest of the hill as it became dark. Sergeant Plants and I climbed into a rock pile. It was too dangerous to advance any further without more support, as we were pretty sure the Germans were only about a hundred yards away in the woods at the top of the hill. Artillery was called in to shell the woods on the top of the hill, but the shells came in a little short and burst very close to us. The concussions were so strong that Plants was bleeding from both his nose and ears and had to be taken down the hill. The shelling probably drove the Germans deeper into the woods, and it was very quiet when the shelling stopped.

"Arthur Clemens crawled up to tell me that my buddy Leroy Edgar had been wounded, so while he relieved me I went down the hill to see him. He was hit in about fifteen places in the lower back and legs. A medic had given him a shot of morphine, so he was dopey and couldn't say too much. I gave him a drink of water and bundled him up real good because it was very cold and shock could set in fast. I hated to leave him, but I had to go back up to the rock pile to help out in case there was a counterattack. Lieutenant Stimson crawled up to my position and asked me how many of my squad were left and I told him I thought there were about four of us left in fighting shape. He told me that since Tommy had been killed I was the new squad leader. A few minutes later our 105s started crashing in again. They were welcome protection, but awfully hard on the nervous system. I spent the rest of the night in the rock pile, cold and weary."

I was astonished at the detail with which Jack recalled the fight. What I thought was going to be an uneventful flight turned into me ordering cup after cup of coffee to listen to Jack complete his story. I had written about the 87th Division and met dozens of veterans from the unit. All my conversations had always been more oriented toward the Battle of the Bulge. Now I was getting details of the 87th Division's earlier combat.

Jack spent all night huddled down behind the rock pile. His life depended on that rock pile—a spot most likely there to this day. As dawn came, L Company was set to relieve K Company so K Company could get much needed food and rest. L Company moved through K Company's positions and attacked the woods at the top of the hill but caught hell in the process, suffering multiple casualties.

Jack's company dropped back down to the town of Obergailbach, which the Germans had now abandoned. They were given some coffee and crackers. The town was full of wounded and shells were still crashing in. There was no real rest.

"PFC Reuben Johnson of Proctor, Minnesota, asked me to visit his folks if he was killed and gave me their address. I did the same with him, as our hometowns were only about twenty miles apart, as I was living just over the border in Wisconsin. Private Ladoucer was crying in a corner of the barn. The combat began to wear on us. I drank water out of a horse trough outside the barn because we had no water, and I regretted it later."

This time to recuperate came to an abrupt end when they received orders around noon to swing around the left end of Hill 360 and attack a town called Gersheim. Jack's company had to wade in a small stream before getting to the town, and the water was very cold. After this crossing their feet remained wet and freezing. All they had was their fairly light combat boots.

"By late afternoon we entered the edge of Gersheim without opposition. We moved into several buildings on the edge of town, as it was getting dark. Private Albert Hall was crying hysterically and saying that he'd never get out of there alive. Haile, my platoon sergeant, was ready to club him, as such sights were bad for morale. It was a quiet, cold night, and when dawn broke we found that the Germans had fled, so we headed for Walsheim, the next town. We dug in twice along the way before we reached the edge of town. Some of our tanks had appeared on the hills beside us and fired ahead into Walsheim to help keep the Germans on the run. The Germans put up some brief resistance but were not very effective, and no one was hit. Our M1s were far superior to their bolt-action rifles," Jack recalled.

Jack's K Company went ahead to secure the far end of town, setting up defensive positions in several houses on the right side of the little village. The Germans were still on three sides of K Company. Eventually, several friendly tanks arrived and parked against the houses the men occupied.

"One parked next to the door of the home I was in, with just the barrels of their 90 mm cannons sticking around the edges of the buildings. We really didn't like them that close to us because they could easily attract fire from the German tanks with their deadly 88s," Jack said.

"A German Tiger tank spotted us from a distance away and blazed away with its 88. The first shell exploded just outside the basement window of our house and knocked both PFC John Lee and myself to the floor. We had been standing by that window watching for the Germans. I thought John was killed but he got up cussing because the explosion had ruined the sandwich he was eating. I was okay, just shaken up pretty good. Things then quieted down for a while and Private Haile and Private Ladoucer caught a chicken and killed it for dinner. I had been getting sicker by the hour, no doubt from drinking out of that horse trough the previous day, so didn't think I could have eaten any of the chicken anyway. They put the chicken and some potatoes in the oven of the wood-burning stove and cranked up the fire. The house we were in had the main floor at street level, but it was built on a sloping lot so most of the back basement wall was aboveground. The Germans saw the smoke coming out of the chimney and decided to ruin our dinner party. The first 88 they fired took out the back basement wall and the second one exploded in the basement, ripping out the kitchen floor and dropping the stove and our chicken dinner into the basement. Fortunately no one was in the kitchen when the second shell hit.

"The basement stairwell had a stone wall on both sides, so when the first shell hit we had quickly moved onto the steps. The stairwell faced away from the exploding shells, so while we were deafened, shocked, and scared by the explosions, we didn't get hit by the shrapnel flying around the basement. Private Juan Torres was sitting on the step below me and while the shells were exploding, he dropped a glass jar of preserved cherries or plums on top of the steel helmet of the soldier sitting just below him. I didn't know if he did it intentionally or not, but when the red juice started running down the other fellow's neck and shoulders, he thought he had been hit and was bleeding. When he realized what had happened he was ready to kill Juan. The last shell also blew up the toilet in the corner of the basement, so that mess added its distinctive flavor to the overall mess we were in."

When the shelling finally ceased, it was dark. K Company had to send out a patrol in order to determine the exact location of the enemy. It was Jack's turn to lead the patrol; however, he was now violently ill, probably from drinking out of the horse trough the day before.

"Corporal Johnny DeFlavio saw how sick I was and said he would take out my patrol and I could handle the next one. The four of them left, but in about twenty or thirty minutes they came back through the front door carrying DeFlavio. They had been attacked just after leaving the edge of town and Johnny had been hit in the shoulder and had lost a lot of blood. I naturally wondered what would have happened to me if I had been healthy enough to lead the patrol." Jack spoke both with remembered regret and relief. "Due to the patrol being attacked, one half of my platoon went up to the north end of town to back up the defenses there."

Jack stayed back with the other half.

"Around 11:00 p.m. that night, the first battalion on our left flank was caught in a German bayonet attack."

This was the only bayonet attack to occur involving the 87th Division during the war. The U.S. soldiers were not dug in or prepared for it. In the dark confusion, Germans inflicted many casualties on the battalion. Jack's company was rushed to relieve them and they dropped back to take care of their wounded and reorganize. Thankfully, the rest of the night was quiet for the men of the Golden Acorns.

"The next day was quiet in our sector, with only a few artillery shells coming in. We could hear a good fight develop at the north end of town and I was told that one BAR man killed or wounded eighteen Germans. Someone said they heard Lieutenant McAllister hollering 'Flush the bastards out!' The next morning we moved back into Walsheim. Everybody seemed to be sick. Shells came in all day, which kept us jumpy and undercover. Private George Gray was hit, but not too seriously. One platoon slaughtered a cow. I was still quite sick and tried to sleep around the stove as much as possible, but every once in a while we had to head back to the basement as shells started coming too close. One shell took off a big part of the roof."

Early the next morning K Company was sent up to the northwest section of Walsheim. Private Arthur Clemens and Jack dug in on a small hill near the edge of some woods. They were aware there were German tanks and riflemen in the woods several hundred yards away. However, without their own artillery support or tanks backing them up, they were not inclined to start an attack.

Luckily, at around ten o'clock that night, Lieutenant McAllister crawled up to Jack's foxhole and told the pair to head back to town. Since no one was relieving them, they wondered why they were giving up their positions. This was when the men of the 87th Division found out they were being pulled out and rushed to Belgium to be thrown into the Battle of the Bulge. A tank battalion met them at the south end of Walsheim and covered their withdrawal from German territory.

"I imagine the Germans reoccupied the town by the next day and wondered what we were doing. It seemed a waste to go up there and lose a lot of good men and then withdraw, but it was felt that stopping the Germans in Belgium was much more important at the moment. We hiked back to Obergailbach and rested for a few hours. We then hiked out of that valley and after about two or three hours reached a large farm where we were allowed to light fires and relax. We stayed there for a few hours and then hiked further down the road to where there were a lot of trucks waiting to take us to Belgium."

The advances of the 87th Division in the Saar Valley had been no better than those of the 26th Division, which they had relieved. In a little less than a week they had advanced about four miles at a heavy cost in dead and wounded. They had inflicted many casualties on the Germans, but that was little consolation when they saw how many of their friends had been wounded or killed.

"Looking back on the first day of battle in Obergailbach, I wondered what my thoughts were on that cold December afternoon when after my buddy Bill Hundley left me I stood alone in that field looking at so many dead American boys from the 26th Division all around me. Johnny DeFlavio, who took my spot on patrol while I was sick, was a good heavyweight boxer and feared no man. But after he was wounded taking out my patrol that night, he was never the same again. The doctors patched him up and sent him back to us in three or four months, but he was very nervous and ended up injuring his leg and being evacuated again. I still wonder what would have happened to me if I hadn't gotten so sick from drinking bad water, and had been leading my patrol instead of Johnny. That little drink of water no doubt had an impact on both our lives," Jack said.

The regimental records indicate that the Golden Acorns had sixty-eight men killed in Obergailbach and on Hill 360. An additional twenty-seven men were killed in the Walsheim area. The wounded were at least double those numbers, possibly higher. Added to that would be the large number of men who'd been evacuated due to trenchfoot—several of whom had to have toes or parts of their feet amputated. Spending so much time in a foxhole in that cold winter weather made it practically impossible to keep one's feet dry or warm.

"I learned a bit later that the Germans had mined some of the rock piles on top of Hill 360, which resulted in several soldiers being wounded and a few being killed. Thank God that the rock pile Sergeant Plants and I jumped into wasn't mined, or he and I might have also been wounded or killed," Jack said.

Survivor's guilt still lurks within him seventy-eight years after the fact. The Saar Valley was a meat grinder. As each day began, the men of the Golden Acorns accepted that more of their friends would likely be wounded or killed before sunset. Jack often wondered if he would be among them. The longer a soldier was exposed to battle, the slimmer became his chances to survive intact. After ten days Company K was down to half strength.

"I mentioned Hugh Gorman being hit in the face and not knowing if he had survived or not. Late in 1999, fifty-five years after that date, I found a long article in the 87th Division magazine regarding Hugh's lengthy recovery from his serious head wounds. He was in military hospitals for several years and ended up having fourteen operations to replace part of his jawbone and correct the scars on his face," Jack said.

Living with death every day was very depressing and stressful, according to Jack. The loss of his friends the first few days was hard to accept on both a conscious and unconscious level. Jack told me the men insulated their feelings and withdrew emotionally, perhaps as a defense mechanism. As many others fell in the subsequent months, the men around Jack rarely gave way to emotion or tears. "We just accepted it as a natural byproduct of warfare and kept on going."

Northern France and the Saar Valley would forever be a part of the Golden Acorn history. The following months would be no better. It brought the Battle of the Bulge. Yet the fight in Obergailbach had hardened Jack for what was to come.

After Jack and I landed in Europe, we found ourselves in the town of Bonnerue, Belgium, where Jack had been surrounded during the Battle of the Bulge. A small informational board marked the area where the fighting had taken place. Jack, now ninety-seven, pulled out his iPhone 13 and took a photo of the tree line. The sight was surreal. Seventy-eight years, a lifetime, had gone by since Jack was last in the Ardennes area of Bonnerue.

He put away his cell phone and turned to me. "This area was called the 'Bloody Crossroads,'" he said. "This wooded area's walkway reminded me of northern Wisconsin. Our orders were to penetrate this forest and kill or capture any Germans we could. Eighty of us entered these woods in a single file."

Back in the present, Jack pulled out his cell phone again, snapping more photos.

As he did so, he continued, "Little did we know we would be stuck here for six days, surrounded. We dug about thirty-five foxholes in a circle. A Jeep came up to us riddled with bullets, and the driver confirmed our fear that the Germans were all around us. The first night was quiet. It was a moonless night and the thick forest made it pitch-black out. However, the next morning a German patrol attacked my side of the perimeter firing burp guns, machine guns, and throwing potato masher grenades." Jack pointed to the trees outside where the fight had gotten hot.

One of the grenades tossed by the Germans landed in PFC Bornside's foxhole, wounding him in the back of the head. Jack and PFC Perry threw lead at the Germans, killing several of them. Jack came across an MG 42, but it only had about twenty rounds of ammo left and wasn't much use.

"As the firefight ceased, everyone began to check themselves and tend to their wounds. I noticed that in the hole next to me my pal Joe Polin was not moving. He was slumped over. We discovered he had caught a bullet between the eyes. All we could do was pull his helmet down over his face and let him sit there for the next six days. Each day I hated to look in his direction," Jack recalled sadly.

In the present, Jack pulled out his cell phone and took one last photo of the woods of Bonnerue, the "Bloody Crossroads." We boarded the bus, and I was exceptionally proud to be accompanying him. It was important to tell his and the men of the Golden Acorns' story accurately. He turned to me on the bus and thanked me for taking him back.

No sooner did we leave than he took out his phone again and began to look at the photos he had so recently taken. He couldn't believe he was back as he scrolled through the pictures. To me, they all looked about the same. But to Jack it was a battlefield. It was sacred ground where the Golden Acorns bled that day in Bonnerue.

CHAPTER NINETEEN

A Silent Eagle

Frank Miniscalco sat in his home in East Boston opening his mail. The year was 1946. He was looking forward to moving on with his life after the war. He'd applied for colleges and jobs, so going through the mail was urgent. But Frank froze when saw a name he recognized on an envelope. The return address indicated the letter was from Los Angeles, California.

It was a name he hadn't heard in three years, "Harrington."

In fact, he hadn't seen that name on paper since D-Day +1. But surely it couldn't be Sergeant Harrington from 1st Squad. Harrington had died on June 7, 1944.

When Frank opened the letter he realized it was from Harrington's wife. She was inquiring as to what had happened to her husband on D-Day. She wanted details. Frank was well aware how Sergeant Harrington had died. He'd been there. It broke his heart, but there was no way he could reply to Harrington's wife. The government had insisted that Sergeant Harrington died on June 6, after parachuting into the countryside of Normandy. The Western Union telegram had no further

Frank Miniscalco, 506th Parachute Infantry Regiment

details other than that he died from wounds in combat during the Longest Day.

It was the same information given to thousands of wives and mothers after D-Day. However, in this case, it wasn't the truth. Sergeant Harrington was killed by one of his own command: Lieutenant Ronald Speirs.

Now at the age of 100, Frank sat in his rocking chair in his Andover, Massachusetts, home. He had just signed the rifle, putting "101st Airborne" underneath his name. Frank was the real deal. He had served with Dog Company of the 506th Parachute Infantry Regiment, a sister company of the famous Easy Company, the "Band of Brothers."

Frank had jumped into Normandy with Speirs as his platoon leader on D-Day, just before Speirs later gained fame (and notoriety) as an eventual commanding officer of Easy Company.

In one way at least, Frank was not like those Screaming Eagles of Easy Company. Frank was a Silent Eagle. He'd turned down interviews and *Band of Brothers* media requests, and had never talked about his experience. He crumpled up Mrs. Harrington's letter that day, threw it away, and didn't look back.

"I didn't want her to know what happened to her husband. Harrington had kids, too. It was a disgraceful way to die in combat. But Lieutenant Speirs had to do what he had to do. All of us kept it under wraps that day. The war went on and many guys there that day ended up being killed anyway," Frank whispered to me.

I had always heard the rumors of Speirs killing German prisoners, and even one of his own soldiers, but to hear it from a veteran who had been there was mind-blowing. He couldn't judge the lieutenant. He also owed Speirs his life.

"How did this all transpire?" I asked.

Frank closed his eyes. It was a loaded question. Frank had never told his story before, so we started at the beginning, when he was a young paratrooper in training at Camp Toccoa in Georgia.

"My best friends during training were Carl Sumner and Thomas Manry," Frank said as he pulled out a photo of the three of them together. The picture had been taken after the trio survived the Normandy invasion. The men posed in their dress uniforms with jump wings in England.

The photo was a tragic reminder for Frank. He would be the only one of the three to survive the war. He studied the picture before putting it down. It was a close-up of their faces, from mid-chest upward. Nearly an entire lifetime had gone by since it had been taken.

While at Camp Toccoa, Frank volunteered to become a machine gunner. "I didn't want to march to the ranges with the riflemen. The riflemen had to march from Toccoa to Clemson College to use the rifle ranges. It was approximately thirty to forty miles. It exhausted the men," he remembered.

The men suffered dozens of blistering forced marches while at Toccoa. Yet this didn't stop Frank, Carl, and Thomas from completing basic training and, later, jump school at Fort Benning.

I had interviewed enough paratroopers to know what they did in England leading up to D-Day. We skipped ahead to Frank's Normandy experience.

After the war, he'd never been back. While so many 101st Airborne veterans had returned to France over the years, Frank refused to.

"Why would I go back? There is nothing there for me. It was not a pleasant experience," Frank told me.

Seventy-eight years before, Frank had stood up to prepare to jump over his drop zone near the town of Sainte-Marie-du-Mont in Normandy. The 101st Airborne objective was to eliminate the Germans to secure Utah Beach for successful landings.

"As we stood up, the plane took several bursts of machine gun fire. We were flying so low and so fast we didn't give the enemy guns much time to get a bead on us. When I finally jumped I landed in water up to my waist. I struggled to get out of my parachute, it was so tight it almost drowned me," Frank recalled.

The Germans had intentionally flooded the fields and marshlands behind Utah Beach. This was a tactic to disrupt airborne invasions but also to isolate the causeways linked to the beach landings.

"As I slid the wet parachute off my face, I could see three other paratroopers in knee-deep water making their way to the road. I thought it was a good idea to join them, so I waded in the water towards their direction."

As the three paratroopers checked their equipment and collected themselves, a German machine gun ripped into them. Frank watched tracer rounds rip off one man's arms as the others hit the ground.

"I halted myself in the water and partially submerged myself so as to not be seen."

Frank then turned around and headed in the other direction, moving further into the flooded marsh.

"I was going deeper when I saw a head above the water just ahead of me. The paratrooper was up to his neck in water, but wasn't saying anything. It was because he was frightened. I told him to follow me. He didn't say anything but followed me out of the water and towards dry land. When we dried ourselves off I turned around and he was gone. It was an odd experience. He said nothing to me the whole time."

Still bewildered by the paratrooper who had disappeared, Frank started walking. He walked for miles alone. He kept going until the sun came up, finally locating and joining other men from D Company.

"By the next day I gathered with some of the men from my company. By luck I'd walked in the right direction. I had walked so far I could see Utah Beach. I was watching the waves of troops and ships landing at the beach," Frank remembered, chuckling at this historic memory.

Some three hundred men from Frank's battalion had assembled at this location. Shortly after, Frank reunited with other men from his 2nd Platoon. That was when Lieutenant Speirs took charge, bringing his men to an assembly point south of the town of Vierville on June 7.

"We came across a patch of woods where there were a decent amount of Germans hunkered down. Our captain went to go get tank support to help flush them out. He requested we remain in position to pick them off. The captain's idea was the tanks would force them to re-deploy elsewhere and get caught in our crossfire," Frank explained.

As Lieutenant Ronald Speirs ran from squad to squad giving the men updates, he encountered an extremely drunk Sergeant Harrington, who was with 2nd Squad. Harrington did not like the captain's idea and was belligerent. He called the plan, which Lieutenant Speirs was enforcing, a "chicken-shit" act of cowardice. Harrington accused Speirs of being afraid and threatened to personally lead his squad to fight the Germans embedded in the woods.

Speirs insisted Harrington fall back to the rear to sober up. At this point, Harrington told the lieutenant to "fuck himself" and continued to insinuate he would take on the Germans with his squad alone.

"I could hear them yelling at one another. I was about thirty meters away down a bend with 1st Squad. We were hunched over the hedgerows waiting for the Germans to be pushed out," Frank remembered.

Back at 2nd Squad, the situation intensified as Harrington's behavior grew more extreme. He continued to insult and refuse to follow Speirs's orders. Finally, the drunken sergeant took it a step further. This would cost him his life.

As Harrington raised himself from a prone position, he swung around his tommy gun. Speirs warned Harrington that if he raised his gun in Speirs's direction then he'd better use it.

In his belligerent, drunken state, Harrington took this as challenge. He gripped his Thompson machine gun and maneuvered his body towards Speirs. Speirs was quicker. He sprayed Harrington with a ten-round burst in the chest. The men of Squad 2 were mortified.

"I heard a 'pop, pop, pop' from their vicinity," said Frank. "We ran over and Sergeant Harrington was bleeding out, with a bottle of some sort of booze in his pants. The bullets had also broken other bottles tucked away in his jump jacket."

Everyone started talking immediately. Speirs meanwhile went to get the company commander, Captain Gross, who immediately determined the act had been self-defense. The next day Captain Gross would also be killed by enemy fire. This relegated the controversial incident to the stuff of legends forever.

"The next operation that stands out in my memory was going into Carentan," Frank said.

Early on the morning of June 13, Frank nearly met his own fate, but at enemy hands.

"We were clearing an area outside the town of Carentan. We were ordered to follow a railroad track for one mile to make sure it was clear. During this patrol a mortar shell landed in the distance," Frank recalled.

"I figured it was far enough away that it shouldn't be an issue, but the Germans started to walk the shells in closer. I began to run, but next thing you know I wound up on my ass. My rifle went flying in one direction, and my helmet in the other."

Frank was soon hit by accurate mortar fire. What was left of D Company was spread out. There was no one to rescue him as he sat in the open.

"It was five o'clock in the morning when that first mortar shell went off. The impact landed way out. The next thing I know I'm sitting on the ground. I didn't know what happened, but when I came to, I was sitting on the ground with my feet out in front of me. I looked over and I saw my helmet about ten feet to the left. I looked the other way, I see my gun about six or seven feet over to the right. I look down at my foot and I see a hole in my boot right where the toe is. I couldn't believe that knocked me down. There was smoke coming out of my boot."

In this manner Frank earned his first Purple Heart.

Frank tried to stand but found himself in immense pain. He could not bend his toes. He had to walk on his heels to reach safety.

"Another fellow placed his shoulders under my arms to assist me. They brought me to a house in Carentan that was loaded with all wounded guys." Yet terror continued to strike the wounded paratroopers. German 88 mm artillery rounds slammed into the land around the home.

"'Jesus Christ,' I said to myself. 'One hit on this house and we are all dead.'" The feeble home rattled, and windows shattered as the 88s landed closer. Above, the ceiling was crumbling on the wounded paratroopers strewn across the floor. As quickly as it had come, suddenly the barrage ceased. Frank and the others were evacuated by boat and taken back to England.

The rest of Frank's platoon moved forward that morning to engage what was left of the 6th Fallschirmjager Regiment and later elements of the 17th SS Panzergrenadier Division. The Battle of Carentan would be won by the Allies, but with a heavy price of American blood.

Frank spent ten days in a hospital in England. His wounds were not significant enough to end his wartime journey just yet. However, he was not thrilled to hear the division would be jumping into Holland on September 17.

"Even though I was reluctant, it was the best jump of my career. The weather was perfect, wind was perfect, elevation was perfect, and my landing was perfect," Frank recalled.

After a month of fighting, Frank's company found itself in a defensive position across a dike in Zetten, Holland. On October 8, 1944, Frank was manning the radio in one of the only buildings. He was northwest of the town and close to the dike. Across the water, the Germans occupied the high ground with an abundant amount of artillery.

"My company was waiting for relief. A couple of guys from the heavy weapons section fired an 81 mm mortar across the dike, and then all hell broke loose in return. The Germans fired counter shells at us. I ran back to the building that had the radio in it to make a transmission from our outpost. As soon as I got on the radio to tell the captain we were under fire, a shell hit the house."

The shell leveled the home and broke Frank's right leg. Two thick pieces of shrapnel pierced the flesh by his knee, tearing through the bone. He folded to the ground like an accordion. Another paratrooper in the house was screaming to Frank for help.

"My back, my back!" the helpless paratrooper screamed.

"I can't help you. I can't even stand," Frank called back.

"As I got up I tried to hobble to the door and fell right over. I couldn't walk an inch. My leg was totally broken. I crawled out of the house and into a slit trench previously dug by occupying Germans. When the barrage ended, a couple of replacements found me and dragged me into the road. Suddenly one last shell came in and they dropped me like a sack of potatoes," Frank recalled.

His legs were devastated. He might potentially need a leg amputated. Suddenly, Lieutenant Ronald Speirs appeared once again. He gave Frank morphine and made sure he was properly placed on a Jeep bound for an aid station. On the Jeep was also a wounded girl, as Frank recalled. She'd been a casualty of collateral damage. Frank's war was over.

"I spent a year in recovery. I had multiple infections to fight and had to learn to walk again. By the grace of God, they did not have to amputate."

Because of his injuries, Frank would miss the Battle of the Bulge. While in the hospital he would learn that both his friends were killed in Bastogne. Thomas Manry and Carl Sumner never saw the finish line of the war.

Frank held on to the picture of Manry and Sumner throughout our conversation. These two men never got to start their lives. Instead, they sacrificed themselves for the betterment of millions of people who will never know their names. They were Toccoa men, Normandy veterans, and Holland survivors. But they died in Bastogne.

Frank came home, got married, and did go to school. After two years of college he landed a job with the telephone company AT&T. He never once attended a 101st Airborne reunion or event. He never owned a hat or T-shirt with a screaming eagle on it. Ours was his first documented interview on paper.

Frank was, and will forever be, the silent eagle.

CHAPTER TWENTY

They Call Me Tag

O n April 12, 1945, the 80th Infantry Division had just assumed responsibility for the security of the Buchenwald concentration camp, which
was located about five miles northwest of the city of Weimar, Germany.
It was in the middle of a forest atop Ettersberg Mountain. Buchenwald
was the largest slave working camp in Germany. It consisted of 140
smaller subcamps as well. Since early April 1945, twenty-eight thousand
inmates of Buchenwald were "evacuated" on death marches or on the
famous death train, which ended up at the concentration camp in
Dachau. Upon its liberation, twenty-one thousand additional prisoners,
mostly political prisoners from the eastern countries and prisoners of
war of the Red Army, were still being monitored. They needed to be
contained for health evaluations and the continued investigation of just
what the hell the American forces had come across.

The 4th and 6th Armored Divisions had been the first units to reach
the camp the day before, but they left the camp in a hurry. Once the
armored divisions breached the gates, they reported what they encountered but did not investigate further. On April 11, 1945, the 4th and 6th

Vincent Tagliamonte, 80th Infantry Division

Armored Divisions were the spearhead of Patton's Third Army. They were ordered to move ahead and attack the city of Jena, thirty miles away. They did not pass much information on to the 80th Division.

The newly liberated inmates were left alone almost twenty-four hours before the 80th Division arrived. The prisoners took over the control of the camp, chasing some SS guards into the forest. They looted nearby villages for food. When elements of the 80th Division arrived at Buchenwald concentration camp in the afternoon of April 12, they had their hands full getting the situation under control. They rounded up prisoners and attempted to organize first aid.

"Tag! Tag, look!" one soldier yelled.

Vincent Tagliamonte, or "Tag" as his buddies called him, was a sergeant with the 80th Division, 319th Regiment, Company F. They were responsible for the security of a satellite camp connected to Buchenwald. Tag leaned against the fence of the camp, his eyes heavy from lack of sleep.

"It's happening again!" the other soldier declared.

Tag turned and peered through the fence. The Jewish prisoners were circling a fellow prisoner. With what little energy they possessed, they pounced on him. Even with their lack of muscle caused by complete malnourishment, the prisoners managed to bludgeon the man severely.

"Open the gate, open the gate!" Tag yelled to some new replacements who looked on with confusion. Within moments the prisoner being beaten was dead, his head caved in. His assaulters scattered into the camp.

A group of Americans stood over the body and watched as a medic pronounced the man deceased. "What the hell was that?" another soldier asked.

"He collaborated with the guards," a prisoner murmured in broken English as he hobbled past on a single crutch. The 6th Armored Division had not mentioned to the 80th Division the need to keep the prisoners separated to prevent revenge killings.

"Even after its liberation, prisoners were still dying at Buchenwald," explained Tag as he sat with me on his front porch seventy-seven years later. The camp his company was assigned to was a subcamp of the main Buchenwald camp. It contained over one hundred starving Russian prisoners and others who were considered undesirables.

It was a beautiful fall day in Melrose, Massachusetts. A gust of wind began to blow branches on the trees across the street. He gazed at the leaves falling and recalled his time at Buchenwald.

I saw this overly upset him, and to distract Tag, I asked him about his childhood growing up in Malden, Massachusetts.

Just a few years before the grisly discovery of the Buchenwald extermination camp, Tag had been a kid living the life of any boy in his early teens in America. "My friend and I would sneak into the town dump for parts of bicycles. One day we finally had enough to build two bicycles," he said cheerfully, momentarily putting aside the horrors we had discussed.

Unlike most of my interviews, I was speaking with him three years after he'd signed the rifle. When we'd first met, he signed my rifle and that was it. Tag had not wanted to talk much about the war at that time. It was after he'd attended a *The Rifle* book signing in August 2021 that he'd finally opened up about his wartime experiences. Over one thousand people were in attendance, as well as fifty World War II veterans. I think this motivated Tag to finally share his story.

Tag was not an ordinary child of the Great Depression, as so many veterans had been. He spoke Italian, German, and English. He was superbly talented in mathematics and was destined to become an engineer. The breakout of World War II delayed that plan. Tag received a draft notice as soon as he turned eighteen. He had not finished high school yet, and his father, a World War I veteran, was able to get him an extension until after graduation.

"The day after I graduated high school, I reported to Fort Devens," Tag said.

After several months of basic, Tag was trained in anti-aircraft artillery. Things seemed to be going at a normal pace, but then the Battle of the Bulge broke out. Every able body with at least basic training complete was rushed to Europe as fast as possible.

"I left through New York City, had a stop in Scotland, then landed in Le Havre, France. We were at a replacement depot not long when I was thrown in the back of a truck. I remember passing through all the destruction. I will never forget crossing the Maginot Line and Siegfried Line without a rifle! That's how desperate they needed replacements," Tag said.

The replacement soldiers went unarmed, transported like cattle to reach the front lines as quickly as possible. U.S. forces were in a dire need of replenishment after the land battle in the Ardennes, which would be the largest of the war.

"This is where I learned I would be joining the 80th Infantry Division," he added. "My unit was just past the Siegfried Line. I hopped out of the truck and saw a pile of weapons so I grabbed myself a BAR," a Browning Automatic Rifle.

There was no time for formation or introductions. It was the middle of February 1945. The 80th Division had crossed the border into Germany. There they faced stiff resistance in their effort to capture one German village after another. While hundreds of German Army regulars surrendered, just as many fanatics held out.

Tag rushed over to meet his company, which had begun digging in. The rest of the 80th Division's regiments were moving north of the town of Wallendorf. "I saw a trench which was already dug. I thought it was my lucky day, so I jumped right in and set up my BAR," Tag said. "Then a corporal ordered me out and to dig my own. He gave the empty trench to two other soldiers who had been with the company longer than me."

Tag climbed out of the trench and moved further down the line to a new foxhole. The same corporal who ordered him out of the trench joined him. "I did not take it personal. Those guys were senior to me. If anyone should get a free foxhole, it should be them," he explained.

Not long after this incident, Tag had his first combat experience of taking incoming fire. Shells began to pound the men of Company F as they cradled into their defensive positions.

"The shelling was deafening. I am not sure how to describe it," he said. "The corporal took out his shovel, ya know, his entrenching tool? And covered his head with it!"

When the bombardment ceased, soldiers went scrambling to find medics and account for casualties. The trench in which Tag had originally set up his BAR had taken a direct hit. The soldiers who had occupied this fighting position were killed in action by the artillery barrage. "What got them was a tree burst!"

The following day was the 319th Regiment's turn to advance. Company F was on the assault to clear pillboxes and anything else in the way. "We started out in a field when the artillery came in again. I hit the deck. I was so scared. I could see the feet of a fella in front of me. He was lying on the ground just a few yards away," Tag recalled.

This time Tag didn't have the false security of his foxhole. He was out in the open and scared stiff of the explosions all around him. It was his first time being this vulnerable. "I had stayed on the ground for so long that when I decided to rise, nobody was around. The whole platoon advanced without me," he said.

"As it turns out, the man who hit the ground next to me was never alive to begin with. It ended up being the legs of a dead German!" Tag had been so frightened by the enemy artillery he was unaware he was hugging the ground next to a corpse, likely killed days before.

"It took me some time to catch up to the platoon. It was not a good feeling," Tag said. His embarrassment would soon evaporate. All the men were thrown into a different kind of war, experiencing long weeks of house-to-house fighting. In the month of March 1945, the unit pushed further into the thickly settled areas of central Germany.

Urban terrain became the most difficult hurdle the 80th Division had to navigate on its route through Germany. "Most of the towns we went into, the German soldiers would be lined up both sides of the streets with their hands up. Yet, other towns, nobody would surrender per order of their mayor or militia. This would lead us to have to clear out every house and building."

Tag explained how urban warfare was conducted in 1945. "The company will break up the neighborhood into sections. Each platoon must move up a different street, clear each home, then all meet on the other side of the city." Tag used his index finger to draw an imaginary map on the kitchen table where we were sitting. As a veteran myself who was trained for military operations in urban terrain, I was reminded by Tag's description of the Battle of Fallujah, Iraq.

"It wasn't just war; it was a battle of survival," he added. American forces were hungry as well. Each home was not only cleared of enemy troops but raided for food. "We used to stick our hands up their fireplaces. Inside many of the chimneys you could pull down meat."

As the American forces occupied each town, children often proved a handful to deal with. Tag took a Nazi dagger from a shoebox while we sat in his kitchen.

"I pulled this away from a member of the Deutsches Jungvolk, German Youth." This was a faction of the Hitler Youth. These kids' ages ranged from ten to fourteen years old. "They would run around towns and stab American Jeep or truck tires that they found parked," said Tag.

Tag was able to catch one and rip away his long knife.

The 80th Division would often march through a German town without a single shot being fired. Prisoners continued to surrender by the hundreds. The resistance got stiffer, however, as the infantry regiments approached the Rhine. The Rhine River was the last natural defense line and last hope of Hitler to stop the American advance into Germany.

"We crossed the Rhine in late March near the town of Mainz," said Tag. "We were given wooden assault boats, all of us with a paddle. It was 1:00 a.m. and I remember the moonlight was so bright that night it may as well have been daytime. I knew this was going to be bad."

Tag's wooden assault boat left the muddy banks of Bischofsheim, Germany, heading for the other side of the Frankfurt area. The men packed light and shifted off into the river. "We were halfway across when tracer rounds began flying all around us," Tag recalled.

"The men were ducking in the boat and hiding behind the wooden frame. I told them it's not going to protect them and we must keep paddling! The men began to paddle nervously until two were hit. Both soldiers died. No one was able to render aid. The remaining soldiers had a job to do, and that was to get across the river—pronto.

"My paddle got shot away from me, so I took the buttstock of my BAR and slapped it in the water and continued to paddle that way," Tag told me. When the assault boat reached the other side of the bank, Tag could see the two men who'd been hit. They were slumped over in their boat and not breathing.

"I went to reach for my backpack for some medical supplies, and it was gone, it was shot off me during the crossing. I didn't realize it."

The mission was not over. "We were told once we got to the other side we had to expand the beachhead." Each of the companies had to move left and right to capture the area. Having a secure riverbank meant the engineers could construct a bridge so the whole division could make it over.

"While I cleared the assigned sector, I noticed there was a boathouse on my side of the river. I moved around the right side of it. When I turned the corner, I was face-to-face with a German soldier." Tag hesitated. I could tell he didn't want to relive what he was about to tell me.

"My BAR was right in his stomach and he had his pistol holstered. It was an SS officer." The officer reached for his pistol and Tag shot the man three times. "After I shot him, I panicked and ran away. I ran so fast, I actually ran through a wooded fence attached to the boathouse. I felt like a cartoon character," Tag recalled.

Shaken, Tag sprinted to the company's command post. He reported to his captain that he believed he'd just killed a German officer. "I got to the CP and told them what happened. Captain Chamberlin, my commanding officer, told me to go get the man's pistol. At first I refused, then he pointed his M1 carbine at me and ordered me to."

Tag cautiously made his way back to the boathouse. He could see where he'd crashed through the wooden fence. It looked like an outline such as those left by Wile E. Coyote. "I went over to his body and removed a Walther P38 from its holster. That is when I noticed the thunder-bolts on his collar."

As the days went on and German cities offered stiffer resistance, Tag and the rest of the men of his company developed a close working relationship with the operators of Sherman tanks. "I was assigned to one tanker, his name was Pappy. The name of his tank was *Tally Whacker*. It was written on the 75 mm barrel. He would toss out ammunition from the inside of his tank to make room for booze that they looted from homes. This guy loved his alcohol.

"One town we tried to enter had much resistance. We came under burp gun fire right away. The Germans had constructed a wooden log wall outside the city. We had to outflank it with the tanks," he said.

As Tag lay down covering fire on an embankment, the tanks began to move around his squad to enter the city. Suddenly, Pappy stopped behind him. "He swung the barrel of his tank over my head and let out two bursts." The tank had engaged enemy targets with Tag caught in between. *Tally Whacker* blew holes into the nearby log fortifications. The way into the city was opened.

"I lost my hearing for two weeks when he fired those shots. It really concerned me," said Tag. "I was pretty out of it. I entered the city pretty deaf, but found a bottle of liquor in the first house I went into. I tried to throw it up to Pappy. He failed to catch it and the bottle shattered all over the turret. It bleached the Army-green paint on his turret white."

The 80th Division continued its blitz through Germany, passing through towns without stopping. "I remember being outside of Kassel,

THEY CALL ME TAG

Germany, and we took refuge in a hospital," Tag recalled. "We assumed we would be safe, but from across a field we could see three Panzer tanks heading our way."

One of the German tank commanders was standing in the turret directing the assault. Totally exposed, the German officer made himself easy to pick off. "My buddy, P.F.C. Schott from New York, positioned himself in the window and with one shot from his M1 Garand hit the tank commander through the face, sending a pink mist into the air."

The German officer was flung back. He dropped into the turret, the head shot killing him instantly. "Suddenly the tank stopped, closed its top hatch, and began to reverse," Tag said.

All three of the tanks accompanying it did the same. "We didn't stick around either," Tag said. They feared there would soon be a major counter-attack of German infantry. But that attack never came. The 80th Division's advance proved unstoppable.

While in the Kassel area, Tag's regiment was able to catch up on rest. "Our chaplain set up Sunday Mass for us. A bunch of us were walking to church when a real dogfight broke out in the sky over our heads. Some P-51 Mustangs were engaged in battle with some Me-109s." Tag's face showed excitement as he recalled the dogfight. Somewhere inside, he was still that nineteen-year-old boy.

American troops crowded the streets rooting for their pilots locked in aerial combat. As the Me-109s began to lose the battle, they broke off from the dogfight and swooped down on the ground troops. They strafed the street Tag was standing on. "Suddenly, it wasn't enjoyable anymore. One of them raked the ground just feet in front of us." The high-caliber bullets impacting the ground nearly killed the church-going soldiers. They took shelter in the homes until the planes left the area.

After recounting so much, Tag finally had to take a break. Not talking about it for a lifetime and then spilling it out had left him exhausted. Soon his story would turn to when his unit began liberating concentration camps.

Tag was not in the same health as he had been when he signed the rifle a few years ago. I was fortunate he'd decided to give me an in-depth interview. He took a deep breath and proceeded to tell me about his entry into the city of Weimar, Germany.

Weimar is a major city rich with German cultural heritage. Musicians and poets like Bach, Herder, Wieland, Goethe, and Schiller lived and worked there in the eighteenth century. The Bauhaus University was founded in Weimar by Walter Gropius in 1919. It was the birthplace of democracy in Germany with the Weimar Republic in 1919. But it was also one of the birthplaces for the rising power of the Nazis. Weimar was one of Hitler's favorite cities. It was the true Nazi capital in central Germany. High-ranking Nazis like Himmler and Göring were guests in the city many times. After taking power, Hitler used the city with its rich tradition in German history for propaganda and political causes. Just outside of the city, at Buchenwald, the Nazis established one of the first and largest concentration camps in the Third Reich.

"I honestly believe I may have been one of the first GIs into Weimar. I was riding on the number one tank into the city," he recalled.

"Weimar had been the political city in which the Third Reich had placed its administration building called the Gauforum. Large Iron Crosses, eagles, and swastikas stood out like gargoyles on the building. We sure did make a mess of this place," Tag remembered. Documents, files, paperwork, and books were scattered about. He was unsure if the Germans did this themselves or someone else. It is most likely that the Germans had attempted to destroy as many documents as possible to keep them from falling into the hands of the U.S. troops. "There was much confusion, but we really didn't stick around too long. We kept advancing."

From Weimar, the 80th Division was sent to what was later known to be the Buchenwald concentration camp. The horrors they witnessed were unimaginable. They found thousands of people in such poor physical state that it was a wonder they possessed a heartbeat. According to Tag, these people were beyond skin and bones. Hundreds were dead, their bodies stacked five feet high in some locations.

Other prisoners were so confused they didn't realize they were being liberated. Some prisoners remained in their wooden bunks, five to a bed without room to turn over. "The Army gave out cots to some of the prisoners of the camp we came across," Tag recalled. "Three of them could fit on one cot. That's how skinny they were. Often you couldn't tell who was still alive and who was dead in the beds around the camp. Our medics gave some of them cheese, but it went right through them. We were instructed not to do that again. It made the prisoners very sick."

Then the 80th Division left Buchenwald and was on the move. The war was not over. The cities closer to Nuremberg proved to be more violent, with civilians taking up arms against the Americans. In one city in particular, a sniper would harass Tag's company for days. "We eventually darted from house to house until we located the home he was in. He was hiding in the attic. We'd moved in to surround his location, when a civilian tossed a potato masher grenade in the home we were in."

The grenade blew up after it was tossed in the window. Tag's squad couldn't chase the civilian assailant, fearing they would be shot by the sniper.

"We set up a counter sniper, who was able to shoot and kill him. I will never forget when we recovered his body that it was a bald old man. He was a senior citizen."

The division moved south towards Nuremberg. According to Tag, this was the most devastated portion of Germany he encountered. "Nuremberg was one city inside of another city. When we patrolled at nighttime, you could hear German civilians under the rubble of their own homes. You could hear voices crying and yelling after the aerial bombings."

In the days ahead, the 80th Division continued to push the remaining enemy forces that opposed them, mostly SS troops, towards Austria. On April 30, 1945, Tag, who was now staff sergeant, advanced with his men at a cocky pace. "We got complacent, thought we had the SS troopers on the run, next thing you know we had a major surprise attack happen to us."

The SS had regrouped across the Isar River in Austria. They unleashed machine guns, small arms, and mortar fire on Tag and the rest of Company F in a well-executed ambush. "We were totally pinned down by the fire coming across the river."

An enemy mortar landed next to Tag. His right hand was peppered with shrapnel fragments and began to turn numb. "The enemy was not going to let up until our tanks came to reinforce us." Four Sherman tanks reached Tag's company and directed their 75 mm guns to the other side of the river. Four .50 caliber machine guns fired in unison and silenced the SS enemy. These die-hard Nazi troopers would surrender the following day. Tag's wounds were barely enough for a bandage, but they did earn him a Purple Heart.

The 80th Division finished its trek through Austria. Towards the end of the movement, they discovered what they thought to be yet another extermination camp. The camp was later identified as Ebensee concentration camp. The hellish compound had been erected as a labor camp, making it slightly less murderous than an extermination camp such as Buchenwald. Ebensee was determined later to be a subcamp of the infamous Mauthausen concentration camp.

"A couple days later and we got news we never thought we would hear: Germany surrendered," Tag recalled. His war was not over, however. Now Staff Sergeant Vincent Tagliamonte fell victim to the controversial point system, which determined when a soldier was allowed to return stateside.

"I was transferred to the Big Red One [1st Infantry Division] for occupation duty, and found myself back in Nuremberg." Forced to remain in Europe, Tag got to witness one of the most historic events in world history, the Nuremberg Trials.

As we temporarily paused our interview, Tag asked his daughter to fetch his Army souvenirs out of the closet. Tag rifled through a small folder until he found what he was looking for. It was a small four-inch ticket stub. The ticket read: "International Military Tribunal Seat Number 81, Session 96."

Tag with the rifle

"This was my balcony seat during the Nuremberg Trials. I looked right down on Hermann Göring, Rudolph Hess, and Joseph Goebbels." Tag spoke of this nonchalantly. "You're the first veteran to sign my rifle who witnessed those trials!" I said excitedly. Tag shrugged his shoulders as if it were no big deal. At the trials, he had only one thing in mind: getting back to his girlfriend, Connie, and marrying her. He did just that.

In the corner of his living room, a beautiful painting was displayed of a young Vincent Tagliamonte in his Army uniform. "A Frenchmen painted that for me when I was on my way home." Next to that painting was a second painting of Connie, his late wife. "He painted that too, but did it from a tiny photo I had in my pocket." The two paintings hung side by side, painted seventy-seven years ago for a marriage that lasted over six decades.

It turned out that the most valuable souvenir Tag brought home wasn't the Nuremberg Trial ticket stub, but these two irreplaceable paintings that represented future generations of remarkable families for our country. I buckled up the rifle and left Tag, grateful that he'd opened up to me in such depth at the end of his eventful life.

CHAPTER TWENTY-ONE

The Final Goodbye

For part one of *The Rifle*, I chose stories of valor. These were stories similar to ones you may have heard, but from the perspective of men now in their late nineties. I chose veterans from lesser-known divisions or units history has overlooked. Those men, most of whom are gone, taught me valuable lessons about being a stand-up veteran, a father, a citizen, and a neighbor.

Of the three hundred men and women who have signed the rifle, not everyone was perfect. That's why I found it important to share those men's outlook on the war as well, and the lives they lived afterwards. Many of our Iraq and Afghanistan veterans are now long into their post-military lives. Some have fallen through the cracks, made mistakes, or suffered mentally.

It is important for them to show that even the Greatest Generation wasn't flawless. While many men in *The Rifle 2* fit the profile of the heroes, I purposely mixed in the poor, the criminals, and the liars for balance. I also included a German veteran, who wrote the foreword.

There are two sides to every story. The victors are often the only ones who get to write history.

I do see similarities between post-9/11 veterans and German World War II veterans. We both served in what were deemed by some "unpopular" wars (especially the Germans, of course). We both were encouraged to fight by our government. Now we are sometimes viewed as charity cases. Yet, we regret nothing. (This does not speak to the special case of Nazi fanatics, but the basic German soldier.)

I am very, very proud to have served in two of my nation's conflicts. I wouldn't change a thing, but the positive future of our veterans requires these kinds of tough talks. The fall of Afghanistan single-handedly made Afghanistan War vets—men who were seeking retribution for September 11—into men on the losing end of a drawn-out war, as Vietnam veterans had been seen by many.

It had been nearly ten years since I was in Afghanistan, yet during the August 2021 suicide attack on the Kabul Airport, I heard the screams of all thirteen service members who were killed that day in my dreams. It became more evident than ever that war would always be a part of me.

The fall of Afghanistan troubled me greatly as I sought out more World War II veterans to fill the rifle. In part this was a therapeutic experience not just for me but for them, too. The rifle created lifelong friendships. Over thirty of these veterans joined me shoulder to shoulder revisiting the battlefields where they or their buddies had once bled.

Visiting Italy, France, the Netherlands, Belgium, Luxembourg, and Germany with these veterans became an addiction of sorts. To see these men, nearly eighty years later, walk into homes they had once occupied, or visit the graves of buddies they hadn't seen since combat, was remarkable. These experiences can never be duplicated.

It was a World War II veteran airman by the name of "Bud" Haedike who helped me see the big picture in the end. Before I took him to Belgium to show him where his B-17 crash-landed, he said to me, "You know Andy, this is going to be a trip of a lifetime for me. But if you told me you were cancelling it to spend time with your kids, I would be just as happy."

These words from a man who watched his life go by like a speeding bullet. He fathered his own kids and outlived a spouse. Basically with those words he'd communicated to me that it was time to finish the rifle mission. After three hundred signatures and a dozen trips to Europe, it was time to focus on my family. My boys needed me.

Both my sons, Andrew and Charles, were born during my rifle signature quest. I was able to conquer much of the task while they were newborns, and I have my wife to thank for that. While I often wasn't present for their infancy, I knew they would never know what it was like to have a conversation with a World War II veteran. By the time they were old enough to have one, all our World War II veterans would be gone. I wanted to make them proud of their father, and perhaps give our family a tradition they could carry.

Despite my misgivings, my police career did not suffer during this seven-year adventure. With a country looking to hang cops, writing my books was a good excuse to lie low and not be so proactive on the streets. Often I would use a work computer to type or conduct research. It was the perfect getaway during the nationwide scrutiny of law enforcement.

As it stands now, some 150,000 World War II veterans remain. America's last Medal of Honor recipient from the Second World War, Hershel "Woody" Williams, has passed away. I was fortunate to attend his funeral in the Capitol Rotunda in Washington, D.C. It was the first time this honor was given. Woody's passing marked a significant milestone in the fading of our country's Greatest Generation.

As I write, one of the first conventional wars in decades is taking place in Europe. Videos show trench warfare once again being conducted. Tank battles and mass executions of prisoners have occurred both on Ukraine and Russia's watch. It is hard to say if more countries will be pulled into the fray, but any historian might recognize building blocks similar to those that sparked World War I. The hope that World

War II would end major country-vs.-country land battles sadly has not come to fruition during World War II veterans' lifetimes.

While this book will mark the end of my World War II research, it will not be the finish line for honoring veterans. There is still an opportunity to bring awareness to veterans of more recent wars. Their stories will be just as important to future generations as the rifle veterans' stories were to me. Some of our nation's greatest leaders came from military backgrounds. To capture their wisdom and experience may be something I will examine when the time is right. What tool I may use to bring light to their sacrifice I'll decide later. Perhaps it will be a camera, a microphone, a pen, or maybe . . . another rifle.

The Rifle Signatures, the Warriors

1. Hershel "Woody" Williams—U.S. Marines
Unit: C Company, 1st Battalion, 3rd Marine Division—Gaum, Iwo Jima
Medals: Medal of Honor, Purple Heart

2. Robert Maxwell—U.S. Army
Unit: HQ Company, 7th Infantry Regiment, 3rd Infantry Division—North Africa, Casablanca, Salerno, Anzio, Monte Cassino, southern France
Medals: Medal of Honor, Silver Star (2x), Bronze Star, Purple Heart (2x), Combat Infantryman Badge

3. Santo DiSalvo—U.S. Army
Unit: G Company, 143rd Infantry Regiment, 36th Division—Salerno, San Pietro, southern France
Medals: Distinguished Service Cross, Purple Heart, Bronze Star, Combat Infantryman Badge

4. Levi Oakes—U.S. Army
Unit: U.S. Army Mohawk Code Talker of the 442nd Signal Battalion—Leyte, Luzon, Philippines
Medals: Silver Star, Bronze Star, Combat Infantryman Badge, Congressional Gold Medal

5. Carl DiCicco—U.S. Army
Unit: G Company, 135th Infantry Regiment, 34th Division—Anzio, North Apennines, Po Valley
Medals: Silver Star, Bronze Star, Purple Heart (4x), Combat Infantryman Badge

6. John Primerano—U.S. Army
Unit: HQ Company, 501st Parachute Infantry Regiment, 101st Airborne—Holland, Belgium, Germany
Medals: Bronze Star, Combat Infantryman Badge, Combat Parachutist Badge

7. Frank Miniscalco—U.S. Army
Unit: D Company, 506th Parachute Infantry Regiment, 101st Airborne—Normandy, Holland
Medals: Bronze Star, Purple Heart (2x), Combat Infantryman Badge, Combat Parachutist Badge (2 Stars)

8. Freeman Johnson—U.S. Navy
Unit: USS *St. Louis*, USS *Iowa*—Pearl Harbor, Okinawa
Medals: Combat Action Ribbon

9. George Hursey—U.S. Army
Unit: Battery G, 64th Coast Artillery—Pearl Harbor, Guadalcanal
Medals: Bronze Star, Purple Heart, Combat Infantryman Badge

10. Bob Noble—U.S. Army
Unit: 347th Infantry Regiment, 87th Division—northern France, Stalag XIB
Medals: Prisoner of War Medal, Bronze Star, Combat Infantryman Badge

11. Robert Nodgren—U.S. Army
Unit: K Company, 329th Regiment, 83rd Infantry Division—Ardennes, Rhineland, Central Europe
Medals: Bronze Star, Combat Infantryman Badge

12. Roy Roush—U.S. Marines
Unit: 2nd Battalion, 6th Marines—Guadalcanal, Tarawa, Saipan, Tinian
Medals: Purple Heart, Combat Action Ribbon

13. William Griffiths—U.S. Marines
Unit: 1st Tank Battalion—Cape Gloucester, Peleliu, Okinawa
Medals: Purple Heart, Combat Action Ribbon

14. Edward E. Parsons—U.S. Army
Unit: 4th Engineer Battalion, 4th Infantry Division—Ardennes, Rhineland
Medals: Bronze Star, Combat Infantryman Badge

15. Jim Baker—U.S. Army
Unit: 15th Infantry Regiment, 3rd Infantry Division—Anzio, southern France
Medals: Purple Heart, Bronze Star, Combat Infantryman Badge

16. Mike Maglio—U.S. Army
Unit: HQ Company, 28th Infantry Regiment, 8th Infantry Division—Normandy, northern France, Rhineland
Medals: Bronze Star, Combat Infantryman Badge

17. Walter Lipinski—U.S. Army
Unit: HQ Company, 20th Armored Infantry, 10th Armored Division—Ardennes, Rhineland, Central Europe
Medals: Bronze Star, Combat Infantryman Badge

18. Quintin Bussolari—U.S. Army
Unit: F Troop, 90th Cavalry, 10th Armored Division—northern France, Rhineland
Medals: Purple Heart, Bronze Star, Combat Infantryman Badge

19. Edwin Swirtek—U.S. Navy
Unit: USS *Wasp* CV18—Saipan, Philippine Sea, Iwo Jima, Chichi Jima, Guam, Rota, Leyte, Luzon

20. Frank Delespro—U.S. Navy
Unit: USS *Cabot*—3 kamikaze strikes—Marianas Island, Philippine Sea,
Iwo Jima, Guam, Wake Island

21. Leo Bruno—U.S. Navy
Unit: ADP 102, USS *Rednour*—2 kamikaze strikes—Okinawa

22. Vinny Tagliamonte—U.S. Army
Unit: HQ Company, 80th Infantry Division—Rhineland, Central Europe
Medals: Bronze Star, Purple Heart, Combat Action Badge

23. Lou San Miguel—U.S. Army
Unit: 103rd Cavalry Reconnaissance, 103rd Infantry Division—Ardennes,
Rhineland, Central Europe
Medals: Purple Heart, Combat Infantryman Badge

24. Anthony Dabrosca—U.S. Army
Unit: 38th Infantry Division—Luzon, Philippines
Medals: Combat Infantryman Badge

25. Enoch Woody Woodhouse—U.S. Army
Unit: Tuskegee Airman
Medals: WWII Victory Medal

26. Delbrook Bins—U.S. Army
Unit: 20th Air Force
Medals: WWII Victory Medal, Korean Service Medal

27. Manuel Almeida—U.S. Army
Unit: 81st Armored Reconnaissance, 1st Armored Division—Tunisia,
North Africa, Sicily, Monte Cassino
Medals: Purple Heart, Bronze Star, Combat Infantryman Badge

28. Rod Hanlon—U.S. Marines
Unit: 2nd Marine Amphibious Corps—Guam
Medals: Purple Heart, Combat Action Ribbon

29. Frances Xie Murphy—U.S. Army
Unit: HQ Company, 83rd Airdrome Squad—Normandy, northern France, Rhineland
Medals: Combat Infantryman Badge

30. Buddy Marino Cuozzo—U.S. Marines
Unit: AA Gunner, 6th Marine Division—Okinawa
Medals: Combat Action Ribbon

31. Bernard Pothier—U.S. Army Air Corps
Unit: Headquarters Squadron, 24th Pursuit Group—Bataan Death March, Camp Fukuoka, Prison Camp #17 Honshu, Japan
Medals: Silver Star, Bronze Star, Prisoner of War Medal, Combat Infantryman Badge

32. Vincent "Bill" Purple—U.S. Army Air Corps
Unit: B-17, 379th Bomber Group, 8th Air Force—England
Medals: Distinguished Flying Cross, Air Medal with four Oak Leaf Clusters

33. Ray Malley—U.S. Army Air Corps
Unit: B-24, 450th Bomber Group, 15th Air Force—Italy
Medals: Distinguished Flying Cross, Purple Heart, Air Medal

34. Steven Vaciliou—U.S. Navy
Unit: USS *Chapultepec*—torpedoed—South America
Medals: Combat Action Ribbon

35. Rocco Telese—U.S. Army
Unit: K Company, 339th Regiment, 85th Infantry Division—Rome-Arno, North Apennines, Po Valley
Medals: Purple Heart, Bronze Star, Combat Infantryman Badge

36. Josiah Benator—U.S. Army
Unit: 20th Armored Infantry, 10th Armored Division—Ardennes
Medals: Bronze Star, Purple Heart, Combat Infantryman Badge

37. Clarence Cormier—U.S. Army
Unit: HQ Company, 422nd Regiment, 106th Infantry
Division—Ardennes
Medals: Bronze Star, Prisoner of War Medal, Purple Heart, Combat
Infantryman Badge

38. Frank Polewarczyk—U.S. Army
Unit: A Company, 315th Regiment, 79th Infantry Division—Normandy,
northern France, Rhineland, Central Europe
Medals: Bronze Star, Purple Heart, Combat Infantryman Badge

39. Francis Gaudere—U.S. Army
Unit: HQ Company, 119th Infantry Regiment, 30th Infantry Division—
Normandy, Holland, Ardennes, Rhineland, Central Europe
Medals: Bronze Star, Combat Infantryman Badge

40. Stanley Sasine—U.S. Army
Unit: 5307th Composite Group, "Merrill's Marauders"—India, Burma
Medals: Bronze Star, Purple Heart, Combat Infantryman Badge

41. Harold Sheffield—U.S. Marines
Unit: 1st Raider Battalion—Solomon Islands, Guadalcanal, Tulagi,
Bougainville
Medals: Combat Action Ribbon

42. Jack Foy—U.S. Army
Unit: A Company, 347th Regiment, 87th Infantry Division—northern
France, Ardennes, Rhineland, Central Europe
Medals: Bronze Star, Purple Heart (3x), Combat Infantryman Badge

43. Chuck Sozio—U.S. Marines
Unit: VMF 525—Ulithi

44. Paul Perry—U.S. Army
Unit: 351st Infantry Regiment, 88th Infantry Division—Sicily, Naples-
Foggia, Rome-Arno
Medals: Bronze Star, Combat Infantryman Badge

45. Larry Kirby—U.S. Marines
Unit: 2nd Battalion, 9th Marines, 2nd Marine Division— Guam, Iwo Jima
Medals: Silver Star, Combat Action Ribbon

46. Alfred Willett—U.S. Army
Unit: 227th Field Artillery, 29th Infantry Division—Omaha Beach, Normandy, northern France, Rhineland
Medals: Bronze Star, Combat Infantryman Badge

47. John McAuliffe—U.S. Army
Unit: M Company, 347th Infantry Regiment, 87th Infantry Division—Ardennes, Rhineland, Central Europe
Medals: Bronze Star, Combat Infantryman Badge

48. Ernest Roberts—U.S. Army
Unit: M Company, 347th Infantry Regiment, 87th Infantry Division—northern France, Ardennes, Rhineland, Central Europe
Medals: Silver Star, Bronze Star, Purple Heart, Combat Infantryman Badge

49. Bernie Ruchin—U.S. Marines
Unit: 2nd Battalion, 2nd Marine Division—Saipan, Tinian
Medals: Purple Heat (2x), Combat Action Ribbon, Korean War Campaign Medal

50. Kenneth Gay—U.S. Army
Unit: 65th Armored Infantry Battalion, 20th Armored Division—Central Europe
Medals: Bronze Star, Combat Infantryman Badge

51. Robert Oliver—U.S. Navy
Unit: LST 309—North Africa, Salerno, Normandy, Japan
Medals: Combat Action Ribbon

52. Joe Milone—U.S. Army
Unit: 701st Tank Destroyer Battalion, 10th Mountain Division—Po Valley
Medals: Bronze Star, Combat Infantryman Badge

53. Nick Francullo—U.S. Army
Unit: HQ Company, 330th Infantry Regiment, 83rd Infantry Division—
Normandy, northern France, Ardennes, Rhineland, Central Europe
Medals: Bronze Star, Purple Heart (2x), Combat Infantryman Badge

54. John Katsaros—U.S. Army Air Corps
Unit: B-17, 401st Bomber Group, 8th Air Force
Medals: Purple Heart, Distinguished Flying Cross, Air Medal with
Cluster, French Resistance and WWII Victory Medals, Prisoner of War
Medal, Bronze Star, British Flying Boot

55. Nelson Bryant—U.S. Army
Unit: D Company, 508th Parachute Infantry Regiment, 82nd Airborne
Division—Normandy, Holland, Ardennes
Medals: Bronze Star, Purple Heart, Combat Infantryman Badge, Combat
Parachutist Badge (2x)

56. Fred Morgan—U.S. Army
Unit: A Company, 505th Parachute Infantry Regiment, 82nd Airborne—
Sicily, Normandy, Holland, Ardennes, Rhineland, Central Europe
Medals: Bronze Star, Purple Heart (2x), Combat Medical Badge, Combat
Parachutist Badge (4x)

57. Edward Hess—U.S. Army
Unit: B Company, 135th Infantry Regiment, 34th Infantry Division—
Anzio, Monte Cassino, Rome-Arno, North Apennines, Po Valley
Medals: Bronze Star, Combat Infantryman Badge

58. Curtiss Burwell—U.S. Army
Unit: HQ Company, 11th Infantry Regiment, 5th Infantry Division—
northern France, Ardennes, Rhineland, Central Europe
Medals: Bronze Star, Purple Heart, Combat Infantryman Badge

59. Sharland Leavitt—U.S. Army Air Corps
Unit: B-17, 95th Bomber Group, 8th Air Force
Medals: Distinguished Flying Cross, Bronze Star, Air Medal

60. John Hymer—U.S. Army
Unit: B Company, 135th Infantry Regiment, 34th Infantry Division—
Anzio, Rome-Arno, North Apennines, Po Valley
Medals: Bronze Star, Combat Infantryman Badge

61. Marshall Heyman—U.S. Army
Unit: 3rd Tank Battalion, 10th Armored Division—Alsace-Lorraine,
Ardennes, Rhineland, Central Europe
Medals: Bronze Star, Purple Heart, Combat Infantryman Badge

62. Peter MacDonald—U.S. Marines
Unit: Navajo Code Talker, 6th Marines—China Occupation

63. Yoshio Nakamura—U.S. Army
Unit: 442nd Regimental Combat Team, Heavy Weapons Platoon—
southern France, Italy
Medals: Bronze Star, Combat Infantryman Badge

64. Lawson Sakai—U.S. Army
Unit: 442nd Regimental Combat Team, 100th Battalion—Rome-Arno,
North Apennines, southern France
Medals: Bronze Star (2x), Purple Heart (3x), Combat Infantryman Badge

65. Eva Wagner—U.S. Army
Unit: Nurse Corps—England
Medals: WWII Victory Medal

66. Masmeno DelRossi—U.S. Army
Unit: B Company, 54th Armored Infantry Battalion, 10th Armored Divi-
sion—Alsace-Lorraine, Ardennes, Rhineland, Central Europe
Medals: Bronze Star, Purple Heart (2x), Combat Infantryman Badge

67. Jerry Gustafson—U.S. Army
Unit: Cannon Company, 442nd Regimental Combat Team—Italy, south-
ern France
Medals: Bronze Star (2x), Purple Heart, Korean War Medal, Vietnam
Campaign Medal, Combat Infantryman Badge (2x)

68. Thomas H. Begay—U.S. Marines
Unit: Navajo Code Talker, 5th Marine Division—Iwo Jima, Chosin Reservoir
Medals: Combat Action Ribbon, Korean War Medal

69. Donald Stratton—U.S. Navy
Unit: USS *Arizona*, USS *Stack*—Pearl Harbor, Leyte Gulf, Lingayen Gulf, Okinawa
Medals: Purple Heart, Combat Action Ribbon

70. Steven Domitrovich—U.S. Army
Unit: 575th Ambulance Company—Ardennes, Rhineland, Malmedy massacre survivor

71. Rocco DiGloria—U.S. Army
Unit: 9th Infantry Division—northern France, Ardennes, Rhineland, Central Europe
Medals: Bronze Star, Purple Heart (2x), Combat Infantryman Badge

72. Charles Sanderson—U.S. Army
Unit: 552nd Heavy Field Artillery Battalion, Red Ball Express—Normandy, Ardennes, Rhineland, Central Europe
Medals: Bronze Star, Combat Infantryman Badge

73. Marvin Gilmore—U.S. Army
Unit: A Company, 458th Anti-Aircraft Battalion—Normandy, Ardennes, Rhineland
Medals: Bronze Star, Combat Infantryman Badge

74. Rod Strohl—U.S. Army
Unit: Easy Company 501st Parachute Infantry Regiment, 101st Airborne—Normandy, Holland, Ardennes, Rhineland, Central Europe
Medals: Bronze Star, Purple Heart, Combat Infantryman Badge, Combat Parachutist Badge (2x)

75. Lawrence Hunewill—U.S. Navy
Unit: Bomber Patrol Squadron, VPB 19—Iwo Jima, various Pacific Island operations

76. Allan Atwell—U.S. Army
Unit: 28th Infantry Division, 28th Military Police Company—Hürtgen
Forest, Ardennes, Rhineland
Medals: Bronze Star, Purple Heart, Combat Infantryman Badge

77. Al Bucharelli—U.S. Army
Unit: HQ Company, 15th Regiment, 3rd Infantry Division—Monte
Cassino
Medals: Bronze Star, Purple Heart, Combat Infantryman Badge

78. Tom Bristol—U.S. Army Air Corps
Unit: 12th Bomber Group; 490th Bomber Squad, 10th Air Force—
China, Burma, India
Medals: Distinguished Flying Cross, Purple Heart, Air Medal

79. James Hackenberg—U.S. Army
Unit: 20th Field Artillery, 5th Infantry Division—northern France,
Ardennes, Rhineland, Central Europe

80. Hank Baggs—U.S. Army
Unit: 359th Regiment, 90th Infantry Division—Ardennes, Rhineland,
Central Europe
Medals: Bronze Star, Combat Infantryman Badge

81. Al Hulstrunk—U.S. Army Air Corps
Unit: glider pilot, 5th U.S. Army, Special Operations Group 12—Operation
Varsity, Rhineland
Medals: Air Medal, Bronze Star, Combat Glider Badge

82. Peter Paicos—U.S. Army Air Corps
Unit: glider pilot, 305th Troop Transport—Operation Varsity, Rhineland
Medals: Air Medal, Bronze Star, Combat Glider Badge

83. Alfred Sidal—U.S. Navy
Unit: USS *Bunker Hill* (severely damaged by two kamikazes)—Okinawa,
Philippine Sea, Solomon Islands, Marshall Islands

84. James Hanley—U.S. Marines
Unit: I Company, 22nd Marines, 6th Marine Division—Okinawa
Medals: Purple Heart, Combat Action Ribbon

85. Russ Lang—U.S. Army
Unit: I Company, 423rd Infantry Regiment, 106th Infantry Division—
Ardennes, Stalag XIIA
Medals: Bronze Star, Prisoner of War Medal, Combat Infantryman
Badge

86. Louise McRoberts—U.S. Army
Unit: 1st Army HQ, present in the hospital when General Patton died

87. Joe Terenzio—U.S. Army
Unit: 169th Infantry Regiment, 43rd Infantry Division—New Guinea,
Philippines
Medals: Silver Star, Bronze Star, Purple Heart (3x)

88. Joe Drago—U.S. Marines
Unit: I Company, 3rd Battalion, 22nd Marines—Okinawa
Medals: Purple Heart, Combat Action Ribbon

89. Sam Yanku—U.S. Army
Unit: D Company, 229th Infantry Regiment, 75th Infantry Division—
Ardennes, Rhineland, Central Europe
Medals: Bronze Star, Combat Infantryman Badge

90. Ernie Deeb—U.S. Army
Unit: 150th Engineer Battalion—Normandy, northern France, Ardennes,
Rhineland
Medals: Bronze Star, Combat Infantryman Badge

91. Anthony DeFusco—U.S. Marines
Unit: I Company, 3rd Battalion, 25th Marines, 4th Marine Division—
Saipan, Tinian, Iwo Jima
Medals: Combat Action Ribbon

92. Allison Blaney—U.S. Army
Unit: 326th Medical Company, 101st Airborne—Normandy, Holland, Ardennes, Rhineland, Central Europe
Medals: Bronze Star, Combat Medical Badge, Combat Parachutist Badge (2x)

93. Herman Streitburger—U.S. Army Air Corps
Unit: 343rd Bomb Squad, 98th Bomb Group, 15th Air Force—Stalag Luft IV
Medals: Distinguished Flying Cross, Air Medal, Bronze Star, Purple Heart, Prisoner of War Medal

94. Alfred Consigli—U.S. Army
Unit: 774th Tank Battalion—Normandy, northern France, Ardennes, Rhineland, Central Europe
Medals: Bronze Star, Combat Infantryman Badge

95. Dan Donovan—U.S. Marines
Unit: 17th Anti-Aircraft Battalion, 2nd Marine Division—Tinian
Medals: Combat Action Ribbon

96. Gerald Glookasian—U.S. Army
Unit: 3rd Tank Battalion, 10th Armored Division—Alsace-Lorraine, Ardennes, Rhineland, Central Europe
Medals: Bronze Star, Purple Heart, Combat Infantryman Badge

97. Dominic Davolio—U.S. Army
Unit: 86th Infantry Division—Central Europe
Medals: Bronze Star, Combat Infantryman Badge

98. Ted Ackroyd—U.S. Army
Unit: 18th Regiment, 1st Infantry Division—Ardennes, Rhineland
Medals: Bronze Star, Combat Infantryman Badge

99. Mike Linquata—U.S. Army
Unit: D Company, 134th Regiment, 35th Division—northern France, Ardennes, Stalag 12A
Medals: Bronze Star, Prisoner of War Medal, Combat Medical Badge

100. Walter Gilbert—U.S. Army
Unit: 101st Infantry Regiment, 26th Infantry Division—northern France, Ardennes, Rhineland, Central Europe
Medals: Silver Star, Bronze Star, Purple Heart (2x), Combat Infantryman Badge

101. Walter "Miz" O'Malley—U.S. Marines
Unit: 2nd Battalion, 27th Marines, 5th Marine Division—Iwo Jima
Medals: Purple Heart, Combat Action Ribbon

102. Louis Zoghby—U.S. Army
Unit: F Company, 194th Regiment, 17th Airborne Division—Ardennes, Operation Varsity, Rhineland, Central Europe
Medals: Bronze Star, Combat Infantryman Badge, Combat Glider Badge

103. Wayne Field—U.S. Army
Unit: 86th Cavalry Reconnaissance, 6th Armored Division—Ardennes, Rhineland, Central Europe
Medals: Bronze Star, Purple Heart, Combat Infantryman Badge

104. Armand Sedgeley—U.S. Army Air Corps
Unit: 97th Bomber Group, 15th Air Force—Italy, North Africa
Medals: Distinguished Flying Cross, Silver Star, Bronze Star, Purple Heart, Air Medal

105. Bob Weber—U.S. Army
Unit: A Company, 54th Armored Infantry, 10th Armored Division
Medals: Bronze Star, Combat Infantryman Badge

106. Bob White—U.S. Army
Unit: HQ Company, 507th Parachute Infantry Regiment, 17th Airborne Division—Ardennes, Operation Varsity, Rhineland, Central Europe
Medals: Bronze Star, Purple Heart, Combat Infantryman Badge, Combat Parachutist Badge

107. Rodney Perkins—U.S. Army
Unit: A Company, 345th Regiment, 87th Infantry Division—Ardennes, Rhineland, Central Europe
Medals: Bronze Star, Purple Heart, Combat Infantryman Badge

108. Len Kieley—U.S. Army
Unit: 8th Tank Battalion, 4th Armored Division—Normandy, northern France, Rhineland, Ardennes, Central Europe
Medals: Silver Star (2x), Bronze Star, Purple Heart, Combat Infantryman Badge

109. Doug Bryant—U.S. Navy
Unit: USS *Dogfish* (SS-350 submarine)—Pacific War patrols, sinking 12 enemy vessels
Medals: Combat Submarine Patrol Badge

110. Winston Patrick Flynn—U.S. Army
Unit: F Company, 157th Regiment, 45th Infantry Division—Anzio, Italy, southern France
Medals: Bronze Star (2x), Purple Heart (3x), Korean War Medal, Vietnam Campaign Medal, Combat Infantryman Badge (3x)

111. Mildred Cox—U.S. Marines
Unit: 1st Marine Division, stenographer (one of the first woman Marines)

112. Russell Erickson—U.S. Army Air Corps
Unit: B-24, 44th Bomb Group, 8th Air Force—Ardennes, Rhineland, Central Europe
Medals: Distinguished Flying Cross (2x), Air Medal (4x)

113. Don Halverson—U.S. Army
Unit: Weapons Company, 168th Regiment, 34th Infantry Division—Monte Cassino, Anzio, Rome-Arno, North Apennines, Po Valley
Medals: Bronze Star, Combat Infantryman Badge

114. Vincent Speranza—U.S. Army
Unit: H Company, 501st Parachute Infantry Regiment, 101st Airborne—Ardennes, Rhineland, Central Europe
Medals: Bronze Star, Purple Heart, Combat Infantryman Badge

115. Clayton Christiansen—U.S. Army
Unit: A Company, 324th Combat Engineer Battalion, 99th Infantry Division—Ardennes, Rhineland, Central Europe
Medals: Bronze Star, Combat Infantryman Badge

116. Robert Thompson—U.S. Army
Unit: A Company, 23rd Infantry Regiment, 2nd Infantry Division—Normandy, northern France, Ardennes, Rhineland, Central Europe
Medals: Bronze Star, Combat Infantryman Badge

117. Raymond Wallace—U.S. Army
Unit: B Company, 507th Parachute Infantry Regiment, 82nd Airborne—Normandy, Stalag 12A
Medals: Bronze Star, Combat Infantryman Badge

118. Chet Rohn—U.S. Army
Unit. C Company, 56th Engineers, 11th Armored Division—Ardennes, Rhineland, Central Europe
Medals: Bronze Star, Combat Infantryman Badge

119. Fred Whitaker—U.S. Army
Unit: B Company, 347th Regiment, 87th Infantry Division—Ardennes, Rhineland, Central Europe
Medals: Bronze Star, Purple Heart, Combat Infantryman Badge

120. Kenneth Gillpatrick—U.S. Army
Unit: HQ Company, Glider Signal Corps, 82nd Airborne—Sicily, Italy, Normandy, Holland, Ardennes, Rhineland, Central Europe
Medals: Bronze Star, Combat Infantryman Badge, Combat Glider Badge (2x)

121. George Arnstein—U.S. Army
Unit: 76th Cavalry Troop, 76th Infantry Division—Rhineland, Ardennes, Central Europe
Medals: Bronze Star, Combat Infantryman Badge

122. Rick Spooner—U.S. Marines
Unit: F Company, 2nd Battalion, 8th Marines, 2nd Marine Division—Saipan, Tinian, Okinawa
Medals: Bronze Star, Purple Heart (3x), Combat Action Ribbon (3x), Korean War Medal, Vietnam Campaign Medal

123. Robert Smith—U.S. Army
Unit: A Company, 746th Tank Battalion—Normandy, northern France, Rhineland, Ardennes, Central Europe
Medals: Bronze Star, Combat Infantryman Badge

124. Vince Terrill—U.S. Army
Unit: C Company, 381st Infantry Regiment, 96th Infantry Division—Okinawa
Medals: Bronze Star, Purple Heart, Combat Infantryman Badge

125. Harvey Segal—U.S. Army
Unit: 37th Field Artillery, 2nd Infantry Division—Normandy, northern France, Ardennes, Rhineland, Central Europe

126. Edwin Waite—U.S. Army
Unit: 259th Infantry Regiment, 65th Infantry Division—Rhineland, Central Europe
Medals: Bronze Star, Combat Infantryman Badge

127. Luigi Pasquale—U.S. Army
Unit: 184th Regiment, 7th Infantry Division—Okinawa
Medals: Bronze Star, Combat Infantryman Badge, Purple Heart

128. Charles Sahagian—U.S. Army
Unit: 347th Regiment, 87th Infantry Division—Ardennes, Rhineland, Central Europe
Medals: Bronze Star, Purple Heart, Combat Infantryman Badge

129. Raymond Goulet—U.S. Army
Unit: 259th Field Artillery, Red Ball Express—Normandy, northern France, Ardennes, Rhineland
Medals: Combat Infantryman Badge

130. Richard Minichiello—U.S. Army Air Corps
Unit: 1333rd Army Air Force Base Unit—India, China, Burma Air Transport
Medals: Air Medal with Oak Leaf Cluster

131. John Leoncello—U.S. Army
Unit: E Company, 345th Regiment, 87th Infantry Division—Ardennes, Rhineland, Central Europe
Medals: Bronze Star, Purple Heart, Combat Infantryman Badge

132. Bennet Bard—U.S. Marines
Unit: 29th Marine Regiment, 6th Marine Division—Okinawa
Medals: Purple Heart, Combat Action Ribbon

133. Charles Swain—U.S. Army
Unit: I Company, 345th Regiment, 87th Infantry Division—Ardennes, Rhineland, Central Europe
Medals: Bronze Star, Combat Infantryman Badge

134. Harold Angle—U.S. Army
Unit: 112th Regiment, 29th Infantry Division—northern France, Ardennes, Rhineland
Medals: Bronze Star, Combat Infantryman Badge

135. Jack Myers—U.S. Army
Unit: 692nd Tank Battalion—Holland, Rhineland, Ardennes, Central Europe
Medals: Bronze Star, Combat Infantryman Badge

136. Thomas Hoke—U.S. Army
Unit: 312th Medical Company, 347th Regiment, 87th Division—northern France, Ardennes, Rhineland, Central Europe
Medals: Bronze, Star Combat Medical Badge

137. John DiClimente—U.S. Army
Unit: 413 Anti-Aircraft Battalion, 1st Infantry Division
Medals: Bronze Star, Combat Infantryman Badge

138. Charles Coggio—U.S. Army
Unit: 88th Infantry Division
Medals: WWII Victory Medal, Occupation Medal

139. Phillip Schwartz—U.S. Army
Unit: 125th Field Artillery, 34th Infantry Division—Salerno, Monte Cassino, Anzio, North Apennines, Po Valley
Medals: Bronze Star, Combat Infantryman Badge

140. Clifford Tenney—U.S. Army
Unit: A Company, 54th Armored Infantry, 10th Armored Division—Rhineland, Central Europe
Medals: Bronze Star, Combat Infantry Badge

141. David Stevens—U.S. Army
Unit: 350th Infantry Regiment, 88th Division—Salerno, Rome-Arno, North Apennines, Po Valley
Medals: Purple Heart, Bronze Star, Combat Infantryman Badge

142. Sam Hanna—U.S. Navy
Unit: LST 308—North Africa, Salerno, Normandy, Japan
Medals: Combat Action Ribbon

143. Sam Boike—U.S. Army
Unit: 740th Field Artillery Battalion—Normandy, northern France, Ardennes, Rhineland, Central Europe
Medals: Purple Heart, Bronze Star

144. Jack Langton—U.S. Navy
Unit: LCI(R) 643— Okinawa
Medals: Combat Action Ribbon

145. Bill Allen—U.S. Navy
Unit: LST 523 (sunk)—Normandy
Medals: Purple Heart, Combat Action Ribbon

146. Rothacker Smith—U.S. Army
Unit: 366th Infantry Regiment, 92nd Infantry Division—Rome, North Apennines
Medals: Purple Heart, Bronze Star, Prisoner of War Medal, Combat Medical Badge

147. Ralph Painter—U.S. Army
Unit: 83rd Armored Field Artillery Battalion—Normandy, northern
France, Rhineland, Ardennes, Central Europe
Medals: WWII Victory Medal

148. Tony Vaccaro—U.S. Army
Unit: 83rd Infantry Division—Normandy, northern France, Rhineland,
Ardennes, Central Europe
Medals: Purple Heart, Bronze Star, Combat Infantryman Badge

149. Edward Hansberry—U.S. Marines
Unit: 1st Marine Division—Cape Gloucester, Peleliu, Okinawa
Medals: Navy Cross, Purple Heart, Combat Action Ribbon

150. Bob Chase—U.S. Army
Unit: 102nd Infantry Division—Holland, Rhineland, Central Europe
Medals: Bronze Star, Combat Infantryman Badge

151. Lawrence Batley—U.S. Army
Unit: 95th Infantry Division—Normandy, Northern France
Medals: Purple Heart, Bronze Star, Combat Infantryman Badge

152. Ray Cardinale—U.S. Army
Unit: C Company, 330th Regiment, 83rd Infantry Division—Ardennes,
Rhineland
Medals: Bronze Star, Purple Heart, Combat Infantryman Badge

153. Charles Ketcham—U.S. Army
Unit: A Company, 54th Armored Infantry Battalion, 10th Armored
Division—Rhineland, Central Europe
Medals: Bronze Star, Combat Infantryman Badge

154. Peter Manna—U.S. Army
Unit: L Company, 163rd Regiment, 41st Division—New Guinea,
Philippines
Medals: Combat Infantryman Badge, Philippine Liberation

155. Anthony Barrasso—U.S. Army
Unit: HQ Company, 101st Regiment, 26th Division—northern France, Ardennes, Rhineland, Central Europe
Medals: Bronze Star, Combat Infantryman Badge

156. Robert Andry—U.S. Army
Unit: B Company, 761st Tank Battalion—northern France
Medals: Bronze Star, Purple Heart

157. Maurice Diamond—U.S. Army
Unit: F Company, 347th Regiment, 87th Division—northern France, Ardennes, Rhineland, Central Europe
Medals: Bronze Star, Purple Heart, Combat Infantryman Badge

158. Norman Menard—U.S. Army Air Corps
Unit: 8th Air Force, 457th Bomb Group
Medals: Air Medal, WWII Victory Medal

159. Peter Cardinale—U.S. Navy
Unit: SS *John Bell*, Armed Guard (torpedoed)—North Africa
Medals: Combat Action Ribbon

160. Mederick Zaher—U.S. Marines
Unit: 1st Marines, Field Artillery
Medals: Combat Action Ribbon

161. Stanley Friday—U.S. Army
Unit: 80th Division, 317th Regiment, HQ Company—northern France, Rhineland, Ardennes, Central Europe
Medals: Bronze Star, Purple Heart, Combat Infantryman Badge

162. John Trezza—U.S. Marines
Unit: 5th Marine Division, 13th Artillery—Iwo Jima
Medals: Purple Heart, Combat Action Ribbon

163. Lawrence Grove—U.S. Army Air Corps
Unit: 15th Air Force, 7th Bomb Group—China, Burma, India, bridge over the River Kwai
Medals: Air Medal (2x)

164. Asa Davison—U.S. Army
Unit: 93rd Infantry Division—Guadalcanal Canal, New Guinea,
Philippines
Medals: Bronze Star, Combat Infantryman Badge

165. Eddie Guaraldi—U.S. Army
Unit: 296th Engineer Battalion—Normandy, northern France, Ardennes,
Rhineland, Central Europe
Medals: European Campaign Medal

166: Curt Shaw—U.S. Army
Unit: 150th Combat Engineer Medics—Normandy, northern France,
Ardennes, Rhineland Central Europe
Medals: Bronze Star, Combat Medical Badge

167. James Sterner—U.S. Army
Unit: K Company, 84th Infantry Division, 333rd Regiment—Ardennes,
Rhineland
Medals: Purple Heart, Bronze Star, Combat Infantryman Badge

168. Bill Halley—U.S. Navy
Unit: USS *Hoggatt Bay*, Avenger Aerial Gunner, Torpedo 14
Medals: Combat Action Ribbon, Air Medal

169. Henry Naruszewicz—U.S. Army
Unit: 276th Armored Field Artillery—northern France, Ardennes, Rhine-
land, Central Europe
Medals: WWII Victory Medal

170. Henry Bengis—U.S. Army Air Corps
Unit: 379th Bomb Group, 8th Air Force
Medals: Air Medal, Prisoner of War Medal

171. Phillip Walsh—U.S. Army
Unit: I Company, 2nd Armored Division, 66th Armored Regiment—
Normandy, northern France, Ardennes, Rhineland
Medals: Bronze Star, Combat Infantryman Badge

172. Arthur Colachico—U.S. Army
Unit: 156th Infantry Regiment, Medical Detachment—northern France
Medals: Combat Medical Badge

173. Emilio Magliacane—U.S. Marines
Unit: 1st Battalion, 5th Marines, 1st Marine Division—Peleliu, Okinawa
Medals: Combat Action Ribbon

174. Dominic Freni—U.S. Army
Unit: 82nd Airborne, 80th Anti-Aircraft Battalion, B Battery—
Normandy, Holland, Ardennes, Central Europe
Medals: Purple Heart, Bronze Star, Combat Infantryman Badge

175. Albert St. George—U.S. Army
Unit: 2nd Armored Division, 82nd Armored Reconnaissance Battalion—
Sicily, Rome, southern France, Rhineland
Medals: WWII Victory Medal

176. Peter Bucci—U.S. Army
Unit: 257th Combat Engineer Battalion
Medals: WWII Victory Medal

177. Jim Martin—U.S. Army
Unit: G Company, 506th Parachute Infantry Regiment, 101st Airborne—
Normandy, Holland, Ardennes, Rhineland
Medals: Purple Heart, Bronze Star, Combat Infantryman Badge

178. Dan McBride—U.S. Army
Unit: F Company, 502nd Parachute Infantry Regiment, 101st Airborne—
Normandy, Holland, Ardennes
Medals: Purple Heart (3x), Bronze Star, Combat Infantryman Badge

179. Tom Rice—U.S. Army
Unit: C Company, 501st Parachute Infantry Regiment, 101st Airborne—
Normandy, Holland, Ardennes
Medals: Purple Heart (2x), Bronze Star, Combat Infantryman Badge

180. Lawrence McCauley —U.S. Army
Unit: 63rd Armored Field Artillery—Normandy, northern France, Ardennes, Rhineland
Medals: WWII Victory Medal, Combat Action Ribbon

181. Charles Davis—U.S. Army
Unit: Signal Company, 17th Airborne Division, 517th Parachute Infantry Regiment—Ardennes, Rhineland
Medals: Glider Badge, WWII Victory Medal

182. Paul Sheaffer—U.S. Army
Unit: 1182nd Combat Engineer Battalion—Rhineland
Medals: WWII Victory Medal

183. Clair Guey—U.S. Army
Unit: 260th Combat Engineer Battalion
Medals: WWII Victory

184. Carl Tringali—U.S. Navy
Unit: USS *Barber* (DE-161)—Pacific

185. Richard Heinl—U.S. Army
Unit: 94th Infantry Division, 376th Regiment
Medals: Bronze Star, Combat Infantryman Badge

186. Angelo Olivari—U.S. Marines
Unit: 29th Regiment, 6th Marine Division—Okinawa
Medals: Combat Action Ribbon, Purple Heart

187. Russell Moulaison—U.S. Navy
Unit: 6th Naval Beach Battalion—Normandy, Rhineland
Medals: Combat Action Ribbon

188. Everett Allen—U.S. Army Air Corps
Unit: 458th Bomb Group, 8th Air Force—Normandy, Holland, Rhineland
Medals: Prisoner of War Medal, Air Medal (2x)

189. David Fisher—Army Air Corps
Unit: 20th Air Force, 39th Bomb Group
Medals: Air Medal

190. Vernon Lopez—U.S. Army
Unit: 214th Military Police—Normandy, northern France, Ardennes
Medals: WWII Victory Medal

191. Jerry Dunham—U.S. Army
Unit 91st Infantry Division—Italy
Medals: Silver Star, Bronze Star

192. Harry N. Whisler—U.S. Army
Unit: 10th Armored Division
Medals: Combat Medical Badge

193. Paul Flynn—U.S. Navy
Medals: WWII Victory Medal

194. Ubert Terrel–U.S. Army Air Corps
Unit: 100th Troop Carrier Squadron, 441st Troop Carrier Group
Medals: Air Medal

195. Anthony Grasso—U.S. Army
Unit: 112th Regiment, 28th Infantry Division
Medals: Purple Heart (2x), Bronze Star, Combat Infantryman Badge

196. Arthur Minichiello—U.S. Navy
Unit: USS *New Jersey*
Medals: Combat Action Ribbon, WWII Victory Medal

197. Arnald Gabriel—U.S. Army
Unit: 175th Regiment, 29th Infantry Division
Medals: Bronze Star, Combat Infantryman Badge

198. Lampton Terrel—U.S. Army
Unit: 1st Engineer Special Brigade
Medals: WWII Victory Medal

199. Joe Crotty—U.S. Navy
Unit: USS *Helena*
Medals: WWII Victory Medal

200. Wallace Mattison—U.S. Army
Unit: 29th Infantry Division, 115th Regiment
Medals: Purple Heart, Combat Infantryman Badge

201. Ed Cottrell—U.S. Army Air Corps
Unit: 48th Fighter Group, 493rd Squadron—Ardennes, Central Europe
Medals: Air Medal

202. Harold Wellington—U.S. Merchant Marine
Unit: MS *John Erickson*
Medals: Merchant Marine Combat Bar

203. James Brush—U.S. Army
Unit: engineer on Manhattan District Project

204. Dorothy Managan—U.S. Army
Unit: Fort Lewis Madigan Hospital Nurse Corps
Medals: WWII Victory Medal

205. Myrl Jean Hughes—U.S. Army
Unit: 334th Station Hospital Nurse Corps—New Guinea
Medals: Pacific Theater Ribbon

206. Verl Luzena—U.S. Army Air Corps
Unit: 4th Combat Camera Unit, 9th Air Force
Medals: WWII Victory Medal

207. George Sarros—U.S. Navy
Unit: LST 515—Normandy
Medals: WWII Victory Medal, Combat Action Ribbon

208. Leo Valente—U.S. Army
Unit: B Company, 284th Combat Engineers—Rhineland, Central Europe
Medals: WWII Victory Medal

209. Jerome Guida—U.S. Army
Unit: 79th Division—Normandy, northern France, Rhineland
Medals: Silver Star, Bronze Star, Purple Heart (2x)

210. Clarence Thorton—U.S. Army
Unit: 14th Armored Division
Medals: WWII Victory Medal

211. Sam Mancuso—U.S. Army Air Corps
Unit: Flight Engineer C-54—China, Burma, India
Medals: Air Medal

212. Nick DiMaria—U.S. Army
Unit: 43rd Division—Okinawa
Medals: Combat Infantryman Badge

213. Frank Marshall—U.S. Army
Unit: E Company, 333rd Regiment, 84th Division
Medals: Purple Heart, Bronze Star, Combat Infantryman Badge

214. John Diperna—U.S. Marines
Unit: H+S Company, 1st Marine Division—Peleliu, Okinawa
Medals: Combat Action Ribbon

215. John Picardi—U.S. Navy
Unit: LST 513—Normandy, Operation Dragoon
Medals: Combat Action Ribbon

216. Arthur Bibeu—U.S. Navy
Unit: LST 543—Normandy, southern France, Okinawa
Medals: Combat Action Ribbon, WWII Victory Medal

217. Bob Chouinard—U.S. Army
Unit: 128th Anti-Aircraft Artillery Gun Battalion—Normandy, northern
France, Rhineland
Medals: WWII Victory Medal

218. Leon Schiff—Merchant Marine
Unit: MS *Sands Point*
Medals: WWII Victory Medal

219. Arthur Butler—U.S. Army
Unit: A Company, 7th Infantry Division, 184th Regiment—Okinawa
Medals: Purple Heart, Combat Infantryman Badge

220. Nunzio Martino—U.S. Navy
Unit: USS *Franklin* (destroyed)
Medals: Combat Action Ribbon, WWII Victory Medal

221. Lawrence Gardner—U.S. Army
Unit: B Company, 43rd Infantry Division, 71st Regiment—Rhineland,
Central Europe
Medals: Bronze Star, Combat Infantryman Badge

222. Charles Gubbish—U.S. Marines
Unit: 3rd Marine Division—Iwo Jima
Medals: Purple Heart, Combat Action Ribbon

223. Dan Elliot—U.S. Army
Unit: 44th Combat Engineer Battalion—Rhineland, Central Europe
Medals: WWII Victory Medal

224. Joseph Cooper—U.S. Navy
Unit: USS *Ommaney Bay*—Philippines
Medals: Combat Action Ribbon

225. Andy Pendleton—U.S. Army Air Corps
Unit: 15th Air Force, 451st Bomb Group—Italy
Medals: Air Medal, WWII Victory Medal

226. John Eakin—U.S. Army
Unit: 34th Division, 168th Regiment—North Apennines, Po Valley
Medals: Bronze Star, Combat Infantryman Badge

227. John Picard—U.S. Army
Unit: C Company, 552nd Heavy Field Artillery Battalion—Normandy, Holland, Ardennes
Medals: WWII Victory Medal

228. Vincent Rabita—U.S. Army Air Corps
Unit: 12th Air Force, 17th Bomb Group, 34th Squadron—Sicily, Italy, southern France
Medals: Air Medal

229. Sid Leavit—U.S. Army
Unit: 17th Airborne, 194th Glider Infantry Regiment—Ardennes, Rhineland
Medals: Bronze Star, Purple Heart, Combat Infantryman Badge

230. Charles Shay—U.S. Army
Unit: 1st Infantry Division—Normandy, northern France, Rhineland, Ardennes
Medals: Silver Star, Purple Heart, Combat Medical Badge, Prisoner of War Medal

231. Richard Weaver—U.S. Army
Unit: 17th Airborne Division, Division HQ—Ardennes, Rhineland
Medals: Combat Infantryman Badge, WWII Victory Medal

232. Oliver Harris—U.S. Army
Unit: 17th Airborne Division, 513th Parachute Infantry Regiment—Ardennes, Rhineland
Medals: Bronze Star, Combat Infantryman Badge

233. Martin Schlocker—U.S. Army
Unit: 17th Airborne Division, 513th Parachute Infantry Regiment—Ardennes
Medals: Combat Infantryman Badge, Prisoner of War Medal

234. Robert Heurgue—U.S. Army
Unit: 82nd Airborne Division, Division HQ—Normandy, Rhineland, Ardennes, Central Europe
Medals: Combat Infantryman Badge, Combat Jump Wings

235. John Althuizen—U.S. Army
Unit: 7th Armored Division—Rhineland, Ardennes, Central Europe
Medals: Purple Heart (2x), Combat Infantryman Badge

236. Cliff Stump—U.S. Army
Unit: 82nd Airborne Division, 80th Anti-Aircraft Artillery Battalion—Normandy, Holland, Ardennes
Medals: Combat Glider Badge

237. Melvin Hurwitz—U.S. Army
Unit: 493rd Bomb Group, 863rd Bomb Squad, 8th Air Force
Medals: Air Medal

238. Neal McCallum—U.S. Army
Unit: 22nd Marines, 29th Regiment, 6th Marine Division—Okinawa
Medals: Purple Heart, Combat Action Ribbon

239. Dick Rung—U.S. Navy
Unit: LCT 539—Normandy
Medals: WWII Victory Medal

240. Wallace King—U.S. Army Air Corps
Unit: 406th Fighter Group, 513th Fighter Squadron, 9th Air Force—Normandy, Rhineland, Central Europe
Medals: Purple Heart, Air Medal

241. Jack Hamlin—U.S. Coast Guard
Unit: rescue swimmer—Omaha Beach

242. Alan Chatwin—U.S. Navy
Unit: guard in Guam

243. Bill Parker—U.S. Army
Unit: 29th Infantry Division, 116th Regiment—Normandy, Rhineland
Medals: Bronze Star, Purple Heart, Combat Infantryman Badge

244. Lester Stoddard—U.S. Army
Unit: 473rd Regiment, 5th Army—Rome, Arno, North Apennines, Po
Valley
Medals: Bronze Star, Purple Heart

245. Fernand Morency—U.S. Army
Unit: U.S. Army Medical Corps—India, Burma
Medals: WWII Victory Medal

246. Dwight Smith—U.S. Navy
Unit: USS *South Dakota*—southern France
Medals: Combat Action Ribbon, WWII Victory Medal

247. Leo Provencal—U.S. Army
Unit: 2nd Infantry Division
Medals: Combat Infantryman Badge

248. Robert Sawyer—U.S. Army Air Corps
Unit: 415th Bombardier Squadron
Medal: WWII Victor Medal

247. Philip Schneider—U.S. Navy
Unit: USS *Pensacola*, LST 925—Pacific Theater
Medals: WWII Victory Medal, Philippine Liberation Ribbon

248. Preston Walsh—U.S. Navy
Unit: Armed Guard for Merchant Vessels
Medals: WWII Victory Medal

249. Taylor Griffin—U.S. Navy
Unit: USNAS—Honolulu, Hawaii
Medals: WWII Victor Medal

250. Charles Tanguay—U.S. Navy
Unit: USS *Woodcock*
Medals: WWII Victory Medal

251. Norman Sanborn—U.S. Merchant Marine
Unit: merchant ship—southern France
Medals: WWII Victory Medal

252. Albert Caldwell—U.S. Navy
Unit: USNTC—Newport, Rhode Island

253. James Lodge—U.S. Army
Unit: 349th Infantry Regiment—Italy
Medals: WWII Victory Medal

254. Allan Hallet—U.S. Army Air Corps
Unit: 389th Bomb Group, 8th Air Force
Medals: Air Medal, WWII Victory Medal

255. In Memory of Avila Sawyer—U.S. Army, KIA, 36th Infantry Division

256. John Burke—U.S. Army
Unit: 387th Regiment, 97th Infantry Division—Central Europe
Medals: Bronze Star, Combat Infantryman Badge

257. Joe Altott—U.S. Army Air Corps
Unit: 500th Bomb Group, 881st Bomb Squad, 20th Air Force—Saipan
Medals: Distinguished Flying Cross, Air Medal

258. Richard Tinsley—U.S. Navy
Unit: Hospital Corpsman—Brooklyn, NY

259. Fred Adams—U.S. Army
Unit: 34th Division, 168th Regiment—North Africa, Italy
Medals: Bronze Star, Combat Infantryman Badge

260. Manny Carvalho—U.S. Army
Unit: HQ Detachment, Intermediate General Depot #2—India, Burma
Medals: WWII Victory Medal

261. George Amaral—U.S. Army
Unit: 27th Combat Engineer Battalion—Rhineland
Medals: WWII Victory Medal

262. Charles Gagnon—U.S. Army
Unit: 7th Signal Corps Company, 7th Infantry Division—Okinawa
Medals: WWII Victory Medal

263. Jim Riley—U.S. Army
Unit: 3003rd Quartermaster Company—Hawaii
Medals: WWII Victory Medal

263. Eddie Neves—U.S. Army
Unit: 408th Ordinance Battalion
Medals: WWII Victory Medal

264. Joann Ipoliti Gallo—U.S. Army
Unit: Nurse Corps—Saipan
Medals: WWII Victory Medal

265. Joseph Poirier—U.S. Army
Unit: C Company, 3rd Infantry Division, 15th Regiment—Anzio
Medals: Bronze Star, Purple Heart, Combat Infantryman Badge

266. Sal Murano—U.S. Army
Unit: 10th Mountain Division—Po Valley
Medals: WWII Victory Medal

267. Ray Celona—U.S. Army
Unit: A Company, 3180th Signal Battalion—Okinawa
Medals: WWII Victory Medal

268. Frank Bellotti—U.S. Navy
Unit: U.S. Navy Scouts and Raiders
Medals: WWII Victory Medal

269. Robert Welsh—U.S. Army
Unit: M Company, 347th Regiment, 87th Division—Ardennes, Rhineland, Central Europe
Medals: Bronze Star, Combat Infantryman Badge

270: Barney Zmoda—U.S. Army
Unit: A Company, 346th Regiment, 87th Division—northern France
Medals: Bronze Star, Combat Infantryman Badge

271. Anthony Pagano—U.S. Army
Unit: 1225th Combat Engineers—Ardennes, Rhineland, Central Europe
Medals: WWII Victory Medal

272. Dan Santagata—U.S. Army
Unit: 5th Infantry Division, 10th Regiment—Normandy, northern France, Ardennes, Rhineland
Medals: Bronze Star, Combat Infantryman Badge

273. Ben Berry—U.S. Army
Unit: 3rd Army Quartermaster Corps
Medals: WWII Victory Medal

274. Joe Landry—U.S. Army
Unit: 776th Anti-Aircraft Artillery Battalion—Normandy, Ardennes, Rhineland
Medals: WWII Victory Medal

275. Jacob Ruser—U.S. Army
Unit: 4th Infantry Division, 12th Regiment—Normandy, northern France, Ardennes, Rhineland
Medals: Purple Heart, Combat Medical badge

276. James Morgia—U.S. Army
Unit: E Company, 84th Division, 334th Regiment—Ardennes, Rhineland, Central Europe
Medals: Silver Star, Bronze Star, Combat Infantryman Badge

277. Gerald White—U.S. Army
Unit: 2nd Infantry Division—Ardennes, Rhineland, Central Europe
Medals: Bronze Star, Combat Infantryman Badge

278. David Bailey—U.S. Army
Unit: 106th Division, 422nd Regiment—Ardennes
Medals: Prisoner of War Medal, Combat Infantryman Badge

279. Lockered Gahs—U.S. Army
Unit: 42nd Infantry Division, 222nd Regiment, Anti-Tank Company—
Ardennes, Rhineland, Central Europe
Medals: Combat Infantryman Badge, Bronze Star

280. Pat Patteson—U.S. Navy
Unit: Lockheed Harpoon Pilot, VPB-135 Lockheed Ventura—Pacific
Medals: Combat Air Medal

281. Jack Moran—U.S. Army
Unit: K Company, 87th Infantry Division, 347th Regiment—Ardennes,
Rhineland, Central Europe
Medals: Bronze Star, Combat Infantry Badge

282. Paul "Bud" Haedike—U.S. Army Air Corps
Unit: 8th Air Force, 452nd Bomb Group, 730th Squadron—Ardennes,
Rhineland, Central Europe
Medals: Air Medal

283. George Ciampa—U.S. Army
Unit: 607th Graves Registration Company—Normandy, northern
France, Rhineland, Ardennes
Medals: WWII Victory Medal

284. Mathias Gutman—U.S. Navy
Unit: LST 553—Peleliu, Leyte, Philippines, Okinawa
Medals: Combat Action Ribbon

285. Lenard Messineo—U.S. Army
Unit: 20th Armored Division—Central Europe
Medals: Combat Infantryman Badge, WWII Victory Medal

286. Gideon Kantor—U.S. Army
Unit: Ritchie Boys—Normandy, Northern France
Medals: WWII Victory Medal

286. Morris Bishaf—U.S. Army
Unit: A Company, 104th Infantry Division, 414th Regiment—Ardennes,
Rhineland
Medals: Bronze Star, Purple Heart, Combat Infantryman Badge

287. James Harvey—U.S. Army Air Corps
Unit: Tuskegee Airman, 332nd Fighter Group—Korea
Medals: First Top Gun

288. Frank Emond—U.S. Navy
Unit: USS *Pennsylvania*—Pearl Harbor survivor
Medals: Combat Action Ribbon

289. Carl Felton—U.S. Navy
Unit: HMS *Ceres*—Normandy
Medals: WWII Victory Medal

290. Ben Lesser—Holocaust survivor
Camps: Auschwitz, Buchenwald, Dachau

291. Caster Salemi—U.S. Army
Unit: 251st Field Artillery, Battery B—Philippines
Medals: WWII Victory Medal, Philippine Liberation Medal

292. Clifford Pierce—U.S. Navy
Unit: USS *Oxford*—Pacific
Medals: WWII Victory Medal

293. James Ingargiola—U.S. Marines
Unit: Company I, 3rd Battalion, 3rd Marine Regiment, 3rd Marine Division—
Iwo Jima, Guam
Medals: Combat Action Ribbon

294. Amelian Pastuszak—U.S. Marines
Unit: 4th Base Depot—Russell Islands
Medals: WWII Victory Medal

295. Walter Paster—U.S. Army
Unit: 2695th Military Police Company—southern France, Rhineland
Medals: WWII Victory Medal

296. Louis Ricci—U.S. Navy
Unit: Naval Base—San Juan, Puerto Rico
Medals: WWII Victory Medal

297. Robert Moran—U.S. Army
Unit: 2nd Infantry Division—Ardennes
Medals: WWII Victory Medal

298. Cletis Bailey—U.S. Army
Unit: 84th Infantry Division—Ardennes
Medals: Bronze Star, Combat Infantryman Badge

299. Richard Marshal—U.S. Army
Unit: 84th Infantry Division—Ardennes
Medals: Combat Infantryman Badge

300. Pasquale Digiovanni—U.S. Marines
Unit: VMF-441, Marine Aircraft Group 31—Okinawa
Medals: WWII Victory Medal

Index